AR

MW00795142

THE
AMERICAN STANDARD
OF PERFECTION

ILLUSTRATED

A COMPLETE DESCRIPTION OF ALL
RECOGNIZED VARIETIES OF FOWLS

AS REVISED BY
THE AMERICAN POULTRY ASSOCIATION, INC.
AT ITS SIXTY-THIRD ANNUAL MEETING
IN NEW YORK CITY
NINETEEN HUNDRED THIRTY SEVEN
AND ITS SIXTY-FOURTH ANNUAL MEETING
IN SAINT PAUL, MINNESOTA
NINETEEN HUNDRED THIRTY-EIGHT

GENERAL INTRODUCTION

The American Poultry Association was organized at Buffalo, New York, February, 1873, by representative poultry breeders from different sections of the United States and Canada. The primary object of the Association was to standardize the varieties of domestic poultry which had become so numerous and were in many cases so similar that there was the greatest confusion in judging and breeding them.

In making standards and determining what breeds were worthy of recognition, it was necessary that the Association should be governed by principles which would be recognized generally as right, for on no other basis was it possible to secure acceptance of its standards as authoritative.

The principles adopted by the Association at that time were, briefly:

First, That in each breed then existing the most useful type should be made the Standard type.

Second, That no more breeds should be recognized as having distinctive breed character than could be identified readily by at least one conspicuous character, or a combination of conspicuous characters, not possessed in the same combination by any other breed.

Third, That recognition of color varieties in a breed should be limited to plainly distinctive color patterns.

In making the first "American Standard of Excellence," issued in February, 1874, the application of these principles was affected somewhat by the character of the material to be standardized. In the ancient breeds, unique and odd features had been developed as the visible marks of superior breeding. It was inevitable that the standardization of breeds distinguished by such features should lead to exaggeration, but it is a notable fact that after the standardization of poultry according to the principles above stated, interest in the making of mere novelties declined and attention turned more and more to the improvement of characters of substantial worth and true beauty.

For more than seventy years prior to the appearance of the first American Standard, poultrymen had been trying to make such blends of European and Asiatic races of fowls as have

6

produced the Plymouth Rock, Wyandotte and Rhode Island Red, yet had failed to produce a breed that could gain wide or lasting popularity. Nor, in all that time, had any old, established breed been so improved that it could win and hold the favor of those who kept poultry for eggs and meat.

Within ten years after the publication of our first Standard, the Plymouth Rock, introduced to the public a few years before, had been accepted by American farmers as their ideal of a general purpose fowl; the Wyandotte was being introduced as an earlier maturing breed of the same type; the American Leghorn was being widely distributed as the most popular laying type, and the American Brahma had become a favorite wherever special attention was given to the growing of poultry for the table. Since that time, other breeds and many varieties of the same general types have appeared and have been bred extensively by all classes of poultry keepers throughout the United States and Canada. Every one of these when presented for admission to the Standard has been subjected to the same severe tests in which the first consideration was to fix the type most serviceable for that breed, and in the periodical revisions of the Standard every request for a change has been considered, first, with relation to its possible effect upon productive values.

Wherever Standard-bred poultry is found lacking in productive or ornamental value, it is because breeders and judges are not interpreting and applying the Standard of Perfection in accordance with the principles governing the making of the Standard.

In regard to the ornamental breeds existing at the time of its organization, the policy of the Association has been to preserve their breed and variety characteristics in the most attractive forms, but it has given no encouragement whatever to the making of new ornamental breeds.

In regard to ornamental characters in poultry generally, this Association maintains that the permanent popularity of any breed or variety bred for economic purposes depends primarily on its material value but is added to and strengthened by the beauty and attractiveness which uniformity of shape and beauty of color lends and which may best be secured by breeding to a universally recognized and accepted Standard.

In the breeds created under its Standard and as far as possible in the breeds previously existing, the American Poultry Association has demanded harmonious development of all characters and qualities; therefore, indifference to productive values and neglect of appearances are equally obnoxious to its principles.

The change of the title, "American Standard of Excellence," to "American Standard of Perfection" was a declaration of the purpose of the Association to exert all its authority and influence to prevent over-development in either direction at the expense of inferiority in the other.

Until 1905 the Standard contained only verbal specifications for ideal types. In the 1905 edition, these were supplemented by reproductions of ideal drawings in pen and ink of the most popular breeds by the best known poultry artists of the time. The value of such illustrations as aids to correct interpretation of the verbal descriptions was demonstrated so clearly by the greater progress made in breeding and by greater consistency in judging under this Standard that, at the next revision, in 1910, the number of illustrations was increased to cover representative varieties in all breeds, except a few of the older ones, in which there was comparatively little interest. The type of illustrations was, however, changed to half-tone reproductions, made to conform fully to the Standard descriptions of the ideal birds.

INTRODUCTION TO THE
1938 EDITION

In accordance with constitutional procedure the Annual Convention of the American Poultry Association, at Topeka in 1936, voted to revise the Standard of Perfection and as a result the revision committee of four members, Mr. George Robertson, Chairman, Mr. Arthur O. Schilling, Mr. Erle Smiley and Mr. Paul P. Ives met in New York for eleven days in June 1937 for the consideration of and action on the vast mass of material which had been submitted by breeders and poultry authorities from all sections of the United States and Canada with reference to changes and additions for the forthcoming revised edition of the American Standard of Perfection.

For some time there had been an increasingly insistent demand in the press and among poultry breeders, fanciers and educators on the need of certain basic and fundamental changes in the relative apportionment of the points in the scale by which poultry is judged as between the fundamentals of size, shape and vigor and the comparatively superficial characters of feather color and pattern.

Voluminous correspondence representing the viewpoints of authorities in every line of poultry breeding work was studied and discussed and the unanimous report of the committee adopted by the unanimous vote of the convention in New York in November resulted in the most basic change in the Standard of Perfection in forty years; the scale of points published in this edition of the Standard which materially increases the evaluation of shape, size and vigor and reduces by the same ratio, the emphasis placed in the scale of points on feather color and pattern.

This 1938 edition of the Standard of Perfection, besides the above, includes many other important changes in descriptions of breeds, instructions to judges, breed classifications, the addition of new breeds recognized as Standard and all recommendations and instructions of the 63rd and 64th Annual Meetings of the American Poultry Association, the final action of the highest authority both as to text and illustration.

TO THE POULTRY ASSOCIATIONS OF AMERICA

Recognizing your loyalty to The American Poultry Association, and believing that a few general rules will be beneficial in conducting poultry exhibitions at which THE AMERICAN STANDARD OF PERFECTION is advertised to govern the placing of awards, we submit the following recommendations with the request that the same importance be attached to them as to other parts of the STANDARD.

Poultry associations at whose exhibitions THE AMERICAN STANDARD OF PERFECTION is used are requested to give preference to judges licensed by the American Poultry Association. Judges who are licensed by this organization are accredited thereby, to the extent of being in good standing and competent; therefore, it is reasonable to conclude that they will apply properly the laws contained in the STANDARD of the Association.

Licensed judges employed by you are required to follow and apply the STANDARD literally, carefully considering each section of every specimen, according to the scale of points provided for the several breeds. No section is to be ignored. Each section is regarded as important. When the judging has been done by score card, protests may be entertained in cases of apparent clerical error in recording or computing the score of a specimen. In such cases, the specimen under dispute shall be rescored by the judge.

When the judging has been done either by score card or by comparison, protests may be entertained in case of apparent dishonesty on the part of a judge, or apparent carelessness that has resulted in the placing of a disqualified specimen. In either case, the judge, together with the president and secretary of the local association, or the judge and two representatives appointed by the management of the association, shall constitute a committee of three, and the majority decision of this committee shall be final.

Protests are not to be entertained except when made in writing, and the person making the protest shall deposit with the secretary of the local association the sum of five dollars, this money to be returned to the person making the protest if his protest is sustained; if protest is not sustained, the deposit becomes the property of the local association.

Should the local association have reason to complain of the work or conduct of the judge, or the behavior of an exhibitor who is a member of the American Poultry Association, the said local association may enter complaint of such work or conduct to the President and Secretary of the American Poultry Association, in which case a full and complete report of the same shall be made, and the charges shall be referred by the President and Secretary of the American Poultry Association to the Judges Licensing Committee for investigation. The judge against whom these charges are made shall be given a hearing before the Judges Licensing Committee of the American Poultry Association and if the charges are proven and sustained at this investigation and the judge found guilty, then the Judges Licensing Committee has the right to suspend or revoke his license.

If the complaint be made against an exhibitor who is a member of the American Poultry Association, the President and Secretary may refer this complaint to the Chairman of the Committee on Welfare, Grievances, and Appeals, for investigation.

The American Poultry Association, through its STANDARD OF PERFECTION, has not only labored for over half a century to standardize and improve the quality of poultry along STANDARD

—beautiful and productive—lines, but the Association has also endeavored to extend the spirit of the fancier and the breeder into a great and broad fellowship, which should create a general sentiment of justice, fairness, and loyalty between all its members and all poultry interests.

The forms of score cards printed in this book are the official score and comparison cards of the American Poultry Association and are copyrighted. All associations are requested to use them.

Consideration is to be given the matter of STANDARD weights and proper sizes at all shows. It is recommended that all specimens having weight clauses be weighed before being judged, and that the correct weight be marked on the coop card.

Any exhibitor found guilty of faking, showing borrowed specimens, or of flagrant misconduct, shall be debarred from competition and shall forfeit any prize or prizes that may have been awarded him.

It is respectfully recommended that local associations, specialty clubs, and other organizations advertise in their premium lists and otherwise that their exhibitions will be conducted under the rules of the American Poultry Association, and that the instructions to judges, general disqualifications, and other provisions and requirements of THE AMERICAN STANDARD OF PERFECTION shall govern.

Fraternally,

THE AMERICAN POULTRY ASSOCIATION, Inc.

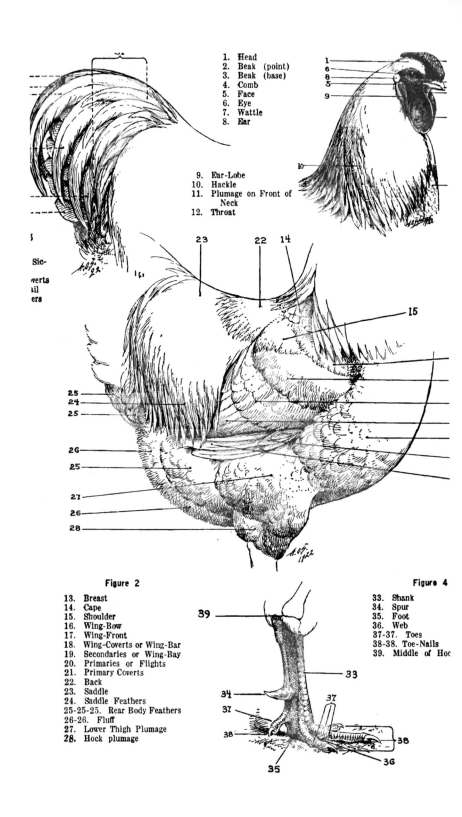

1. Head
2. Beak (point)
3. Beak (base)
4. Comb
5. Face
6. Eye
7. Wattle
8. Ear

9. Ear-Lobe
10. Hackle
11. Plumage on Front of Neck
12. Throat

Figure 2

13. Breast
14. Cape
15. Shoulder
16. Wing-Bow
17. Wing-Front
18. Wing-Coverts or Wing-Bar
19. Secondaries or Wing-Bay
20. Primaries or Flights
21. Primary Coverts
22. Back
23. Saddle
24. Saddle Feathers
25-25-25. Rear Body Feathers
26-26. Fluff
27. Lower Thigh Plumage
28. Hock plumage

Figure 4

33. Shank
34. Spur
35. Foot
36. Web
37-37. Toes
38-38. Toe-Nails
39. Middle of Hoc

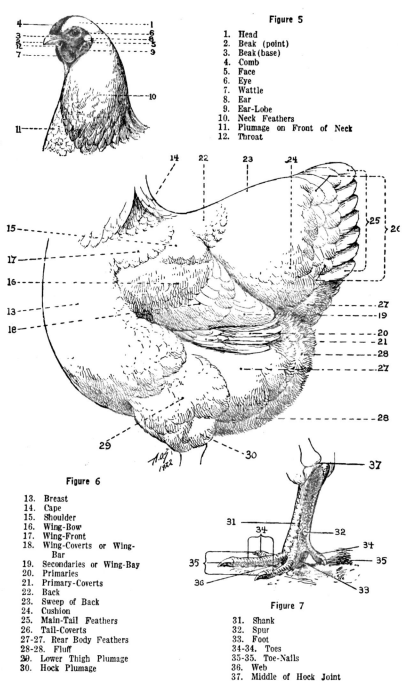

Figure 5

1. Head
2. Beak (point)
3. Beak (base)
4. Comb
5. Face
6. Eye
7. Wattle
8. Ear
9. Ear-Lobe
10. Neck Feathers
11. Plumage on Front of Neck
12. Throat

Figure 6

13. Breast
14. Cape
15. Shoulder
16. Wing-Bow
17. Wing-Front
18. Wing-Coverts or Wing-Bar
19. Secondaries or Wing-Bay
20. Primaries
21. Primary-Coverts
22. Back
23. Sweep of Back
24. Cushion
25. Main-Tail Feathers
26. Tail-Coverts
27-27. Rear Body Feathers
28-28. Fluff
29. Lower Thigh Plumage
30. Hock Plumage

Figure 7

31. Shank
32. Spur
33. Foot
34-34. Toes
35-35. Toe-Nails
36. Web
37. Middle of Hock Joint

NOMENCLATURE OF FEMALE

13

GLOSSARY OF TECHNICAL TERMS

BARRING: Bars or stripes extending across a feather. (See page 65, figures 43, 44, and 45.)

BEAN: A hard, bean-shaped protuberance growing in the tip of the upper mandible of a waterfowl. (See page 14, figure 3.)

BEAK: The projecting mouth parts of chickens and turkeys, consisting of upper and lower mandibles. (See pages 12, and 13, figures 1, and 5.)

BEARD: In chickens, a group of feathers pendant from the throat, on Houdans and some varieties of Polish. (See page 16, figure 7.) In turkeys, a tuft of coarse, bristly hairs projecting from the upper part of breast. (See illustrations of Turkeys.)

BILL: The projecting mouth parts of water fowl, consisting of upper and lower mandible. (See page 14, figure 3.)

BLADE: The rear part of a single comb, usually extending beyond the crown of the head; should be smooth and free from serrations. (See page 16, figure 4.)

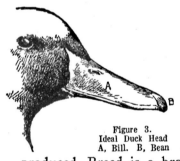

Figure 3.
Ideal Duck Head
A, Bill. B, Bean

BOW-LEGGED: A deformity in which the legs are too far apart at the hock and are bent inward laterally below the knees. (See General Disqualifications, page 63.)

BRASSINESS: Having the color of brass, metallic yellow.

BREED: A race of domestic fowls which maintains distinctive characteristics of shape, growth, temperament, and shell-color of eggs produced. Breed is a broader term than variety. Breed includes varieties, as, for example, the Barred, White, and Buff varieties of the Plymouth Rock breed.

BREEDER: A broad, general term that designates the poultry raiser who produces fowls for any special purpose with the object of improving their value or in conformity with an agreed standard of excellence.

BUFF: A medium shade of orange color having a rich, golden cast. A color term used in describing the plumage of all Standard buff varieties of poultry, that is not so intense as to show a reddish cast, or so pale as to appear brassy or light yellow.

(The term orange, used in this definition, refers to the primary color of the spectrum.)

BUTTERCUP COMB: A comb set firmly on the center of skull, with a single leader from base of beak to a deep cup-shaped crown formed by a complete circle of regular points.

Note: The cavity within the circle of points should be deep; the texture of comb, fine and smooth. (See page 22, figure 24.)

CAPE: The short feathers on the back underneath the hackle, collectively shaped like a cape.

CAPON: An unsexed male, readily distinguished by the undeveloped comb and wattles; the profusion of long, narrow hackle and saddle feathers, and low tail.

CARRIAGE: The attitude, bearing, or style of a bird.

CARUNCLES: Small, fleshy protuberances—as on the head of a turkey or Muscovy duck.

CARUNCULATED: Having caruncles.

CAVERNOUS: Applied to the hollow, protruding nostrils of some breeds.

CHICKENS: (a) Used as a general term to designate all domestic fowls, except turkeys, ducks, and geese; (b) specifically, domestic fowls under one year old.

CHICKS: Young of the domestic hen while in the downy stage.

COCK: A male fowl one year old or more.

COCKEREL: A male fowl less than one year old.

COMB: The fleshy protuberance growing on top of a fowl's head. The Standard varieties of combs are: Single, rose, pea, V-shaped, strawberry, cushion, and buttercup, all others being modification of these. (See pages 16 and 22, figures 4 to 9, and figure 24.)

CONDITION: The state of a fowl in regard to health, and in regard to state and cleanliness of plumage, head, and legs.

COVERTS: See tail, flight, and wing-coverts. (See pages 12 and 13, figures 2 and 6.)

CREAMINESS: Having the color of cream; light yellow.

CREST: A crown or tuft of feathers on the head of a fowl. (See page 16, figure 7.)

CROP: The receptacle in which a fowl's food is accumulated before it passes to the gizzard.

Figure 4.
1, Base; 2, 2, 2, 2, 2, Points; 3, Blade.
For ideal types see illustrations of breeds
and varieties.

Figure 5.
Rose-Comb.
1, Base; 2, Rounded Points; 3, Spike.
For ideal types see illustrations of breeds
and varieties.

Figure 6.
Pea-Comb.
For ideal types see illustrations of breeds
and varieties.

Figure 7.
Sultans Head, Male (Ideal).
1-1, V-shaped Comb; 2, Crest; 3-3, Muffs,
4, Beard.
For ideal types see illustrations of breeds
and varieties. For example, Houdans and some
varieties of Polish.

Figure 8.
Cushion-Comb (Ideal).

Figure 9.
Strawberry-Comb (Ideal).

DIFFERENT FORMS OF COMBS

Figure 10.
Over Refined.
(Too small.)

Figure 11.
Standard or Medium Size.
(Side view.)

Figure 12.
Standard or Medium Size.
Firm and even on head.
(Front view.)

STANDARD AND DEFECTIVE COMBS

CUSHION: The mass of feathers at the rear or back of a fowl, partly covering the tail; most pronounced in Cochin females. (See Cochin illustrations and page 13, figure 6.)

CUSHION COMB: A solid, low comb set firmly on head; the upper surface smooth, free from points and wrinkles; the front, rear and sides nearly straight. (See page 16, figure 8.)

DARK SLATE: A very dark gray, approaching black.

DEFECT: A departure from perfection as described by the Standard. (See chapter, "Cutting for Defects.")

DEWLAP: A pendulous skin development under throat.

DISQUALIFICATION: A deformity or one or more serious defects that excludes a fowl from an award or score, or from use in the breeding pen. A fowl so excluded is said to be disqualified.

DISQUALIFIED: Applied to a fowl that is unworthy of an award or score.

DOWN: The first hairy covering of chicks; also the tufts of feather-like growth that are sometimes found on the shanks, toes, feet, or webs of feet of fowls. (Note: If the quill and web are discernible to the eye, it is called a "feather.")

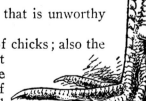

Figure 13.
Duck Foot (A Disqualification).

17

DRAKE: A male of the duck family.

DROOPING WING: A wing carried loosely folded against the body with wing points carried below the horizontal.

DUBBING: Cutting off the comb, wattles, or ear-lobes, so as to leave the head smooth.

DUCK: A female of the duck family.

DUCKLING: The young of the duck family in the downy stage of plumage.

DUCK-FOOTED: The fourth, or hind toe, carried forward. (See page 17, figure 13.)

EAR-LOBES: The formation of bare skin just below the ears. Ear-lobes of different breeds vary in color, being red, white, purple, cream, etc.; they also vary greatly in size and shape. (See pages 12 and 13, figures 1 and 5.)

ENAMEL: The quality of white found in the ear-lobes of Mediterranean varieties.

EXCRESCENCES: A disfiguring, abnormal or superfluous outgrowth.

FACE: The bare skin on the head of a fowl around and below the eyes. (See page 62, figure 42.)

FAKING: An attempt on the part of an exhibitor to deceive the judge.

FANCIER: A breeder of poultry who seeks to produce chickens, turkeys, ducks, or geese in conformity with an ideal or prescribed standard.

FAWN: A soft, grayish tan.

FEATHER: A growth formed of a discernible quill and a vane (called "web") upon each side. Quality of feather depends upon size and tex-

Figure 14.

Cochin Leg and Toe Feathering.

A, Upper Thigh; B-B, Lower Thigh; C-C, Shank; D-D, Toe.

Figure 15.

Sections of a Feather.

turé. Smooth, hard texture of feather is secured when the barbs in the web are hooked completely together. When the hooklets on the barbs or ribs of the web are reduced in number or size, the web is more split, stringy, transparent or curling. (See page 18, figure 15, and paragraph "Quality of Feather," under "Instructions to Judges.") Note: When the quill is not discernible to the eye, it is "down."

FEATHER-LEGGED: Term used to designate those breeds having feathers on shanks and toes. (See page 18, figure 14, and definition of "Leg-feathers.")

FLIGHTS: See Primaries.

FLIGHT-COVERTS: The short, moderately stiff feathers located at the base of the wing primaries, or flight feathers, and partly covering their quills. (See pages 12 and 13, figures 2 and 6.)

FLUFF: The soft feathers about thighs and posterior part of fowl, also the soft, downy part of a feather. (See pages 12 and 13, figures 2 and 6.)

FOREIGN COLOR: Any color that differs from the basic color prescribed by the Standard for the specimen under consideration.

FOWL: Generally, a term applied to all poultry; specifically, applied to designate mature domestic cocks and hens.

FOWLS: Plural of fowl.

FROSTING: A marginal edging or tracing of color on feather of laced, spangled, and peniciled varieties. (See page 66, figure 50.)

GIPSY COLOR: Very dark purple.

GROUND COLOR: The ground color is the predominating or basic color of the web of a feather.

HACKLE: The neck plumage of males formed of the hackle feathers. (See page 12, figure 1.)

HACKLE FEATHERS: The long, narrow feathers growing on the neck of males. (See page 12, figure 1.)

HANDLING: (Applied to Games) Refers to the development and firmness of muscle.

HARDNESS OF FEATHER: A term used in describing the plumage of Games. Hardness of feather depends on the closeness of webbing and the amount of fluff in the feather; consequently in a hard feathered specimen, the feather will be webbed closely and will possess very little fluff.

19

HEAD: That part of a fowl composed of skull and face, to which the comb, crest, beak, wattles, and ear-lobes are attached.

HEN: Any domestic female fowl one year old or more.

HEN-FEATHERED: A male bird that resembles a hen in feather structure and color markings.

HOCK: The joint between the thigh and the shank. (See pages 12 and 13, figures 4 and 7.)

IRIDESCENT: A prismatic play of color.

KEEL: In ducks, the deep, pendant fold of skin suspended from the entire under side of the body, including the breast and abdomen. In geese, the word "abdomen" is used to distinguish the posterior portion of the underbody from the keel, hence the keel in geese is the loose, pendant fold of skin suspended from the under part of the body in front of the legs.

KEEL-BONE: Breast bone or sternum. (See pages 30 and 31.)

KEY-FEATHER: Short feather growing between primaries and secondaries; usually more pronounced in turkeys.

KNEE-JOINT: See "Hock."

KNOCK-KNEED: A deformity in which the legs come too near together at the hocks and are bent outward laterally below the hocks. (See General Disqualifications, page 63.)

LACED-LACING: A feather edged or bordered with a band of color, different from the ground color of feather. (See page 66, figures 49 and 51.)

LEAF-COMB: A combination of two small single combs, having serrated, leaflike edges; the original Houdan comb, now replaced in America by the V-shaped comb. (See page 16, figure 7.)

LEG: Includes thigh, lower thigh, and shank. (See pages 12 and 13.)

LEG-FEATHERS: Feathers growing on the thighs, lower thighs, or shanks.

LESSER SICKLES: See "Sickles."

LOPPED COMB: A comb falling over to one side. See "General Disqualifications."

LUSTER: The special brightness of plumage that gives brilliancy to the surface color.

MEALY: Applied to the plumage of buff or red varieties if the ground color is stippled with a lighter color. (See "Stipple"; also page 66, figure 52.)

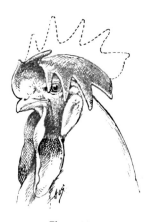

Figure 16.

Lopped Single-Comb.

(A Disqualification.)

Figure 17.

One Form of Side Sprigs.

(A Disqualification.)

Figure 18.

Lopped Rose-Comb.

(A Disqualification.)

Figure 19.

Split Comb.

Showing the tendency of the blade to divide perpendicularly.
(A Disqualification.)

Figure 20.

Common Faults of Head and Adjuncts:

1. Twisted Comb in front.
2. Double Points.
3. Coarse, Wrinkled Wattles.
4. Loosely-Fitting Lobes.

Figure 21.

Thumb Marks in Comb, Rear Turning to One Side.

(Defects.)

FAULTY COMBS. HEADS AND ADJUNCTS

Figure 22.

A Desirable Type of Single-Comb Head, Wattles, and Ear-Lobes. (Plymouth Rocks.)

Figure 23.

Undesirable Type of Single-Comb. Head, narrow, shallow, over-refined. (Crow-Head.)

Figure 24.

Buttercup-Comb (Ideal).

Figure 25.

A Desirable Type of Rose-Comb. Head, Wattles and Lobes. (Wyandottes.)

Figure 26.

Comb, coarse; Wattles, coarse and wrinkled; Lobes, too loosely-fitted.

DESIRABLE AND UNDESIRABLE HEADS AND HEAD ADJUNCTS

Mossy: Irregular dark markings appearing in feathers and destroying the desirable contrast of color. (See page 65, figure 46.)

Mottled: (1. A Standard requirement.) (a) Feathers marked at the end with a broad white tip. (b) Feathers with a neat, clear, sharply-defined, white tip (as in Anconas and Mottled Houdans). (See page 67, figure 62.) (2. A defect.) The surface spotted with colors or shades that differ from that required by this Standard.

Muffs: The cluster of feathers covering the sides of the face below the eyes, extending from the beard to the ear-lobes. Found only on bearded varieties. (See page 16, figure 7.)

Nostrils: Openings beginning at base of beak and extending into the head.

Pair: A male and female of one variety.

Parti-Colored: Fowls having feathers of two or more colors or shades of color. For examples, Silver-Laced Wyandottes, Blue Andalusians.

Pea-Comb: A triple comb of medium length, resembling three straight single combs placed parallel with one another and joined at base, each having short but distinctly divided serrations, the serrations of the two outer rows being lower and smaller than those of the middle row, and those of each row being somewhat larger and thicker at the middle than at the front and rear of the comb. (See page 16, figure 6.)

Pen: (Exhibition.) A male and four females of the same variety.

Penciling: Small markings or stripes on a feather. They may run straight across, as in the Penciled Hamburgs, in which case they frequently are called "Bars," or may follow the outline of the feather, taking a crescentic form, as in the Dark Brahmas, Partridge Cochins, etc. (See pages 65 and 68, figures 47 and 48.)

Peppered-Peppering: Sprinkled with gray or black.

Pinion Feathers: The feathers attached to the segment of the wing that is most remote from the body.

Plumage: The feathers of a fowl.

Poult: The young of the domestic turkey, properly applied until sex can be distinguished, when they are called cockerels and pullets.

POULTRY: Domestic fowls.

PRIMARIES: The longest feathers of the wing, growing between the pinions and secondaries, hidden when wing is folded; otherwise known as flight feathers. (See pages 12 and 13; also page 55, figure 39.)

PROFILE: A direct side view of a fowl. Applied to live specimens and to illustrations.

PULLET: A female fowl less than a year old.

QUILL: The hollow, horny, basal part or stem of a feather. (See "Shaft"; also page 18, figure 15.)

RICH: (As applied to color.) Sound, vivid, full.

ROSE-COMB: A solid, low comb, the upper surface covered with small, rounded points and free from hollow center. This comb terminates in a well-developed spike which may turn upward as on Hamburgs; be nearly horizontal, as on Rose-Comb Leghorns; or turn downward as on Wyandottes. (For various types see pages 16, 21, and 22; figures 5, 18, 25, and 26; also Standard descriptions.)

RUMP: The rear portion of the back of a duck or other fowl.

SADDLE: The rear part of the back of a male bird, extending to the tail and covered by the saddle feathers. (See page 12, figure 2.)

SADDLE-FEATHERS: The feathers growing out of the saddle. (See page 12, figure 2.)

SCALY LEGS: Incrustations or deposits upon and beneath the scales of a fowl's shanks or toes.

SCOOP BILL: A basin-like cavity in the center of bill of a waterfowl. (See page 24, figure 27.)

SECONDARIES: The long, large quill feathers that grow between the first and second joints of the wing, nearest the body, that are visible when wing is folded. (See pages 12 and 13, figures 2 and 6.)

SERRATED: Notched along the edge like a saw.

SERRATION: A V-shaped notch between the points of a single comb.

Figure 27.
Head of Duck Showing
Scoop-Bill.
(Disqualification.)

24

SEX FEATHERS: A term used to designate the feathers characterizing the mature males of most breeds of ducks, and which correspond to the sickle feathers of a domestic cock. These two top tail feathers usually extend a little more than half the length of the tail when they take a turn upward and forward, making a pronounced curl, which gives a jaunty and attractive appearance.

SHAFT: The stem of a feather, especially the part filled with pith, which bears the barbs. (See page 18, figure 15.)

SHAFTING: The shaft of the plume portion of a feather that is lighter or darker in color than the web of the feather. (See page 66, figure 53.)

SHANK: The portion of a fowl's leg below the hock, exclusive of the foot and toes. (See pages 12, and 13; also pages 30, and 31.)

SHANK-FEATHERING: The feathers growing on the outer side of the shank.

SICKLES: The long, curved feathers of the male's tail; also properly applied to the prominent tail-coverts of males, which are called "lesser sickles."

SIDE SPRIG: A well-defined, pointed growth on the side of a single comb. (See page 21, figure 17.)

SINGLE COMB: A comb consisting of a single, fleshy, serrated formation, extending from the beak backward over the crown of the head. (For various types, see pages 16 and 17; also Standard descriptions.)

SLATY-BLUE: A grayish blue, shades of which are required for the surface and under-color of Blue varieties; also found in the under-color of Light Brahmas and Columbian varieties.

SLIP: A male on which the operation of caponizing has been incompletely performed; readily distinguished from the capon by greater development of comb and wattles. (See "Capon.")

SLIPPED WING: A wing of a fowl not closely folded and not held up in proper position; a defect resulting from injury or from weakness of the muscles of the wing. (See page 26, figure 28.)

SOLID COLOR—SELF COLOR: A uniform color, unmixed with any other color or shade of color.

SPANGLE: A clearly defined marking of a distinctive color, located at the end of a spangled feather. (See page 67, figures 55, 58, and 61.)

Figure 28.
Slipped Wing and Twisted Feather.
(Disqualifications.)

SPANGLED: Plumage made up of spangled feathers.

SPLASHED FEATHER: A feather with colors scattered and irregularly intermixed. (See page 67, figure 56.)

SPLIT COMB: A single comb which is divided perpendicularly with two parts overlapping. (See page 21, figure 19.)

SPLIT TAIL: A tail showing a decided gap between top main-tail feathers at their base, the result of subnormal feather development, disarrangement, or improper placement of quills of feathers. (See page 59, figure 41.) (See General Disqualifications, page 61.)

SPLIT WING: A wing so irregularly formed as to show a decided gap between primaries and secondaries. (See page 59, figure 40.)

SPUR: A horn-like protuberance, growing from the inner side of the shank of a fowl; knob-like or pointed, according to the age of the fowl and the sex. (See page 12, figure 4.)

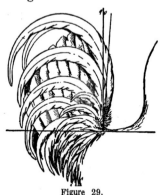

Figure 29.
Squirrel Tail.
(A Disqualification except in Japanese Bantams.)

SQUIRREL-TAIL: A fowl's tail, any portion of which projects forward beyond a perpendicular line drawn through the juncture of tail and back. (See page 26, figure 29.)

STATION: Ideal pose, embodying Standard style; notably height and reach as applies to Games.

STERN: The lower or under part of the posterior section of a fowl.

STIPPLE: Verb, to execute in stipple, i. e., to draw, paint or engrave by means of dots instead of lines. Noun, the effect obtained in color work by use of dots instead of strokes or lines. (See page 66, figure 54.)

STRAIN: A family of any variety of poultry that possesses, and reproduces with marked regularity, common individual characters which distinguish this from other families of the same variety.

26

STRAWBERRY COMB: Approaching in shape the outline and surface of a strawberry. (See page 16, figure 9.)

STRIPE: A stripe of color in the web of neck feathers of both sexes, and the saddle of males of some parti-colored varieties, that differs from the color of the edge of the same feather, or set of feathers. In most instances the stripe should extend through the web, running parallel with the outer edges of the feather and tapering to a point near the lower extremity of the feather. (See pages 67 and 72, figures 59 and 60.)

STRIPED FEATHER: A feather the surface of which shows a stripe. (See definition of "Stripe.")

STUB: The quill portion of a short feather.

SURFACE COLOR: The color of that portion of the plumage of a fowl that is visible when the feathers are in their natural position.

SYMMETRY: Perfection of proportion; the harmony of all parts or sections of a fowl, viewed as a whole with regard to the Standard type of the breed it represents.

SWEEPSTAKE PRIZE: A prize awarded to a specimen or group of specimens winning the highest honor in either a variety, breed, class, or combination of classes.

TAIL-COVERTS: The curved feathers in front of and at the sides of the tail. (See pages 12 and 13, figures 3 and 6.)

TAIL FEATHERS, MAIN: The stiff feathers of the tail. (See pages 12 and 13, figures 3 and 6.)

THIGH: That part of the leg above the shank.

THIGH, LOWER: The section between the hock and the joint next above. (See pages 12 and 13, figures 2 and 6.)

THUMB-MARKS: A disfiguring depression which sometimes appears in the sides of a single comb. (See page 21, figure 21.)

TICKING: (a) The specks or small spots of black color on the tips of neck feathers of Rhode Island Red females. (b) Small specks of color on feathers that differ from the ground or body color.

TIPPED: A term applied to a feather, the web end of which differs in color from the main portion of the feather. (See page 67, figures 58 and 61.)

TOE FEATHERING: The feathers on the toes of fowls required to have feathered shanks and toes. (See page 18, figure 14.)

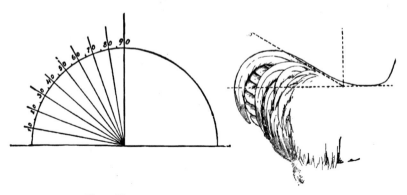

Figure 30.
Diagram Showing Degrees from Horizontal.

Figure 31.
Method of Measuring Tail Angles.

TRIO: One male and two females of the same variety.

TWISTED COMB: An irregularly shaped single comb. (See page 21, figure 20.)

TWISTED FEATHER: Feather with quill or shaft twisted. (See page 26, figure 28.)

TYPICAL: Expressing a characteristic in color or form, representative of a breed or variety; for example, typical shape, meaning the form singular to a breed.

UNDER-COLOR: The color of the downy portion of feathers, not visible when the feathers are in natural position. (See page 18, figure 15.)

VARIETY: A subdivision of a breed (see definition of "Breed"), a term used to distinguish fowls having the Standard shape and other characteristics of the breed to which they belong, but differing in color of plumage, shape of comb, etc., from other groups of the same breed.

V-SHAPED COMB: A comb formed of two well-defined, horn-shaped sections. (See page 16, figure 7.)

VULTURE-HOCK (VULTURE-FEATHERED): The stiff quill feathers growing on the thighs, extending backward, straight beyond the hock. To disqualify, they must be without a sufficient quantity of fluffy feathers to relieve the stiff appearance and to fill up the sharp angles, viewed in profile. (See page 29, figure 32.)

Figure 32.
Vulture-like Hocks.
(As shown, a Disqualification, except in Sultans and some breeds of feather legged bantams.)

WATTLE: The pendant growths at the sides and base of beak.

WEB—WEB OF FEATHER: The flat portion of a feather, made up of a series of barbs on either side of the shaft. (See page 18, figure 15.) Web of Feet: The flat skin between the toes. Web of Wings: The triangular skin attaching the three joints of the wing, visible when wing is extended.

WING-BAR: The stripe or bar of color extending across the middle of the wing, formed by the color or marking of the wing coverts. (See pages 12 and 13, figures 2 and 6.)

WING-BAY: The triangular section of the wing, below the wing-bar, formed by the exposed portion of the secondaries when the wing is folded. (See pages 12 and 13, figures 2 and 6.)

WING-BOW: The upper part of the wing, below the shoulder and wing-front and above the wing-bar. (See pages 12 and 13, figures 2 and 6.)

WING-COVERTS: The small, close feathers clothing the bend of the wing and covering the roots of the secondary quills. (See pages 12 and 13, figures 2 and 6.)

WING-FRONTS: The front edge of the wing at the shoulder. This section of the wing is sometimes called "wing-butts." The term wing-fronts is recommended, thus avoiding confusion. (See pages 12 and 13, figures 2 and 6.)

WING-POINTS: The ends of the primaries. (See pages 12 and 13, figures 2 and 6.)

WRY TAIL: Tail of fowl permanently carried to one side.

Figure 33.
Wry-Tail.
(A Disqualification.)

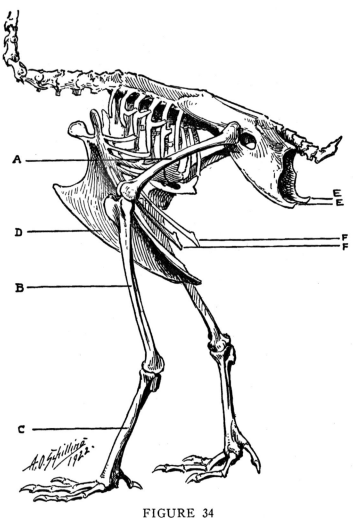

FIGURE 34

SKELETON SHOWING FRAMEWORK OF FOWLS

A. Thigh or upper thigh (femur)
B. Lower thigh (tibia)
C. Shank (metatarsus)
D. Breast or keel bone (sternum)
E.E. Pubic bones
F.F. Lateral processes of sternum

30

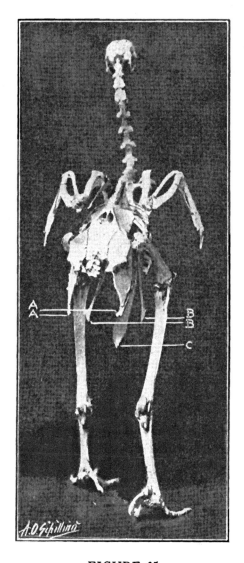

FIGURE 35

SKELETON OF FOWL (REAR VIEW)

A.A. Pubic bones   B.B. Lateral processes of sternum
C. Rear of keel bone (sternum)

Showing width carried well back. Spread between pubics and between pubic points and rear of sternum indicates laying condition.

31

INSTRUCTIONS TO JUDGES

FOR ECONOMIC QUALITIES OF STANDARD-BRED FOWLS

Standard-bred poultry is practical poultry, because most of the different breeds produce eggs, or meat, or both, to greater economic advantage than non-Standard stock. The purpose of the STANDARD OF PERFECTION is to establish those ideal types that are not alone the most beautiful and symmetrical but also the most useful and productive.

It should be understood that every Standard breed and variety produces both meat and eggs. Some breeds excel in egg production and some in the production of meat. The most rapid and economic producers of meat are often economic producers of eggs, while on the other hand, the meat of the highest egg producers is ultimately consumed as food.

The breeder cannot afford to sacrifice the economic qualities of his breed. It is important that he should maintain the size, type and color that are characteristic of the breed and variety, and it is vitally important that he should maintain that soundness of constitution which is necessary if vigor, size, type, color, and production are to be developed to their highest perfection.

Over emphasis of undercolor of plumage should be avoided.

The desired surface color is essential to the beauty of the specimen but undercolor is primarily a breeder's consideration; it should not be given undue consideration in judging.

The head is of great importance as it is indicative of the temperament and vigor, or lack of vigor, of the specimen. In all breeds where high egg production is especially desirable, particular emphasis should be laid on the character of the head and eye. The head should be fairly strong, inclined to be flat on top, rather than round, fairly long but well enough filled in forward of the eyes to avoid any appearance of crow-headedness. The face should be clean-cut, free from wrinkles, skin fine in texture, comb of fair substance. The over-refined, thin type of comb is not only liable to buckle or show thumb marks but is indicative of lack of constitutional vigor. The eye should be bright, full

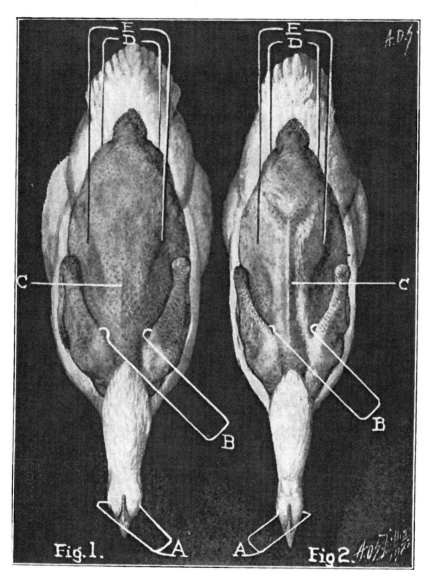

Figure 36
DESIRABLE HEAD AND BODY CHARACTERISTICS

DEFECTIVE HEAD AND BODY CHARACTERISTICS

Figure 1, left—Desirable Head and Body Characteristics.
Figure 2, right—Undesirable Head and Body Characteristics.
Compare: A, for width of skull; B, point at which heart girth is measured;
    C, showing width of back; E, hips, and D, at end of pubic points.

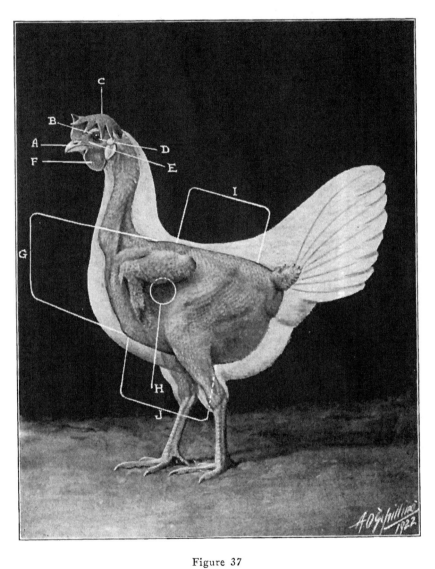

Figure 37

HEAD AND BODY CHARACTERISTICS INDICATIVE OF
VIGOR AND PRODUCTIVENESS

EXPLANATION OF FIGURE 37

A, Beak—properly proportioned.

B, Skull—properly proportioned.

C, Comb—thick at base, properly developed.

D, Eye—expressing vigor and alertness.

E, Face—full and of smooth texture.

F, Wattles—properly developed.

G, Body—deep, broad, well-developed.

H, Heart girth—of ample circumference, most easily measured by span of thumb and fingers over back extended downward back of wings.

I, Back—broad, flat.

J, Keel—of good length.

Note: Compare with Figure 38, page 36, showing defective head and body characteristics.

Figure 38

HEAD AND BODY CHARACTERISTICS SHOWING A LACK OF
VIGOR AND PRODUCTIVENESS

EXPLANATION OF FIGURE 38

A, Beak—shallow, narrow, long—improperly proportioned.

B, Skull—narrow.

C, Comb—thin, undeveloped.

D, Eye—small, sunken, showing lack of vigor.

F, Wattles—undeveloped.

E, Face—small, sunken.

G, Body—shallow, undeveloped.

H, Heart Girth—small.

I, Back—narrow, sloping.

J, Keel—short, making breast too flat.

Compare with Figure 37, page 34, for indication of Vigor and Productiveness.

and very prominent, with a keen, alert expression, indicative of vigor. This must not be interpreted to mean that breed type is to be disregarded. In judging classes such as Brahmas and Wyandottes the foregoing description must be considered relatively, rather than literally, as these breed types demand a more massive type of head than do many of the others. (See pages 16, 17, and 22.)

Judges are instructed to recognize those characteristics of body-shape that are typical of a useful and productive fowl and give full consideration to those fundamental qualities of body-type that are necessary to maintain vigor, usefulness and productiveness at the highest point consistent with true breed type.

Judges shall consider not only the external appearance, which is somewhat dependent upon plumage development, but shall also handle each specimen in order to ascertain the true conformation of body as determined by the actual shape of the carcass and to ascertain its condition as to health and fleshing. Irreparable damage may be done by failing to do this and awarding prizes to birds that may appear to the eye good in color and excellent in type, but that are in reality poorly fleshed and emaciated to the point of being a danger to the race.

In breeds in which the back shape is described as "broad" the judge shall handle the bird to determine if the carcass actually carries the desired breadth. Where the back is described as "broad its entire length," the carcass should actually carry the desired width not only at the shoulders and hips, but from the hips to the stern, and a specimen whose carcass narrows decidedly from hips to stern is just as faulty as though it was narrow across the saddle or cushion. In other words, this Standard description of back, "broad its entire length," applies to the carcass (or body shape) and to the appearance of specimen in plumage (or typical shape). (See pages 33, 34, and 36.)

A large heart girth is necessary for adequate lung capacity and for the proper functioning of the heart, upon both of which depend the maintenance of vigor and productivity. Heart girth is measured by determining the width of the back and the depth of the body immediately behind he wings. (See page 34.)

A large abdomen or body cavity is necessary for large intestinal development, which is essential for the rapid digestion and assimilation of that quantity of food and nutrients required for heavy egg production. Judges are, therefore, instructed that they shall determine the depth and fullness of this section by handling when the Standard description of body reads "deep and full"; and as a convenient form of measurement the judge may place his thumb on the hip bone and span the sides of the body to the keel bone back of legs with his hand and fingers. A shallow body as determined by handling shall be adjudged deficient in shape characteristics when the Standard says that the body shall be "deep and full." (See pages 34 and 36.)

The period of moulting and degree of pigmentation are valuable aids in culling operations and are largely dependent upon the kind and amount of feed supplied and the seasonal conditions, but are not of fundamental breed character. Many rules that may be applicable in culling should not be confused with judging.

FOR CAPON CLASSES

CAPONS: Capons should be shown in but one class and judged by comparison only. Capons less than one year old should have at least the weight required by the Standard for cockerels of the variety shown. Capons over one year old should have at least the Standard weight required of cocks of the variety shown.

Capon classes should be judged for conformity with their particular Standard breed-type and variety characteristics.

A capon which shows development of comb, wattles or earlobes must be classed as a "slip" and disqualified.

The tendency of a capon is to put on flesh and settle down. Such development affects the type; therefore, all capons should be judged for the quality and proper distribution of flesh; for weight, as proportionate to breed, and for breed-type and other breed characteristics. Capons which show impurity of breeding or that are decidedly lacking in breed or variety characteristics must be disqualified. Merely technical disqualifications that do not interfere with market quality shall not apply.

FOR THE BABY CHICK CLASSES

The growing importance of the Baby Chick industry with the increasingly large numbers produced and sold has made it imperative that accurate color descriptions of the different breeds and varieties be provided.

Because of the variations in color and markings of baby chicks of the different Standard breeds and varieties, as well as the possible variations of markings in the same variety due to ancestral blood lines, the color descriptions following should assist materially in identifying the purity of breed characters of baby chicks.

These descriptions present in a general way the color characteristics of chicks of the Standard breeds and varieties. It must be understood that variations, when they do appear, do not necessarily indicate impure blood.

RULES FOR CUTTING FOR DEFECTS

VIGOR:

Deduct from one-half to one point for each chick not showing the maximum of alert, snappy, lively activity upon arrival.

CONDITION:

Deduct from one to two points for each deformity.

Deduct from one-half to two points for each imperfectly healed navel.

Deduct from one-half to one point for each pasty vent.

Deduct from one-half to one point for each chick showing signs of a sticky hatch.

TRUENESS TO VARIETY COLOR:

Deduct from one-fourth to one-half point for each chick whose down color varies decidedly from the Standard color for the breed or variety.

Deduct from one-half to one point for each chick with shank color differing from that required for the breed or variety.

UNIFORMITY OF COLOR:

Deduct one-fourth point for each chick whose down color or shank color differs from that of the majority of the entry.

UNIFORMITY OF SIZE:

Deduct one-fourth point for each chick that varies in size from the average of the entry.

WEIGHT:

The Standard weight for an entry of 25 chicks is two pounds net. Deduct one point for every ounce the entry falls below this weight.

DEAD CHICKS:

Deduct five points from the total score of the entry for each chick dead upon arrival at the show.

STANDARD COLOR FOR BABY CHICKS

BARRED PLYMOUTH ROCKS

GENERAL COLOR: Slaty black, most densely black on back, shading lighter on sides of body, which is creamy white underneath, this color extending up on breast and part way up on front of neck. The wings sometimes show light spots at ends and the top of the head sometimes has a more or less distinct spot of creamy white.

BEAK, SHANKS AND TOES: Yellow to dark slate. Bottoms of feet, yellow.

WHITE PLYMOUTH ROCKS

GENERAL COLOR: Bluish gray, creamy white, or white.

BEAKS, SHANKS AND TOES: Yellow, sometimes shading to light gray.

BUFF PLYMOUTH ROCKS

GENERAL COLOR: Buff, varying from rich or dark to a light shade of buff.

BEAK, SHANKS AND TOES: Yellow.

SILVER-PENCILED PLYMOUTH ROCKS

GENERAL COLOR: Light gray, with a distinct, fairly broad stripe of rich chestnut down covering the center of back, bordered with two narrow distinct stripes of a lighter color along the sides of back; the gray on the sides of body and breast shading lighter gradually towards the under part of body where it approaches a creamy white; a spot of rich chestnut on top of head.

BEAK, SHANKS AND TOES: Yellow, but shades may vary.

PARTRIDGE PLYMOUTH ROCKS

GENERAL COLOR: Varying shades of brown; light chestnut with a distinct and fairly broad band of rich chestnut covering

The following is the official score card of the American Poultry Association for judging exhibits of baby chicks:

OFFICIAL SCORE CARD

of

THE AMERICAN POULTRY ASSOCIATION

for

BABY CHICKS

Entry No. ....Class.................. ....

Exhibitor ....

Address ....

Chicks dead on arrival..Total Score................................

		Cuts	Remarks
Vigor	25		
Condition	25		
Trueness to variety color	15		
Uniformity of color..	15		
Uniformity of size.......	10		
Weight	10		
Dead chicks			
Total	100		

DISQUALIFICATIONS FOR BABY CHICKS

The following imperfections, because of their serious nature, disqualify the entry:

(1)   Comb of type foreign to the breed or variety.

(2)   In all breeds required to have unfeathered shanks, any down, feather or feathers. stub. stubs. or feather-like growth on shanks, feet, toes, or hocks; or unmistakable indications of down, feather, feathers, stub, or stubs having been plucked from same.

(3)   Side sprig on single combs.

(4)   Web feet in any breed of chickens, or abnormal number of toes for the breed or variety.

top of head and running through center of back to tail, bordered along sides of back with two narrow, distinct stripes of lighter color; a distinct, dark stripe on each side of face running from beak to back of head in line with the eyes, thus dividing the face; sides of body light chestnut gradually shading to a creamy white on breast and under-body.

BEAK, SHANKS AND TOES: Yellow, but shades may vary.

COLUMBIAN PLYMOUTH ROCKS

GENERAL COLOR: Bluish slate, some approaching creamy yellow, bluish slate color intensified on back; black spots on heads of some chicks.

BEAK, SHANKS AND TOES: Yellow, but shades may vary.

BLUE PLYMOUTH ROCKS

GENERAL COLOR: An even medium shade of slaty blue; breast and under part of body much lighter, approaching bluish white; tips of wings, light blue, approaching gray.

BEAK, SHANKS AND TOES: Varying between yellow and slate.

Note: White, black and speckled sports frequently come from Blue matings.

SILVER-LACED WYANDOTTES

GENERAL COLOR: Dark slate or gray; back, dark slate with a distinct stripe of gray on each side; breast, light gray shading to creamy white, then to gray under the body; wings, powdery gray shading to same shade as breast at ends; head, powdery gray, sprinkled with brown on top and showing patches of gray on face and sides of neck.

BEAK, SHANKS AND TOES: Yellow, but shades may vary.

GOLDEN-LACED WYANDOTTES

GENERAL COLOR: Reddish-brown and gray; back, chestnut, or black shaded with dark chestnut; breast and body, dark gray shading lighter toward the rear; head, rich chestnut shading to mahogany on neck with a tendency to show a ring of chestnut at base of neck.

BEAK, SHANKS AND TOES: Yellow, but shades may vary.

WHITE WYANDOTTES

GENERAL COLOR: Bluish gray, creamy yellow, or varying shades of yellow; some chicks show a distinct collar of darker yellow at base of neck.

BEAK, SHANKS AND TOES: Yellow, but shades may vary.

BLACK WYANDOTTES

GENERAL COLOR: Dark slate or black; front of neck, ends of wings, and fluff, white. Some chicks have white ring around the eyes.

BEAK, SHANKS AND TOES: Yellow, more or less shaded with darker color; bottoms of feet, yellow.

BUFF WYANDOTTES

See color description of Buff Plymouth Rock chicks.

PARTRIDGE WYANDOTTES

See color description of Partridge Plymouth Rock chicks.

SILVER-PENCILED WYANDOTTES

See color description of Silver-Penciled Plymouth Rock chicks.

COLUMBIAN WYANDOTTES

See color description of Columbian Plymouth Rock chicks.

BLACK JAVAS

See color description of Black Wyandotte chicks.

DOMINIQUES

GENERAL COLOR: Slaty black, most densely black on back, shading lighter on sides of body, which is creamy white underneath, which color extends up on breast and part way up on front of neck; wings of some chicks show light spots at ends; top of head, more or less distinctly spotted with creamy white.

BEAK, SHANKS AND TOES: Yellow to dark slate; bottoms of feet, yellow.

RHODE ISLAND REDS

GENERAL COLOR: Red, richest on back, with some chicks showing spots on head and stripes on back; the richer and more uniform the color, however, the better.

BEAK, SHANKS AND TOES: Yellow, but shades may vary.

RHODE ISLAND WHITES
GENERAL COLOR: Creamy white or yellow of varying shades.
BEAK, SHANKS AND TOES: Yellow, but shades may vary.

CHANTECLER
GENERAL COLOR: Creamy white or yellow of varying shades.
BEAK, SHANKS AND TOES: Yellow, but shades may vary.

JERSEY BLACK GIANTS
See color description of Black Wyandotte chicks.

LAMONAS
GENERAL COLOR: Creamy white or yellow of varying shades.
(See Chantecler.)

ASIATIC CLASS

LIGHT BRAHMAS
See color description of Columbian Plymouth Rock chicks.
SHANKS AND TOES: Down on outer sides of shanks, on outer toes, or on both outer and middle toes.

DARK BRAHMAS
See color description of Silver-Penciled Plymouth Rock chicks.
SHANKS AND TOES: Down on outer sides of shanks, on outer toes, or on both outer and middle toes.

BUFF COCHINS
See color description of Buff Plymouth Rock chicks.
SHANKS AND TOES: Down on shanks and outer and middle toes.

PARTRIDGE COCHINS
See color description of Partridge Plymouth Rock chicks.
SHANKS AND TOES: Down on shanks and outer and middle toes.

WHITE COCHINS
See color description of White Plymouth Rock chicks.
SHANKS AND TOES: Down on shanks and outer and middle toes.

BLACK COCHINS
See color description of Black Wyandotte chicks.
SHANKS AND TOES: Down on shanks, outer and middle toes.

BLACK LANGSHANS

PLUMAGE: See color description of Black Wyandotte chicks.

BEAK, SHANKS AND TOES: Flesh color with darker markings, but shades may vary; bottoms of feet pink; down on outer sides of shanks and outer toes.

WHITE LANGSHANS

PLUMAGE: See color description of White Plymouth Rock chicks.

BEAK, SHANKS AND TOES: Color, light slate; bottoms of feet, pink; down on outer sides of shanks and outer toes.

MEDITERRANEAN CLASS

DARK BROWN LEGHORNS

GENERAL COLOR: Dark reddish brown, some chicks with a lighter stripe on each side of back; breast, lighter in shade.

BEAK, SHANKS AND TOES: Dark horn.

LIGHT BROWN LEGHORNS

See color description of Partridge Plymouth Rock chicks.

WHITE LEGHORNS

GENERAL COLOR: Creamy white or yellowish white, the yellowish shades accentuated in spots on some chicks.

BEAK, SHANKS AND TOES: Yellow, but shades may vary.

BUFF LEGHORNS

See color description of Buff Plymouth Rock chicks.

BLACK LEGHORNS

See color description of Black Wyandotte chicks.

COLUMBIAN LEGHORNS

See color description of Columbian Plymouth Rock chicks.

RED LEGHORNS

See color description of Rhode Island Red chicks.

BLACK MINORCAS

PLUMAGE: See color description of Black Wyandotte chicks.

BEAK, SHANKS AND TOES: Dark horn; bottoms of feet, white.

WHITE MINORCAS

GENERAL COLOR: Creamy white in varying shades.

BEAK, SHANKS AND TOES: Shading from yellow to pinkish white; bottoms of feet, white.

BUFF MINORCAS

GENERAL COLOR: Buff; back, breast and body, light golden buff; head and neck, a darker shade of buff, dark spots showing on top of head of some chicks.

BEAK, SHANKS AND TOES: Shading from yellow to pinkish white; bottoms of feet, white.

BLUE ANDALUSIANS

See color description of Blue Plymouth Rock chicks.

BEAK, SHANKS AND TOES: Flesh color with darker shading.

ANCONAS

GENERAL COLOR: Black and white; back, black or rusty black shading to dark slate on body; breast, under part of body, and fluff, creamy yellow shading to white; end of wings, creamy yellow shading to yellow.

BEAK, SHANKS AND TOES: Yellow or dusky yellow.

BUTTERCUPS

GENERAL COLOR: Light golden buff; more or less of black markings on head, neck, back and wings; some chicks with black markings around eyes.

BEAK: Light to dark horn.

SHANKS AND TOES: Varying from pale yellow to dark green.

ENGLISH CLASS

BUFF ORPINGTONS

GENERAL COLOR: Light buff, some chicks with brown spots or stripes on head.

BEAK, SHANKS AND TOES: Shaded yellow to pinkish white. Bottoms of feet, pinkish white.

BLACK ORPINGTONS

PLUMAGE: See color description of Black Wyandotte chicks.

BEAKS, SHANKS AND TOES: Dark horn, bottoms of feet white.

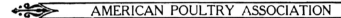

White Orpingtons

PLUMAGE: See color description for White Plymouth Rock chicks.

BEAK, SHANKS AND TOES: Shaded yellow to pinkish white; bottoms of feet, pinkish white.

Dark Cornish

GENERAL COLOR: Smoky or reddish buff; back on some chicks divided by two black stripes; head and neck smoky to dark reddish buff, accentuated on top of head; breast and under part of body, white or smoky white.

BEAK, SHANKS AND TOES: Yellow, but shades may vary.

White-Laced Red Cornish

GENERAL COLOR: White.

BEAK, SHANKS AND TOES: Yellow, but shades may vary.

White Cornish

See color description for White Plymouth Rock chicks.

Speckled Sussex

GENERAL COLOR: Creamy white or light buff, shading to light chestnut on back; chestnut spot on top of neck and shoulders; breast and under part of body, light buff or creamy white.

BEAK, SHANKS AND TOES: Shaded yellow to pinkish white; bottoms of feet, pinkish white.

FRENCH CLASS

Houdans

GENERAL COLOR: Black and yellowish white; back, sides of body including outer thighs, back of neck, markings below and back of eyes, and on some chicks front of crest, black. Crest, throat, breast, fluff and outer half of wings, lemon yellow.

COMB: V shaped, visible on careful examination.

NOSTRILS: Broad, highly arched, cavernous—highly characteristic.

BEAK, SHANKS AND TOES: Pink, beak on some chicks marked with black. Shanks on some chicks marked with black.

CREVECOEUR

GENERAL COLOR: Black on upper surface, white or creamy white on under surface.

NOSTRILS: Broad, highly arched.

BEAK, SHANKS AND TOES: Black.

LA FLECHE

GENERAL COLOR: Black on upper surface; breast may vary from black to almost pure white.

COMB: V shaped, the two points usually falling forward.

BEAK, SHANKS AND TOES: Black.

NOSTRILS: Noticeably broad, highly arched, cavernous.

SALMON FAVEROLLES

GENERAL COLOR: White, some chicks with dark markings on back; long down on upper throat extending well back of eyes indicating the characteristic beard and muffs.

BEAK, SHANKS AND TOES: Down on shanks and outer toes. Color, pink.

CONTINENTAL CLASS

CAMPINES

Golden

GENERAL COLOR: Medium brown; top of head, neck and center of back, medium brown bordered with a black stripe, balance of back and extending under body and breast, brownish white with black stripe extending along each side of back. Wings, a mixture of gray, brown and black.

FACE: Spotted brown and black.

BEAK, SHANKS AND TOES: Pinkish white to pinkish gray.

Silver

GENERAL COLOR: Gray; top of head, neck and center of back, medium gray, bordered with black stripe; balance of back and extending under body and breast, grayish white with a black stripe extending along each side of back. Wings, a mixture of gray and black, face spotted black and light gray.

BEAK, SHANKS AND TOES: Pinkish white to pinkish gray.

SUMATRAS

See color description of Black Wyandottes.

FOR JUDGING IN GENERAL

BRASSINESS: In White varieties, brassiness on surface of plumage is a serious defect and is to be discounted accordingly.

COLOR DEFECTS: A few very small, grayish specks in white fowls shall not debar a specimen that is otherwise superior in color from winning over one less typical in shape and sound in color; provided, however, that the gray specks do not appear prominently in the primary, secondary, or main-tail feathers.

Brown or black in quills of primaries or secondaries of white varieties should not be confused with the color often found on the under side of the feather, due to coagulation of blood, which causes stains visible on the upper side of the feather.

DATED SCORE CARDS: All score cards made out by judges applying the Standard are to be dated with ink, indelible pencil, or stamp on the date the specimens are scored.

DEFECTIVE SCORE CARD: It shall be considered irregular for a judge to sign a score card unless the weight of all breeds and varieties having Standard weights is considered, regardless of the season.

EXPLANATION OF TERMS IN SHAPE DESCRIPTION: When such words as "broad," "medium," "deep," etc., are used in the Standard descriptions of the breeds, these descriptive terms shall be interpreted as meaning broad, medium, or deep in proportion to the size and character of the breed described. In other words, "medium" as applied to the size of the Orpington male and female combs does not mean that the comb on the male should be of the same size as the comb on the female but that the male's comb should be medium in size in proportion to the characteristic size of the male sex; again, "medium" as applied to the combs of both the Plymouth Rock and Orpington males does not mean that the Standard Orpington should carry a Plymouth Rock comb, but should carry a medium sized comb in proportion to the size and bulk of the Orpington breed. (See page 212 and page 213.)

FAKING: As applied to exhibition poultry, "Faking" refers to the employment of artificial means to create the appearance of merit which the specimen does not possess naturally. Subjecting a specimen to one or more of the following processes constitutes "Faking" and shall debar the specimen so treated from competition: The obvious bending or breaking down of sickles or maintail feathers; the crimping or bending back of saddle feathers; the artificial coloring of lobes, faces, beaks, shanks, toes or plumage; the removal of white from lobes or faces required to be red; removing red in faces or lobes required to be white; evidence of any alteration to cover up a disqualification; evidence of removing a feather or feather-like growth as confirmed by a hole or indication of such in shanks or toes; the singeing or dyeing of feathers; the use of artificial coloring on any part or parts of the specimen; cutting, trimming, or mutilating any section except the dubbing of Games and Game Bantams; subjecting any white specimen to any process or treatment which leaves the skin in an irritated or inflamed condition, the feathers brittle, or which destroys the natural life and appearance of the feathers; or subjecting any colored or parti-colored specimen to any process that has resulted evidently in deepening, softening, intensifying or altering the shade or tone of the color of plumage. And, furthermore, the appearance and condition of the plumage shall constitute sufficient evidence to justify the action by the judge, as will be found specified under "General Disqualifications," (page 61).

JUDGING DUCKS AT SUMMER OR FALL SHOWS: In judging Rouen or Call drakes at the summer or fall exhibitions, due allowance should be made for the summer moult common to males of those varieties.

MERIT: The merit of specimens shall be determined by a careful examination of all sections in the "Scale of Points," beginning with weight or size and continuing through the list, deducting from the full value of each section of a perfect specimen for such defects as are found. Judges must familiarize themselves with the Scale of Points of each breed they are to pass upon to award prizes intelligently. It must be understood that no more and no less value can be placed on any section than is provided for in the Scale of Points. It shall be understood further that the requirements of the Standard of Perfection must be applied whether judged by score card or comparison.

The minimum cut for any section shall be one-fourth of one point.

In awarding prizes, judges must consider carefully each and every section of the specimen according to the Scale of Points and not allow color alone, or any one or two sections, to determine their decisions. The vital importance of typical shape is to be borne constantly in mind, though at the same time due consideration is to be given to color in all sections, including undercolor. All specimens in competition must be handled and examined by the judge, except those that show decided inferiority as seen in coops.

In judging it is imperative that Shape be considered of greatest importance. Specimens lacking in this essential breed characteristic shall not be awarded first honors, even though there be no competition.

OLD AND YOUNG SPECIMENS: All other points being equal, when prizes are offered on old and young specimens competing together, the former shall be awarded the prizes.

PRIVATE SCORING: Private scoring of specimens, except by licensed A. P. A. judges using American Poultry Association Score Cards, is not advisable and members of this Association are directed not to lend their support to the practice as a selling method.

QUALITY ENTITLING SPECIMENS TO PRIZES: To receive a first prize, the specimen must, in the opinion of the judge, score 90 points or more, except cocks of all parti-colored varieties, which may be awarded first prize, provided they score 88 points or more. For each receding prize, drop one point. A pen to win first prize must score 180 points or more, unless it contains a cock of a parti-colored variety, in which case 178 points or more may win first prize, but first prize shall not be given on a pen if the male in pen scores less than 88 points, or any female less than 85 points.

Judges shall not be required to score turkeys or water fowls.

FEATHER QUALITY: Feather formation is important in all varieties as an indication of health and vigor as adding to the beauty and attractiveness of the specimen and especially is this true in the formation of the portions defined as "web." In this section the barbs should be closely and completely hooked together, giving the appearance of a smooth, fine surface. This applies to both males and females.

The following feather description applies to females and such sections of the male as conform generally to the feather type of the female.

In Cochins, the feathers should be broad, long, soft, carried loosely on body. Fluff, long and abundant.

In Brahmas the plumage is more compact than in Cochins. Extreme fluffiness should be avoided.

In Langshans, the American, the English except Cornish, and the French varieties, the feathers should be moderately long and broad, carried fairly close to the body.

In Mediterranean, Hamburg, Polish and Continental varieties, the feathers should be moderate in length and breadth, fitting rather closely to body.

In Games and Game Bantams, Malay and Malay Bantams, feathers short, rather narrow, hard and firm, little fluff, held very close to body.

In Cornish, the feathers should be close fitting as in the Game varieties but wider.

Wherever size of feather is described in the Standard text of a variety, judges are to consider and value' this character of the feather in relation to feather pattern. Wherever size of feather is referred to in the shape description of a breed, it shall be considered a shape characteristic in all varieties of that breed. Judges should familiarize themselves with quality of feather. (See definition of "Feather," page 18.)

VARIATION OF PIGMENTATION: Fading from the color described as Standard in beak, skin or leg color shall not be considered a defect when such fading is the natural result of heavy egg production or age.

Scaly Legs: A fowl whose legs and toes are so deformed by what is called "Scaly Legs" as to hide, or appear to have destroyed, the color shall not be awarded a first prize.

Score of Exhibition Pen: To ascertain the score of an exhibition pen, add the scores of the females together and divide the sum by the number of females in the pen; to the quotient thus obtained add the score of the male and this sum shall be the score of the exhibition pen.

Size and Weight: To determine size, the judge shall decide by comparing the specimens in competition, or by demanding the weighing of such specimens, in case weight is required by the Standard. In all varieties (except Call and East India Ducks), having a section termed "Size" and not being subject to weight clauses, the largest specimen, other things being equal, shall win; in Call and East India Ducks, this rule is reversed and the smallest specimens shall win, except those abnormally small.

Sweepstake Prize: In awarding sweepstake prizes, only specimens in such classes as are recognized by and described in the Standard of Perfection can be considered.

All Standard fowls, including Bantams, Water Fowls, and Turkeys, are eligible to compete for Sweepstake Prizes.

Ties: In case of ties between two or more specimens that cannot be broken by any of the rules stated in the following paragraph—(Weight)—the specimen receiving the smallest total sum of cuts for shape shall be awarded the prize. In case of ties on exhibition pens at score card shows, when one of the tying pens contains all old and the other all young specimens, the adult pen shall win; when the tying pens are both adult or both young, the pen containing the highest scoring male shall win; when the tying pens contain females of mixed ages, the pen containing the highest scoring male shall win; when one of the pens contains all hens or all pullets while the other contains females of mixed ages, the pen having the females either all adult or all young shall win; when the tie cannot be broken by any of the above rules, the pen containing the lowest total of shape cuts in the five main shape sections shall win. In deciding ties at score card shows, or by comparison judging, the specimen or pen showing superior merit in uniformity of shape and color shall be awarded the prize.

Weight: (a) All specimens shall be judged according to

their Standard weights, provided, however, that the disqualifying weight for young specimens, except Bantams and those ducks prized for their smallness, shall not apply until December 1st of each year. It shall be understood that disqualifying weights on adult specimens are to apply at all times. (b) In all breeds having weight clauses, except Bantams and those ducks prized for their smallness, deduct two points per pound up to limit of section for amount lacking from Standard weights, and in that proportion for any fractional part of a pound, using one-fourth pound as a minimum, the specimen to have the benefit of any fraction less than one-fourth pound. (c) In all varieties of Bantams, deduct one-half point per ounce for any excess over Standard weights. (d) In all varieties having weight clauses, except Bantams and Ducks prized for their smallness, deduct two points per pound for any excess over Standard weight, using one-fourth pound as a minimum; providing, however, that one pound of excess over Standard weight be allowed on fowls and Ducks, and two pounds on Geese and Turkeys. (e) In all varieties, except Bantams and Ducks prized for their smallness, when adult specimens are equal in score and are above or below Standard weight, the one nearest Standard weight shall be awarded the prize, except when one specimen is cut for weight and the others are not, the specimen that is Standard weight or above shall be awarded the prize. (f) All chicks or immature specimens, except Bantams and those varieties prized for their smallness, having an equal score, when one or more are cut for lack of weight, the one of less weight shall be awarded the prize; but when each of such specimens are of Standard weight, or over, the one nearest Standard weight shall be awarded the prize. (g) In all varieties of Bantams, and those varieties of Ducks

Figure 39
1, Front. 2, Bow. 3, Bar. 4, Secondary.
5, Primaries. 6. Primary Coverts.

prized for their smallness, other things being equal, the specimen nearest Standard weight shall win.

(*Caution*—The weight clause must not be understood to mean that a small but over-fat specimen is within the spirit of the meaning of the Standard; the size must be proportionate to the weight, preserving the ideal shape and type of the Standard specimen.)

WING DIVISION: In discounting the color of wings, due consideration shall be given to all sections as shown in Figure 39, page 55.

CUTTING FOR DEFECTS

These cuts should not be confused with nor take precedence over the valuation given each section in the Scale of Points of all varieties.

Judges, in applying the score card or in awarding prizes by the comparison method, are to discount for the more common defects, as follows:

COMBS

	Points
Frosted combs	½*
Too many or too few points on single combs, each	½
Thumb mark on comb, not less than	1
Rear of comb turning around	½ to 1
Coarse texture of comb	½ to 1
Roughness, irregularity, hollow-center, over-size and ill-shape in comb of rose-comb varieties, each defect	½ to 2
More than one spike on rear of rose-comb, each	1½

Inverted or telescope rear portion on combs not less than two points.

HEAD AND ADJUNCTS

Coarse texture of wattles	½ to 1
For black in bean or bill of white ducks (females) when not a disqualification	½ to 2
Color of eyes not as described for the different varieties, each	¼ to 1½

Red eye in Campines. Cut to color limit.

If eye is destroyed, leaving only the socket	1½

Red in comb, face or wattles of Silkies ½ to 1 in each section where found.

*To shape limit.

If eye shows permanent injury, but retains its form..... ½ to 1
Red markings directly above the eyes of White-Faced
    Black Spanish .... ½ to 2½
For positive white in face of cocks and hens of Medi-
    terranean class, except in White-Faced Black
    Spanish .... ½ to 2
For dewlap (excessive development of throatiness)
    when not a required breed characteristic.................... ½ to 1

WINGS

For missing feather or part of feather in primaries or
    secondaries, where foreign color disqualifies.......... 1   to 2
When feather is broken, but not detached, in prima-
    ries or secondaries where foreign color disqualifies ½
For broken or missing feather in primaries or second-
    aries of buff or parti-colored varieties, where for-
    eign color does not disqualify .... ½ to 1

TAILS

Absence of sickles, where foreign color disqualifies,
    for each sickle 1½
Absence of sickles, where foreign color does not dis-
    qualify, for each sickle 1
Absence of one or more main-tail feathers in varieties
    subject to color disqualifications, each 1
Absence of one or more main-tail feathers in varieties
    not subject to color disqualifications, each.............. ½
Pinched or "Gamy" tails in Leghorn females.................. ½ to 2
If tail in any specimen shows not to exceed three-
    fourths development 1
If tail in any specimen shows not to exceed one-half
    development 2
If tail in any specimen shows not to exceed one-fourth
    development 3
Split Tail (in young birds) 2   to 2½
    (in old birds a disqualification)

LEGS AND TOES

Feathered middle toes in Langshans............................... ½ to 1½
For each bare middle toe in Brahmas and Silkies.............. 1
Crooked toes, each .... ½ to 2
Double spurs in all varieties except Sumatras, each........ ½

Horny, well-defined spurs on females, each.................... ½
For dark spots on shanks or toes in all breeds and
   varieties required to have yellow, white or pinkish
   white shanks and toes, except Anconas and
   Houdans .... ¼ to 2

DEFORMITIES

Crooked breast or keel-bone in all fowls except Tur-
   keys .... ½ to 2
Crooked breast or keel-bone in turkeys under "Deform-
   ities of shape and plumage" page 61

COLOR OF PLUMAGE

Brassiness in all varieties, in each section where found 1   to 2
Creaminess of plumage or quill in white varieties,
   except where specified creamy white, in each
   section where found .... ¼ to 1½
Gray specks in any part of plumage of white varieties,
   in each section where found .... ¼ to 2
Purple barring in plumage of any variety, in each
   section where found .... ½ to 2
Lack of luster on surface plumage of all varieties, in
   each section calling for luster....................................... ½ to 1
Irregular barring in Barred Plymouth Rocks, in each
   section where found .... ¼ to 2
In Barred Plymouth Rocks, for black feather or
   feathers (See color disqualifications for this
   variety) in each section where found........................... ¼ to 2
Metallic, brassiness, or any foreign cast on surface of
   Barred Plymouth Rocks, in each section where
   found .... ½ to 2
Bronze or brassiness in plumage of red varieties, in
   each section where found .... ½ to 2
Irregular or deficient penciling in penciled varieties,
   in each section where found .... ¼ to 2
Irregular, indistinct, crescentic or too heavy lacing in
   laced varieties, in each section where found............ ¼ to 1½
Frosty edging in any laced section of laced or spangled
   varieties, in each section where found....................... ¼ to 1½
Mossy-centered feathers in laced varieties, in each
   section where found .... ½ to 2½

Mealiness in plumage of buff or red varieties, in each section where found .... ½ to 2

Light colored shafting in buff or red varieties, in each section where found .... ½ to 1½

Black or white in buff varieties, in each section where found, cut from one-half to the color limit of the sections.

Slate under-color in Rhode Island Reds, in each section where found .... ¼ to 1½

Slate under-color in buff varieties, in each section where found .... ½ to 2

Gray or white in any except disqualifying sections of plumage of all Partridge varieties and Brown Leghorns, cut .... ½*

White or gray barring in main-tail feathers of Bronze turkeys when not a disqualification (See Disqualifications for Turkeys) .... ½ to 2

*To color limit.

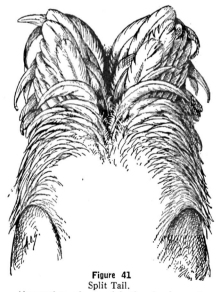

Figure 40
Split Wing
(A Disqualification.)

Figure 41
Split Tail.
Abnormal or sub-normal feather development.
In young birds a defect—in old birds a disqualification.

AMERICAN POULTRY ASSOCIATION

OFFICIAL SCORE OR COMPARISON JUDGING CARD
of
AMERICAN POULTRY
ASSOCIATION

Exhibitor .... Weight......................

Address ....

Variety .... Sex...........................

Entry No. .... Band No. .... Coop No. ....

Remarks	Shape	Symmetry	Remarks	Color
		Weight or Size		
		Condition and Vigor		
		Comb		
		Beak		
		Head		
		Eyes		
		Wattles		
		Ear-Lobes		
		Neck		
		Wings		
		Back		
		Tail		
		Breast		
		Body and Fluff		
		Legs and Toes		
		†Crest and Beard		
		*Hardness of Feather		
Total Shape Cuts......			Total Color Cuts......	
TOTAL CUTS			TOTAL SCORE.......	

Disqualified for ....

Award ....

Date .... Place...............................

.... Judge

.... Secretary

NOTE:—For scoring, each section receives its numerical cut. For comparison the Judge checks as follows: v, excellent; xxxx, good; xxx, fair; xx, poor; x, very poor.
†Applies to Crested Breeds.   *Applies to Games and Game Bantams.
Copyright, 1926, American Poultry Association.

60

GENERAL DISQUALIFICATIONS

If, in applying the Standard of Perfection, judges find any of the defects described below, they shall disqualify the specimen and state on the proper card or blank the nature of the disqualification; though it must be understood that under all disqualifying clauses, the specimen shall have the benefit of the doubt.

These general disqualifications are, for the most part, defects which are transmitted from the parents to the progeny. Some of them have been shown to be definitely inherited in a Mendelian manner. Although these defects, with the exception of disqualifications for weight requirements and color of skin, may not interfere with the utilitarian purpose of the fowl, they are, nevertheless, objectionable from the viewpoint of appearance. Furthermore, continued selection against these defects in the breeding stock soon results in the birds raised each year being comparatively free of disqualifications.

GENERAL INFERIORITY

Specimens unworthy of a score or lacking in breed characteristics.

Faking in any manner shall disqualify the specimen. (See definition of faking page 18 and instructions to judges page 51.)

DEFORMITIES OF SHAPE AND PLUMAGE

Deformed beaks.

Crooked or otherwise deformed backs.

A wing showing clipped flights or secondaries, or both, except clipped flights in Canada or Egyptian Geese, or Muscovy, Call or East India Ducks.

A split wing. (See Glossary, page 59, figure 40.)

A slipped wing. (See Glossary, page 26, figure 28.)

Twisted feather or feathers in primaries or secondaries of wing and sickles or main-tail feathers or split tails in cocks of any variety.

Entire absence of main-tail feathers.

Wry tails.

A squirrel tail, in any breed except Japanese Bantams.

Crooked breast or keel bone in turkeys.

A scooped or deformed bill in drakes and ducks. (See Glossary, page 24, figure 27.)

Hen feathered males except in Sebright Bantams, Campines and Hennie Games.

Duck foot in all varieties.

Weight Requirements

In all breeds having weight clauses, except Leghorns, Anconas, Bantams, and Turkeys, any specimen falling more than two pounds below standard weight.

In Leghorns and Anconas males falling more than one and one-half pounds, and females more than one pound, under Standard weight.

In all varieties of Bantams, specimens more than four ounces above Standard weight.

In all varieties of Turkeys, specimens falling more than six pounds below Standard weight.

Comb

Lopped single or pea-comb, except in Mediterranean, Continental, New Hampshire, Lamona, Dorking and Frizzle females.

Lopped rose-comb falling to one side sufficiently to obstruct the sight; rose-combs sufficiently large to obstruct sight. Combs foreign to the breed.

Figure 42.
Showing Face Section.
(Any positive enamel white in this Section disqualifies Mediterranean cockerels and pullets except White-Faced Black Spanish.)

Split comb. (See page 21.) *Note*: A comb which merely turns over a trifle from the natural upright position is not to disqualify. To disqualify, a single-comb must fall below the horizontal plane where the comb begins to lop; a pea-comb must fall below the horizontal plane on level with top of head. (See page 21, figure 16.)

Side sprig or sprigs on all single-comb varieties. (See page 21, figure 17.)

Absence of spike in all rose-comb varieties.

A spike or spikes on a cushion comb.

Head and Adjuncts

Positive enamel white in the face of Mediterranean cockerels and pullets except White-Faced Black Spanish.

Positive enamel white in the ear-lobe of males or females of all American, Asiatic and English varieties, except Dorkings, Red-caps and Lamonas.

In varieties in which positive enamel white in ear-lobes disqualifies, it must be understood that judges shall not disqualify for mere paleness of lobe due to the general condition of the specimen.

In varieties in which positive enamel white is a disqualification, judges shall disqualify for unmistakable evidence of an attempt to remove the defect.

Black in the bill or bean of the drake of any white variety of Ducks.

Absence of crest, beard, or muff in any variety described as Crested, Bearded or Muffed. Any appearance of crest, beard, or muff in any variety for which it is not required.

SHANKS AND TOES

Decided bow-legs or knock-knees.

In all breeds required to have unfeathered shanks, any feather or feathers, stub or stubs, or feather-like growth on shanks, feet or toes; or unmistakable indications of feather, feathers, stub, stubs, or down having been plucked from same.

Entire absence of spurs on cocks.

Any down, stub or stubs, feather or feathers, or feather-like growth on shank, disconnected from feathers on thigh and below the hock joint. (See pages 12 and 13, figures 4 and 7.)

Plucked hocks.

Web feet in any breed of chickens.

In four-toed breeds, more or less than four toes on either foot. In five-toed breeds, more or less than five toes on either foot.

COLOR

Shank, shanks, foot, feet, or toes of color foreign to the breed.

Red or yellow in the plumage of any black variety. (See variety disqualifications.)

Black in quills of primaries or secondaries of white varieties. (See "Color Defects," Instructions to Judges.)

Foreign color in any part of the plumage of white varieties, except slight gray ticking.

DESCRIPTIONS OF COMMON PLUMAGE COLORS AND COLOR PATTERNS

WHITE

Color of Male and Female

PLUMAGE: Web, fluff, and quills of feathers, in all sections, pure white.

BLACK
Color of Male and Female

PLUMAGE: Surface, lustrous, greenish black; under-color, dull black, except otherwise specified.

BUFF
Color of Male and Female

PLUMAGE: Surface throughout an even shade of rich golden buff, the head, neck, hackle, back, wing, bows and saddle richly lustrous in male and hackle of female showing some luster. Under-color matching surface as near as possible. See "Definition of Buff."

SILVER-PENCILED
Color of Male

HEAD: Plumage, silvery white.

NECK: Hackle, web of feather, solid, lustrous, greenish black, of moderate width, with a narrow edging of silvery white, uniform in width, extending around point of feathers; shafts, black; plumage on front of neck, black.

WINGS: Fronts, black; bows, silvery white; coverts, lustrous, greenish black, forming a well-defined bar of this color across wings when folded; primaries, black except a narrow edging of white on lower edge of lower webs; secondaries, black, except lower half of lower webs, which should be white, except near end of feathers at which point the white terminates abruptly leaving end of feathers black; the secondaries when folded forming a white wing-bay between the wing-bar and tips of secondary feathers.

BACK AND SADDLE: Silvery white on surface, free from brown; saddle, silvery white, with black stripe in each feather, tapering to a point near its lower extremity. A slight shafting of silver white permissible.

TAIL: Main-tail feathers, black; sickles and coverts, lustrous, greenish black; smaller coverts, lustrous, greenish black edged with white.

BREAST: Lustrous black.

BODY AND FLUFF: Body, black; lower body feathers, black slightly tinged with gray; fluff, black, slightly tinged with gray.

LEGS AND TOES: Lower thighs, black.

UNDER-COLOR OF ALL SECTIONS: Slate, shading lighter toward base of feather.

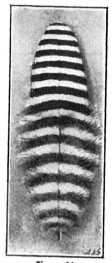

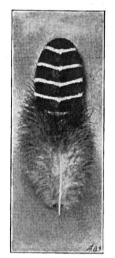

Figure 44

Barring, at right angle with
length of feather.
Feather of Female.
Example:
Barred Plymouth Rocks.

Figure 45

Barring, Slightly V-Shaped.
Example: Campines.

Figure 43

;, at right angle with
ength of feather.
Feather of Male.
Example:
d Plymouth Rocks.

Figure 46

Mossy (Defective) Feather.
Occurs most often in laced
varieties.

Figure 47

A Penciled Feather.
(Crescentic Form.)
Examples: Partridge; Silver-
Penciled Varieties.

Figure 48

A Penciled Feather.
(Parallel Form.)
Example: Hamburgs.

STANDARD AND DEFECTIVE COLOR PATTERNS

Figure 49
Laced Feather (Silver).
Examples:
Silver-Laced Wyandottes.

Figure 50
Frosting (A Defect).
Faulty in Laced Varieties.

Figure 51
Laced Feather.
Examples: Blue Varieties.

Figure 52
Mealy (Defective) Feather.
Occurs in Red and Buff
Varieties.

Figure 53
One Form of Shafting.
(A Defect.)
Occurs in Stippled Varieties.

Figure 54
A Stippled Feather.
Examples: Brown Leghorns
and Silver-Grey Dorkings, etc.

STANDARD AND DEFECTIVE COLOR PATTERNS

Figure 55
Spangled Feather.
(Hamburgs.)

Figure 56
Splashed Feather.
(A Defect.)
Occurs in Spangled
and Mottled Vari-
eties.

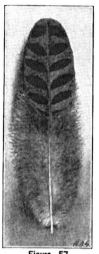

Figure 57
A Feather with Elon-
gated, Diagonal
Spangles.
(Buttercups.)

Figure 58
Feather Tipped with
Spangle.
(Speckled Sussex.)

Figure 59
A Striped Feather.
Male Hackles.

Figure 60
A Striped Feather
with Diamond-Shaped
Center.
(Saddles of Laced
Wyandottes.)

Figure 61
A Feather Tipped
with a Spangle.

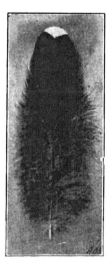

Figure 62
A Mottled Feather.
(Anconas, Mottled
Houdans.)

STANDARD AND DEFECTIVE COLOR PATTERNS

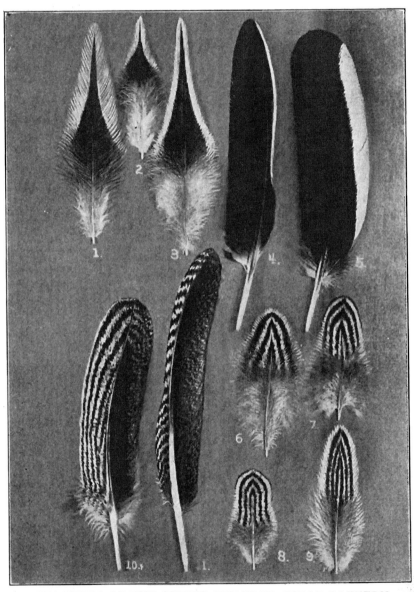

FEATHERS OF THE SILVER PENCILED COLOR PATTERN

Male feathers: 1, Hackle; 2, Back; 3, Saddle; 4, Primary; 5, Secondary.
Female feathers: 6, Back; 7, Wing-Bow; 8, Breast; 9, Neck; 10, Secondary; 11, Primary.

Color of Female

HEAD: Plumage, silvery gray.

NECK: Silvery white; center portion of feathers, black slightly penciled with steel gray; feathers on front of neck, same as breast.

WINGS: Fronts, bows and coverts, steel gray with distinct, soft black pencilings, outlines of which conform to shape of feathers; primaries, black with narrow edge of steel-gray penciling on lower webs; secondaries, upper webs, black, lower webs steel-gray with distinct, soft black pencilings extending around outer edge of feathers.

BACK: Steel-gray, with distinct, soft black pencilings, outlines of which conform to shape of feather; feathers, free from white shafting.

TAIL: Main-tail feathers, black, except the two top feathers, which are gray on upper web, and penciled with soft black; coverts, steel-gray with distinct, soft black pencilings, outlines of which conform to shape of feather.

BREAST: Steel-gray, with distinct, soft black pencilings, outlines of which conform to shape of feather.

BODY AND FLUFF: Body, steel-gray, with distinct, soft black pencilings, reaching well down on lower thighs; fluff, steel-gray, penciled with a darker shade.

LEGS AND TOES: Lower thighs, steel-gray, with distinct pencilings.

UNDER-COLOR OF ALL SECTIONS: Slate.

Note: Each feather in back, breast, body, wing-bows, and thighs to have three or more distinct pencilings. A sharp contrast between the dark pencilings and ground color is highly desirable.

PARTRIDGE
Color of Male

HEAD: Plumage, bright red.

NECK: Hackle, web of feather, solid, lustrous, greenish black of moderate width, with a narrow edging of a medium shade of rich, brilliant red, uniform in width, extending around point of feather; shaft, black; plumage on front of neck, black.

WING: Fronts, black; bows, a medium shade of rich, brilliant red; coverts, lustrous, greenish black, forming a well-defined bar of this color across wings when folded; primaries, black, lower edges, reddish bay; secondaries, black, outside webs, reddish bay, terminating with greenish black at end of each feather; the secondaries when folded forming a reddish bay wing-bay between the wing-bar and tips of the secondary feathers.

BACK AND SADDLE: A medium shade of rich, brilliant red, with lustrous, greenish black stripe down the middle of each feather, same as in hackle. A slight shafting of rich red permissible.

TAIL: Main-tail feathers, black; sickles and lesser sickles, lustrous greenish black; coverts, lustrous, greenish black, edged with a medium shade of rich, brilliant red.

BREAST: Lustrous black.

BODY AND FLUFF: Body, black; lower body feathers, slightly tinged with red; fluff, black, slightly tinged with red.

LEGS AND TOES: Lower thighs, black.

UNDER-COLOR OF ALL SECTIONS: Slate.

Color of Female

HEAD: Plumage, deep, reddish bay.

NECK: Reddish bay; center portion of feathers black; slightly penciled with deep reddish bay; feathers on front of neck, same as breast.

WINGS: Fronts, bows, and coverts, deep reddish bay, with distinct pencilings of black, outlines of which conform to shape of feathers; primaries, black with edging of deep, reddish bay on outer webs; secondaries, inner webs, black, outer webs deep, reddish bay, with distinct pencilings of black extending around outer edge of feathers.

BACK: Deep reddish bay, with distinct pencilings of black, the outlines of which conform to shape of feathers.

TAIL: Main-tail feathers, black, except the two top feathers, which are deep reddish bay on the upper web penciled with black; coverts, deep reddish bay penciled with black.

BREAST: Deep reddish bay, with distinct pencilings of black, the outlines of which conform to shape of feathers.

BODY AND FLUFF: Body, deep reddish bay, penciled with black; fluff, deep, reddish bay.

LEGS AND TOES: Lower thighs, deep reddish bay penciled with black.

UNDER-COLOR OF ALL SECTIONS: Slate.

Note: Each feather in back, breast, body, wing-bows, and thighs to have three or more distinct pencilings.

COLUMBIAN
Color of Male

HEAD: Plumage, white.

NECK: Hackle, web of feather, solid, lustrous, greenish black, moderately broad, with a narrow edging of silvery white, uniform in width, extending around point of feather; greater portion of shaft, black; plumage on front of neck, white.

WINGS: Fronts, white, may be partly black; bows and coverts, white; primaries, black, with white edging on lower edge of lower webs; secondaries, lower portion of lower webs, white, sufficient to form a white wing-bay, the white extending around ends of feathers and lacing upper portion of upper webs, this color growing wider in the shorter secondaries, sufficient to show white on surface when wing is folded; remainder of each secondary, black.

BACK AND SADDLE: Surface, white; cape, black and white; saddle, white except lower saddle feathers, which should be white with a narrow V-shaped black stripe at end of each feather, tapering to a point near its lower extremity and extending from points of wing to root and sides of tail. This V-shaped stripe increasing in width, length and density as it nears the tail-coverts.

TAIL: Main-tail feathers, black; the curling feathers underneath, black laced with white; sickles and coverts, lustrous, greenish black; smaller coverts, lustrous, greenish black edged with silvery white.

BREAST: White.

BODY AND FLUFF: Body, white, except under wings, where it may be bluish slate; fluff, white.

LEGS AND TOES: Lower thighs, white.

UNDER-COLOR OF ALL SECTIONS: Light bluish slate.

Color of Female

HEAD: Plumage, white.

NECK: Feathers beginning at juncture of head, web a broad, solid, lustrous, greenish black, with a narrow lacing of silvery white extending around the outer edge of each feather; greater portion of shaft, black; feathers on front of neck, white.

WINGS: Fronts, bows, and coverts, white; primaries, black with white edging on lower edge of lower webs; secondaries,

FEATHERS OF THE COLUMBIAN COLOR PATTERN

Male plumage: 1, Back; 2, Saddle adjoining Back; 3, Lower Saddle; 4, Upper Saddle adjoining Tail-Coverts; 5, Lower Hackle.

Female plumage: 6, Secondary; 7, Primary; 8, Tail-Covert; 9, Back; 10, Lower Neck.

lower portion of lower webs, white, sufficient to secure a white wing-bay, the white extending around the end and lacing upper portion of upper webs, this color growing wider in the shorter secondaries, sufficient to show white on surface when wing is folded; remainder of each secondary, black.

BACK: White; cape, black and white.

TAIL: Main-tail feathers, black, except the two top feathers, which are slightly edged with white; coverts, black with a narrow lacing of white.

BREAST: White.

BODY AND FLUFF: Body white, except under wings where it may be bluish slate; fluff, white.

LEGS AND TOES: Lower thighs, white.

UNDER-COLOR OF ALL SECTIONS: Light bluish slate.

BLUE

Color of Male

HEAD: Plumage, very dark, lustrous blue.

NECK: A clear, even, medium shade of slaty blue, each feather sharply laced with very dark, lustrous blue.

WINGS: Fronts and bows, a clear, even, medium shade of slaty blue, each feather sharply laced with very dark, lustrous blue; coverts, a clear, even, medium shade of slaty blue, each feather having a sharply-defined lacing of darker blue; primaries, a clear, even, medium shade of slaty blue laced with darker blue; secondaries, inner webs, a clear, even shade of slaty blue, outer webs, slaty blue, each feather sharply laced with darker blue.

BACK AND SADDLE: A clear, even, medium shade of slaty blue, each feather sharply laced with very dark, lustrous blue.

TAIL: Main-tail feathers, a clear, even, medium shade of slaty blue, each feather sharply laced with dark, lustrous blue; sickles, a clear, even, medium shade of slaty blue, each feather sharply laced with very dark, lustrous blue; tail-coverts, a clear, even, medium shade of slaty blue, each feather sharply laced with very dark, lustrous blue.

BREAST: A clear, even, medium shade of slaty blue, each feather having a sharply defined lacing of darker blue.

BODY AND FLUFF: Body, a clear, even, medium shade of slaty blue, each feather having a sharply defined lacing of darker blue; fluff, slaty blue, laced with darker blue.

73

LEGS AND TOES: Lower thighs, a clear, even shade of slaty blue, each feather having a sharply defined lacing of darker blue.

UNDER-COLOR OF ALL SECTIONS: Slaty blue.

Color of Female

HEAD: Plumage, slaty blue.

NECK: A clear, even, medium shade of slaty blue, sharply laced with darker blue.

WINGS: Fronts, bows and coverts, a clear, even, medium shade of slaty blue, each feather having a sharply defined lacing of darker blue; primaries, a clear, even, medium shade of slaty blue; remainder of wing an even shade of slaty blue, darker than that of primaries; feathers in all sections except primaries, sharply laced with darker blue.

BACK: A clear, even, medium shade of slaty blue, each feather having a sharply defined lacing of darker blue.

TAIL: A clear, even, medium shade of slaty blue, each feather laced with a darker blue.

BREAST: A clear, even, medium shade of slaty blue, each feather having a sharply defined lacing of a darker blue.

BODY AND FLUFF: Body, a clear, even, medium shade of slaty blue, each feather having a sharply defined lacing of darker blue; fluff, a clear, even, medium shade of slaty blue.

LEGS AND TOES: Lower thighs, slaty blue, each feather sharply laced with a darker blue.

UNDER-COLOR OF ALL SECTIONS: Slaty blue.

Note: All Blue varieties are considered as parti-colored varieties.

Note: Blue is not and cannot be an established pure color. It is a result of blending Black and White and occurs in a definite Mendelian manner. When Blues are mated together, the offspring will occur approximately in the proportion of one white splashed, to two blue to one black.

BREEDS AND VARIETIES OFFICIALLY RECOGNIZED BY THE AMERICAN POULTRY ASSOCIATION

CLASS 1

AMERICAN

Breeds	*Varieties*
PLYMOUTH ROCKS	Barred White Buff Silver-Penciled Partridge Columbian Blue
WYANDOTTES	Silver-Laced Golden-Laced White Black Buff Partridge Silver-Penciled Columbian
WYANDOTTE BANTAMS	White Black Buff Partridge Silver-Penciled Columbian
JAVAS	Black Mottled
DOMINIQUES	
RHODE ISLAND REDS	Single-Comb Rose-Comb
RHODE ISLAND WHITES	
CHANTECLERS	White Partridge
JERSEY BLACK GIANTS	
LAMONAS	
NEW HAMPSHIRES	

SCALE OF POINTS

American, Asiatic, Mediterranean, English, Continental, Hamburg, French Classes, Sumatras, Old English Games and Frizzles—All varieties of Bantams except Modern Games, Japanese and Polish.

	Solid Color White		Solid Color Other than White		Parti Color	
	Shape	Color	Shape	Color	Shape	Color
1. Symmetry	4		4		4	
* 2. Weight or size	4		4		4	
3. Condition and Vigor	10		10		10	
* 4. Comb	5		5		5	
5. Beak	2	1	2	1	2	1
* 6. Head	3	1	3	1	3	1
7. Eyes	2	2	2	2	2	2
8. Wattles	2		2		2	
* 9. Earlobes	2	2	2	2	2	2
10. Neck	3	3	2	4	1	5
11. Wings	5	3	4	4	3	5
*12. Back	8	4	7	5	6	6
13. Tail	5	3	4	4	4	4
14. Breast	7	3	5	5	5	5
15. Body and Fluff	5	3	5	3	4	4
16. Legs and Toes	5	3	5	3	5	3
	72	28	66	34	62	38

*Note: For the French class, substitute for sections 4, 6, 9 (parti color) the following:

Houdans and Crevecoeurs: Crest—shape 4, color 1; Comb 1; Head—shape 1; Beard—shape 2, color 1; Earlobes—shape 1, color 1.

Faverolles: Comb 4; Head—shape 1, color 1; Beard—shape 3, color 1; Earlobe—shape 1, color 1.

For Hamburgs

For Hamburgs: From section two, deduct 2 points and from section twelve, back shape, deduct 2 points. Add 2 points allotted in section 9, making it read "lobes—shape 4, color 4."

ROSE COMB BANTAMS

Rose Comb Bantams: Take 1 from section sixteen, shape of leg; 1 from fourteen, color of breast; 1 from twelve, color of back, and add 2 to shape of earlobe and 1 to color of earlobe. Take 1 from section 15, body and fluff, shape, and add to section four, comb, making it read, "comb 6."

SILKIES

Silkies: Take 2 points from section four, shape of comb, 2 from eleven, color of wings, and 1 from fourteen, color of breast, and add section Crest, 5 points, making shape 4, color 1.

PLYMOUTH ROCKS

The first breed of poultry to bear this name was first exhibited at America's first poultry show, held at Boston, Mass., 1849. It is believed that these fowls lost their identity and that the progenitors of our present Barred Plymouth Rocks were first exhibited at Worcester, Mass., in 1869. This breed is a composite of several blood lines. The first and most prominent cross was that of a Dominique male with Black Cochin or Black Java females, which was originally made at Putnam, Conn. The Dominique male used was not the American or Rose-Comb Dominique which became a Standard breed in 1874, but a single-combed, hawk-colored bird commonly kept in that locality. This was after the birth of the present-day Plymouth Rock, which already had been recognized as a distinctly new breed and was admitted to the first American Standard of Excellence, published at Buffalo, N. Y., January 15, 1874.

Whether the Plymouth Rock originated from a Dominique-Black Cochin or from a Dominique-Black Java cross was for a time a much mooted question. The historical fact that "Black Cochin" or "Black Java" had been used synonymously in show classifications before the first poultry standard was made in 1873 may have led to confusing the Java with the Cochin.

White Plymouth Rocks were admitted to the American Standard of Perfection in 1888. They were white sports of the Barred variety, though some strains trace their ancestry to other white fowls.

Buff Plymouth Rocks became a Standard variety in 1892. The earliest strains originated in Rhode Island, not far from Fall River, Mass., and were first exhibited as Golden Buffs. Buff Cochin blood was introduced in some strains produced in New York State.

Silver-Penciled Plymouth Rocks originated in the State of New York in 1894. Dark Brahma and Silver-Penciled Wyandotte blood lines produced this variety, which was admitted to the Standard in 1907.

Partridge Plymouth Rocks became a Standard variety in 1909. They originated in Indiana, in 1898, by the crossing of Partridge Cochin females with a dark Cornish male; the female offspring being mated (in 1899) to a Single-Comb Golden Wyandotte male.

Other strains were produced in the Eastern States in which the blood of Partridge Cochins, Brown Leghorns, Golden-Laced Wyandottes and Barred Plymouth Rocks was amalgamated to form the new variety. The variety, as we have it, is the result of later combinations of all strains.

Columbian Plymouth Rocks originated in Ohio in 1902, as the result of crosses between Light Brahmas, Barred Plymouth Rocks, White Plymouth Rocks, and Columbian Wyandottes. They were admitted to the Standard in 1910.

Blue Plymouth Rocks were admitted to the Standard at Kansas City, Missouri, in 1920.

ECONOMIC QUALITIES: Dual purpose fowls for the production of eggs and meat. Color of skin, yellow; color of egg shells, brown. There may be considerable difference in the shades or tints of the shells, which vary from a very light to a dark brown, depending on the strain and on the stage of production. Due attention should be paid to the Standard weights for Plymouth Rocks in order to insure vigorous breeding and laying females that will produce eggs weighing not less than twenty-four ounces per dozen. Texture of the feathers is also of paramount importance in both exhibition and utility specimens.

Disqualifications

(See General Disqualifications and Cutting for Defects, page 56, and fleshing qualities, page 38.)

STANDARD WEIGHTS

Cock	9½ lbs.	Hen	7½ lbs.
Cockerel	8 lbs.	Pullet	6 lbs.

SHAPE OF MALE

COMB: Single, rather small in proportion to size of specimen; set firmly on head; straight, upright; evenly serrated, having five well-defined points, those in front and at rear a little smaller than the other three, giving the comb a semi-oval appearance when viewed from the side; fine in texture; blade not conforming too closely to head. (See Standard illustration, page 80.)

BEAK: Stout, comparatively short, regularly curved.

HEAD: Moderately large; face, smooth. (See description of Head, page 22; see Standard illustration, page 80.)

EYES: Large, full, prominent.

WATTLES: Moderately long, nicely rounded at lower edges, uniform, fine in texture, free from folds or wrinkles.

EAR-LOBES: Oblong, smooth, hanging about one-third the length of wattles.

NECK: Rather long, moderately well-arched, having abundant hackle flowing well over shoulders.

WINGS: Of medium size, well folded and carried without drooping; fronts, well covered by breast feathers and points well covered by saddle feathers; primaries and secondaries, broad and overlapping in natural order when wing is folded.

BACK: Rather long, broad its entire length, flat at shoulders, nearly horizontal from neck to saddle, where there is a slight concave sweep to tail; saddle feathers, rather long, abundant, filling well in front of tail; feathers moderately broad.

TAIL: Of medium length, moderately well-spread, carried at an angle of thirty degrees above the horizontal (see illustrations and figures, pages 28 and 80), forming no apparent angle with the back; main-tail feathers, broad and overlapping; sickles, well-curved, covering tops of main-tail feathers, conforming to the general shape of the tail; lesser sickles and tail-coverts, of medium length, nicely curved and sufficiently abundant to almost hide the stiff feathers of the tail when viewed from front or side.

BREAST: Broad, full, moderately deep, well-rounded.

BODY AND FLUFF: Body, rather long, broad, deep, full, straight, extending well forward, connecting with breast so as to make no break in outline; fluff, moderately full.

LEGS AND TOES: Legs, set well apart and straight when viewed from front; lower thighs, large, of medium length and well-feathered, smooth; shanks, of medium length, smooth, straight, stout; toes, of medium size and length, straight, well-spread.

SHAPE OF FEMALE

COMB: Single, small, proportionate to size of specimen; set firmly on the head; straight, upright; evenly serrated, having five well-defined points, those in front and at rear being somewhat smaller and shorter than the other three. (See Standard illustration, page 81.)

BEAK: Comparatively short, regularly curved.

HEAD: Moderately large and broad, medium in length; face, smooth. (See Standard illustration, page 81.)

EYES: Large, full, prominent.

BARRED PLYMOUTH ROCK MALE

BARRED PLYMOUTH ROCK FEMALE

WATTLES: Small, well-rounded, uniform, fine in texture, conforming to size and shape of head.

EAR-LOBES: Oblong in shape, smooth.

NECK: Medium in length, nicely curved and tapering to head, where it is comparatively small; neck feathers moderately abundant, flowing well over shoulders with no apparent break at juncture of neck and back.

WINGS: Of medium size, well-folded and carried without drooping; fronts, well covered by breast feathers and points well covered by back feathers; primaries and secondaries, broad, and overlapping in natural order when wing is folded.

BACK: Rather long, broad in its entire length, flat at shoulders, rising with a slightly concave incline to tail; feathers moderately broad.

TAIL: Of medium length, fairly well-spread, carried at an angle of twenty degrees above the horizontal (see pages 28 and 80), forming no apparent angle with the back; tail-coverts, well-developed; main-tail feathers, broad and overlapping.

BREAST: Broad, full, moderately deep, well-rounded.

BODY AND FLUFF: Body, rather long, moderately deep, full, straight from front to rear and extending well forward, connected with the breast so as to make no break in outline; fluff, full, of medium length.

LEGS AND TOES: Legs, set well apart and straight when viewed from front; lower thighs, large, of medium length and well-feathered, smooth; shanks, of medium length, smooth and stout; toes, of medium size and length, straight, well-spread.

Note: See Instructions to Judges and paragraph "Quality of Feather," page 53.

BARRED PLYMOUTH ROCKS

Disqualifications

Red or yellow in any part of plumage; two or more solid black primaries, or two or more solid black secondaries, or two or more solid black main-tail feathers; shanks other than yellow. (See General Disqualifications and Cutting for Defects.)

COLOR OF MALE

COMB, FACE, WATTLES, AND EAR-LOBES: Bright red.

BEAK: Yellow.

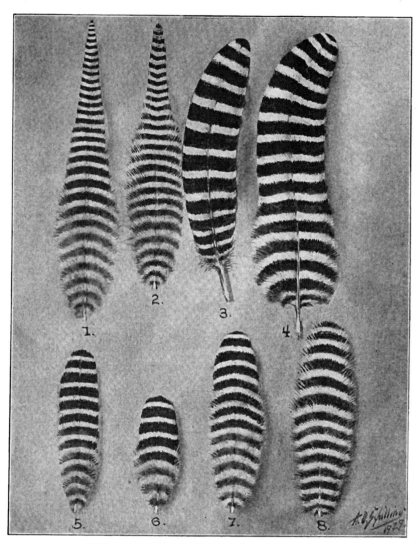

BARRED PLYMOUTH ROCK FEATHERS

Male: (1) Hackle, (2) Saddle. Female: (3) Secondary, (4) Main-tail, (5) Neck, (6) Breast, (7) Back, (8) Body.

WHITE PLYMOUTH ROCK MALE

WHITE PLYMOUTH ROCK FEMALE

BUFF PLYMOUTH ROCK MALE

BUFF PLYMOUTH ROCK FEMALE

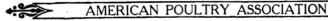

Eyes: Reddish bay.

Shanks and Toes: Yellow.

Plumage: Grayish white, each feather crossed by regular, parallel, sharply defined, dark bars that stop short of positive black; free from shafting, brownish tinge or metallic sheen; the light and dark bars to be of approximately equal width, in number proportionate to the length and width of the feathers, and to extend throughout the length of feathers in all sections of the fowl; each feather ending with a narrow, dark tip; the combination of overlapping feathers giving the plumage a bluish appearance and of an even shade throughout.

COLOR OF FEMALE

Plumage: Grayish white, each feather crossed by regular, parallel, sharply defined, dark bars that stop short of positive black; free from shafting, brownish tinge or metallic sheen. The light bar being approximately one-half the width of the dark bar; the bars, in all sections of the fowl shall be in numbers proportionate to the length and breadth of the feathers; each feather ending in a narrow, dark tip; the combination of over-lapping feathers giving the plumage a bluish appearance and of an even shade throughout.

Note: The barred color pattern as found in the Barred Plymouth Rocks is due to a sex-linked factor for barring so that the male receives twice the amount of light barring as the female. Therefore, if the male with light and dark bars of approximately even width is accepted as desirable, it is necessary for the female to which he is mated to have light bars approximately one-half as wide as the dark bars, if standard-bred males and females are to be produced by a single mating.

Note: This color description to go into effect March 1st, 1942. Color standard for Light and Dark Barred Rocks as published in supplement to 1930 edition to be in effect until then.

WHITE PLYMOUTH ROCKS

Disqualifications

Shanks other than yellow. (See General Disqualifications and Cutting for Defects.)

COLOR OF MALE AND FEMALE
COMB, FACE, WATTLES, AND EAR-LOBES: Bright red.
BEAK: Yellow.
EYES: Reddish bay.
SHANKS AND TOES: Rich yellow.
PLUMAGE: See description of White plumage color, page 63.

BUFF PLYMOUTH ROCKS
Disqualifications
Shanks other than yellow. (See General Disqualifications and Cutting for Defects.)

COLOR OF MALE AND FEMALE
COMB, FACE, WATTLES, AND EAR-LOBES: Bright red.
BEAK: Yellow.
EYES: Reddish bay.
SHANKS AND TOES: Rich yellow.
PLUMAGE: See description of Buff plumage color, page 64.

SILVER-PENCILED PLYMOUTH ROCKS
Disqualifications
Shanks and Toes other than yellow or dusky yellow. (See General Disqualifications and Cutting for Defects.)

COLOR OF MALE
COMB, FACE, WATTLES, AND EAR-LOBES: Bright red.
BEAK: Dusky yellow, shading to yellow at point.
EYES: Reddish bay.
SHANKS AND TOES: Yellow.
PLUMAGE: See description of Silver-Penciled plumage color, page 64.

COLOR OF FEMALE
COMB, FACE, WATTLES, AND EAR-LOBES: Bright red.
BEAK: Dusky yellow, shading to yellow at point.
EYES: Reddish bay.
SHANKS AND TOES: Dusky yellow.
PLUMAGE: See description of Silver-Penciled plumage color, page 69.

SILVER-PENCILED PLYMOUTH ROCK MALE

SILVER-PENCILED PLYMOUTH ROCK FEMALE

PARTRIDGE PLYMOUTH ROCK MALE

PARTRIDGE PLYMOUTH ROCK FEMALE

COLUMBIAN PLYMOUTH ROCK MALE

COLUMBIAN PLYMOUTH ROCK FEMALE

PARTRIDGE PLYMOUTH ROCKS

Disqualifications

Positive white in main-tail feathers, sickles, or secondaries; shanks other than yellow or dusky yellow. (See General Disqualifications and Cutting for Defects.)

COLOR OF MALE

COMB, FACE, WATTLES, AND EAR-LOBES: Bright red.
BEAK: Dark horn, shading to yellow at point.
EYES: Reddish bay.
SHANKS AND TOES: Yellow.
PLUMAGE: See description of Partridge plumage color, page 69.

COLOR OF FEMALE

COMB, FACE, WATTLES, AND EAR-LOBES: Bright red.
BEAK: Dark horn, shading to yellow at point.
EYES: Reddish bay.
SHANKS AND TOES: Yellow.
PLUMAGE: See description of Partridge plumage color, page 70.

COLUMBIAN PLYMOUTH ROCKS

Disqualifications

One or more solid black or brown feathers on surface of back; dark spots or mossiness in surface of back or saddle appearing in approximately 15 per cent of the feathers of this section, except narrow black stripes extending not over half the length of feather in saddle and near tail of male, or dark markings in cape of either sex; red feathers in plumage; shanks and toes other than yellow. (See General Disqualifications and Cutting for Defects.)

COLOR OF MALE

COMB, FACE, WATTLES, AND EAR-LOBES: Bright red.
BEAK: Yellow, with dark stripe down upper mandible.
EYES: Reddish bay.
SHANKS AND TOES: Yellow.
PLUMAGE: See description of Columbian plumage color, page 71.

COLOR OF FEMALE
COMB, FACE, WATTLES, AND EAR-LOBES: Bright red.
BEAK: Yellow, with dark stripe down upper mandible.
EYES: Reddish bay.
SHANKS AND TOES: Yellow.
PLUMAGE: See description of Columbian plumage color, page 71.

BLUE PLYMOUTH ROCKS

Disqualifications

Red, yellow, or positive white in plumage; shanks other than yellow. (See General Disqualifications and Cutting for Defects.)

COLOR OF MALE
COMB, FACE, WATTLES, AND EAR-LOBES: Bright red.
BEAK: Horn shading to yellow at point.
EYES: Reddish bay.
SHANKS AND TOES: Yellow.
PLUMAGE: See description of Blue plumage color, page 73.

COLOR OF FEMALE
COMB, FACE, WATTLES, AND EAR-LOBES: Bright red.
BEAK: Horn shading to yellow at point.
EYES: Reddish bay.
SHANKS AND TOES: Yellow.
PLUMAGE: See description of Blue plumage color, page 74.

WYANDOTTES

The Silver-Laced Wyandotte is the parent variety of the Wyandotte family. It originated in New York State, where it was first known under several names of which "American Sebrights" possibly fitted its general appearance more closely than did the name "Sebright Cochins". In 1883, "American Sebrights" became a Standard breed under the name Silver-Laced Wyandottes. The true origin is shrouded in mystery. That Dark Brahma-Spangled Hamburg blood was used by the originator of the "American Sebright" was evident in some of the earlier Eastern strains, by the cropping out of the Hamburg combs and Dark Brahma color markings.

Golden-Laced Wyandottes originated in Wisconsin in 1880. They were produced by mating Silver-Laced Wyandotte females with a cross-bred Partridge Cochin-Brown Leghorn cockerel. They were admitted to the Standard in 1888.

The color pattern of the Sebright Bantam has been more or less of an ideal for breeders of Silver and Golden-Laced Wyandottes. It is one, however, that should conform to the larger size of the fowl by having more sharply defined and wider black lacing to harmonize with the broader oval center of the feather.

White Wyandottes originated from sports of the Silver-Laced variety, in New York State in 1887, and were admitted to the Standard in 1903. Texture of feather is all important in Wyandottes, especially so in the White variety, where broad feathers and smooth fitting plumage are necessary to preserve the characteristic curvilinear breed type of the true Wyandotte.

Buff Wyandottes made their first appearance in 1891. These were light colored Rhode Island Reds, but though lacking in type and off in color, they laid the foundation of a Buff Wyandotte that would be such in breed, type and color. Golden and White Wyandotte crosses, and Buff Cochin-White and Golden Wyandotte crosses dominated in other strains. The Buff variety was admitted to the Standard in 1893.

Black Wyandottes became a Standard variety in 1893. They originated from black sports of the Silver-Laced variety.

Partridge Wyandottes were admitted to the Standard in 1901. They originated about the same time in the East and West, the Partridge Cochin furnishing the color patterns for both the

Eastern and Western strains, but the varieties with which the Cochins were crossed were somewhat different. The Eastern strain was the result of a Partridge Cochin-Golden Wyandotte cross; the Western strain was produced from Partridge Cochin-Cornish-Golden Wyandotte crosses.

Silver-Penciled Wyandottes were produced by blending two strains; one, a Partridge Wyandotte-Dark Brahma cross, the other, a cross of Silver-Laced Wyandottes and Silver-Penciled Hamburgs. They were admitted to the Standard in 1902.

Columbian Wyandottes were first exhibited in 1893 at the Columbian Exposition or World's Fair held in Chicago that year, which gave them the name they now hold. This variety was produced by crossing a White Wyandotte and a Barred Plymouth Rock. Columbian Wyandottes were admitted to the Standard in 1905.

Economic Qualities: Medium weight, dual purpose fowl for the production of meat and eggs. Color of skin, yellow; color of egg shells, varying from very light to a rich brown, depending on individual, strain, and the stage of production.

Disqualifications

(See General Disqualifications and Cutting for Defects.)

STANDARD WEIGHTS

Cock	8½ lbs.	Hen	6½ lbs.
Cockerel	7½ lbs.	Pullet	5½ lbs.

WYANDOTTE BANTAMS

Disqualifications

The disqualifications for all Wyandotte Bantams shall be the same as for the larger Wyandottes of the corresponding varieties except weight. (See General Disqualifications and Cutting for Defects.)

STANDARD WEIGHTS

Cock	30 oz.	Hen	26 oz.
Cockerel	26 oz.	Pullet	24 oz.

SHAPE AND COLOR OF MALE AND FEMALE

The shape and color of the Wyandotte Bantams shall conform to the description of the large Wyandottes.

SILVER-LACED WYANDOTTE MALE

SILVER-LACED WYANDOTTE FEMALE

SHAPE OF MALE

COMB: Rose; low, firm on head; top, free from hollow center, oval, surface covered with small, rounded points; tapering to a well-defined point at rear; the entire comb curving to conform to the shape of skull. (See Standard illustration, page 100.)

BEAK: Short, well-curved.

HEAD: Short, round, crown broad; face, smooth and free from small feathers. (See description of Head, page 22; see Standard illustration, page 100.)

EYES: Full, round, prominent.

WATTLES: Moderately long, nicely rounded at lower edges, uniform, fine in texture, free from folds or wrinkles.

EAR-LOBES: Oblong, well-defined, hanging about one-third the length of wattles; smooth.

NECK: Short, well-arched; hackle, abundant, flowing well over shoulders.

WINGS: Medium in size, well-folded; carried not too closely to body, and without drooping; sides, well-rounded; primaries and secondaries, broad and overlapping in natural order when wing is folded.

BACK: Medium in length, broad its entire length, flat at shoulders; saddle, broad, full, rising with concave sweep to tail; saddle feathers, abundant.

TAIL: Short, well spread at base, carried at an angle of forty degrees above the horizontal (see page 28, figures 30 and 31); sickles, moderately long, curving gracefully and closely over tail; coverts, broad, abundant, filling out well in front, hiding the stiff feathers; main-tail feathers, broad and overlapping.

BREAST: Broad, deep, round.

BODY AND FLUFF: Body, medium in length, deep, round; fluff, fairly well developed but not so abundant as to hide profile of hocks.

LEGS AND TOES: Legs, set well apart and straight when viewed from front; lower thighs, short, stout, showing outlines when viewed sideways, well-covered with smooth feathers; shanks, moderately short, stout, well-rounded; toes, straight, well-spread.

SHAPE OF FEMALE

COMB: Rose, similar to that of male, but much smaller. (See Standard illustration, page 101.)

BEAK: Short, well-curved.

HEAD: Short, round; crown, broad; face, smooth and free

102

from small feathers. (See Standard illustration, page 101.)

EYES: Full, round, prominent.

WATTLES: Fine in texture, well-rounded.

EAR-LOBES: Oblong in shape, well-defined.

NECK: Short, well-arched; neck feathers, abundant.

WINGS: Medium in size, well-folded; carried not too closely to body and without drooping; sides well-rounded; primaries and secondaries, broad and overlapping in natural order when wing is folded.

BACK: Medium in length, broad its entire length, flat at shoulders; rising in a concave sweep to a broad, slightly rounded cushion, which extends well on to main-tail; plumage abundant.

TAIL: Short, well-spread at base, carried at an angle of thirty degrees above horizontal (see page 28, figure 30); coverts, broad, abundant; main-tail feathers, broad and overlapping.

BREAST: Broad, deep, round.

BODY AND FLUFF: Body, medium in length, deep, round; fluff, fairly well developed but not so abundant as to hide profile of hocks.

LEGS AND TOES: Legs, set well apart and straight when viewed from front; lower thighs, short, stout, showing outlines when viewed sideways, well-covered with smooth feathers; shanks, moderately short, stout, well-rounded; toes, straight, well-spread.

Note: See Instructions to Judges and paragraph "Quality of Feather," page 53.

SILVER-LACED WYANDOTTES

Disqualifications

Shanks other than yellow. (See General Disqualifications and Cutting for Defects.)

COLOR OF MALE

COMB, FACE, WATTLES, AND EAR-LOBES: Bright red.

BEAK: Dark horn, shading to yellow at point.

HEAD: Plumage, silvery white, each feather having a black stripe tapering to a fine point near its extremity.

EYES: Reddish bay.

NECK: Hackle, web of feather lustrous, greenish black with a narrow edging of silvery white, uniform in width, extending around point of feather; shaft of feather, white; plumage on front of neck, same as breast.

WINGS: Fronts, black with white centers; bows, silvery white; coverts, a broad, oval white center in each feather, laced with a narrow, lustrous, greenish black lacing, conforming to the shape of feather, forming a double bar of laced feathers across wings; primaries, black, lower edges white; secondaries, black, lower half of outer webs, white with narrow black edgings wider at the tips, upper webs, edged with white.

BACK AND SADDLE: Silvery white on surface; saddle, silvery white in appearance, a black stripe through each feather, laced with white, conforming to shape of center, the black stripe having a long diamond-shaped center of white.

TAIL: Main-tail feathers, black; sickles and coverts, lustrous, greenish black; smaller coverts, black, with diamond-shaped centers, feathers laced with white.

BREAST: A broad, oval center of white in each feather, laced with a narrow, sharply-defined, lustrous, greenish black lacing, conforming to edge of feather.

BODY AND FLUFF: Body, a broad oval center of white in each feather, laced with a narrow, sharply-defined, lustrous, greenish black lacing, conforming to edge of feather; fluff, slate.

LEGS AND TOES: Lower thighs, web of each feather, white, laced with a narrow, sharply-defined, lustrous, greenish black lacing, conforming to edge of feather; shanks and toes, yellow.

UNDER-COLOR OF ALL SECTIONS: Slate, shading to lighter slate at base.

COLOR OF FEMALE

COMB, FACE, WATTLES, AND EAR-LOBES: Bright red.

BEAK: Dark horn, shading to yellow at point.

HEAD: Plumage, silvery gray.

EYES: Reddish bay.

NECK: Silvery white in appearance, with a black center through each feather, laced with white; shafts of feathers, white; feathers on front of neck, same as breast.

WINGS: Fronts, bows, and coverts, a broad, oval center of white in each feather, laced with a narrow, sharply-defined, lustrous, greenish black lacing, conforming to edge of feather; primaries, black, lower edges white; secondaries, black, lower half of outer webs, white with narrow black edging wider at tips.

BACK: A broad, oval center of white in each feather, laced with a narrow, sharply-defined, lustrous, greenish black lacing, to conform to edge of feather.

TAIL: Main-tail feathers, black; coverts, and lesser coverts, black with white centers.

BREAST: A broad, oval center of white in each feather, laced with a narrow, sharply-defined, lustrous, greenish black lacing, to conform to edge of feather.

BODY AND FLUFF: Body, a broad, oval center of white in each feather, laced with a narrow, sharply-defined, lustrous, greenish black lacing, to conform to edge of feather; fluff, slate.

LEGS AND TOES: Lower thighs, each feather white, edged with a narrow, sharply-defined, lustrous, greenish black lacing, to conform to edge of feather; shanks and toes, yellow.

UNDER-COLOR OF ALL SECTIONS: Slate.

GOLDEN-LACED WYANDOTTES

Disqualifications

Shanks other than yellow or dusky yellow. (See General Disqualifications and Cutting for Defects.)

COLOR OF MALE

COMB, FACE, WATTLES, AND EAR-LOBES: Bright red.

BEAK: Dark horn, shading to yellow at point.

HEAD: Plumage, rich golden bay, each feather having a black stripe, tapering to a fine point near its extremity.

EYES: Reddish bay.

NECK: Hackle, web of feather, lustrous, greenish black, with a narrow edging of rich golden bay, uniform in width, extending around point of feather; shaft of feather, golden bay; plumage in front of neck, same as breast.

WINGS: Fronts, black with golden bay centers; bows, rich golden bay; coverts, a broad oval center of rich golden bay in each feather, with a narrow, lustrous, greenish black lacing, conforming to shape of feather, forming a double bar of laced feathers across the wings; primaries, black, lower edge, rich golden bay; secondaries, black, lower half of outer webs, rich golden bay, with a narrow black edging wider at the tip, upper webs, edged with rich golden bay.

BACK AND SADDLE: Rich golden bay on surface; saddle, rich golden bay in appearance, a black stripe through each feather, laced with rich golden bay, conforming to shape of center, the black stripe having a long, diamond-shaped center of rich golden bay.

TAIL: Main-tail feathers, black; sickles and coverts, lustrous, greenish black; smaller coverts, black with diamond-shaped, rich golden bay centers, feathers laced with rich golden bay.

BREAST: A broad, oval center of rich golden bay in each feather, laced with a narrow, sharply-defined, lustrous, greenish black lacing, conforming to edge of feather.

BODY AND FLUFF: Body, a broad, oval center of rich golden bay in each feather, laced with a narrow, sharply-defined, lustrous greenish black lacing, conforming to edge of feather, fluff, slate.

LEGS AND TOES: Lower thighs, web of each feather rich golden bay, laced with a narrow, sharply-defined, lustrous, greenish black lacing which conforms to edge of feather; shanks and toes yellow.

UNDER-COLOR OF ALL SECTIONS: Slate shading to red at base.

COLOR OF FEMALE

COMB, FACE, WATTLES, AND EAR-LOBES: Bright red.

BEAK: Dark horn, shading to yellow at point.

HEAD: Plumage, rich golden bay.

EYES: Reddish bay.

NECK: Rich golden bay in appearance, with a black center through each feather, laced with rich golden bay; shafts of feathers, golden bay; feathers on front of neck, same as breast.

WINGS: Fronts, bows and coverts, a broad oval center of rich golden bay in each feather, laced with a narrow, sharply-defined, lustrous greenish black lacing which conforms to edge of feather; primaries, black, lower edges, rich golden bay; secondaries, black, lower half of outer webs, rich golden bay with narrow, black edgings wider at tips.

BACK: A broad, oval center of rich golden bay in each feather, laced with a narrow, sharply-defined, lustrous, greenish black lacing which conforms to edge of feather.

TAIL: Main-tail feathers, black; coverts and lesser coverts, black with rich golden bay centers.

BREAST: A broad, oval center of rich golden bay in each feather, laced with a narrow, sharply-defined, lustrous, greenish black lacing which conforms to edge of feather.

BODY AND FLUFF: Body, a broad, oval center of rich golden bay in each feather, with a narrow, sharply-defined, lustrous, greenish black lacing which conforms to edge of feather; fluff, slate.

LEGS AND TOES: Lower thighs, each feather rich golden bay, edged with a narrow, sharply-defined, lustrous, greenish black lacing which conforms to edge of feather; shanks and toes, yellow.

UNDER-COLOR OF ALL SECTIONS: Slate.

WHITE WYANDOTTES

Disqualifications

Shanks other than yellow. (See General Disqualifications and Cutting for Defects.)

COLOR OF MALE AND FEMALE

COMB, FACE, WATTLES, AND EAR-LOBES: Bright red.
BEAK: Yellow.
EYES: Reddish bay.
SHANKS AND TOES: Rich yellow.
PLUMAGE: See description of White plumage color, page 63.

BLACK WYANDOTTES

Disqualifications

More than one-half inch of positive white in any part of plumage, except one inch or less of white in under-color of hackles and saddles of cocks; two or more feathers edged or tipped with positive white; beak or shanks other than yellow or yellow shaded with black; bottoms of feet showing complete absence of yellow. (See General Disqualifications and Cutting for Defects.)

COLOR OF MALE AND FEMALE

COMB, FACE, WATTLES, AND EAR-LOBES: Bright red.
BEAK: Yellow.
EYES: Reddish bay.
SHANKS AND TOES: Yellow; bottoms of feet, yellow.
PLUMAGE: See description of Black plumage color, page 64.

BUFF WYANDOTTES

Disqualifications

Shanks other than yellow. (See General Disqualifications and Cutting for Defects.)

WHITE WYANDOTTE MALE

WHITE WYANDOTTE FEMALE

BUFF WYANDOTTE MALE

BUFF WYANDOTTE FEMALE

PARTRIDGE WYANDOTTE MALE

PARTRIDGE WYANDOTTE FEMALE

COLOR OF MALE AND FEMALE

COMB, FACE, WATTLES, AND EAR-LOBES: Bright red.
BEAK: Yellow.
EYES: Reddish bay.
SHANKS AND TOES: Rich yellow.
PLUMAGE: See description of Buff plumage color, page 64.

PARTRIDGE WYANDOTTES
Disqualifications

Positive white in main-tail feathers, sickles, or secondaries; shanks other than yellow or dusky yellow. (See General Disqualifications, and Cutting for Defects.)

COLOR OF MALE

COMB, FACE, WATTLES, AND EAR-LOBES: Bright red.
BEAK: Dark horn, shading to yellow at point.
EYES: Reddish bay.
SHANKS AND TOES: Yellow.
PLUMAGE: See description Partridge plumage color, page 69.

COLOR OF FEMALE

COMB, FACE, WATTLES, AND EAR-LOBES: Bright red.
BEAK: Dark horn, shading to yellow at point.
EYES: Reddish bay.
SHANKS AND TOES: Yellow.
PLUMAGE: See description Partridge plumage color, page 70.

SILVER PENCILED WYANDOTTES
Disqualifications

Shanks and toes other than yellow or dusky yellow. (See General Disqualifications, and Cutting for Defects.)

COLOR OF MALE

COMB, FACE, WATTLES, AND EAR-LOBES: Bright red.
BEAK: Dusky yellow, shading to yellow at point.
EYES: Reddish bay.
SHANKS AND TOES: Yellow.
PLUMAGE: See description of Silver-Penciled plumage color, pages 64 and 68.

COLOR OF FEMALE
COMB, FACE, WATTLES, AND EAR-LOBES: Bright red.
BEAK: Dusky yellow, shading to yellow at point.
EYES: Reddish bay.
SHANKS AND TOES: Dusky yellow.
PLUMAGE: See description of Silver-Penciled plumage color, pages 68 and 69.

COLUMBIAN WYANDOTTES
Disqualifications
One or more solid black or brown feathers on surface of back; dark spots or mossiness in surface of back or saddle appearing in approximately 15 per cent of the feathers of this section, except narrow black stripes extending not over half the length of feather in saddle and near tail of male, or dark markings in cape of either sex; red feathers in plumage; shanks and toes other than yellow. (See General Disqualifications and Cutting for Defects.)

COLOR OF MALE
COMB, FACE, WATTLES, AND EAR-LOBES: Bright red.
BEAK: Yellow, with dark stripe down upper mandible.
EYES: Reddish bay.
SHANKS AND TOES: Yellow.
PLUMAGE: See description of Columbian plumage color, pages 71 and 72.

COLOR OF FEMALE
COMB, FACE, WATTLES, AND EAR-LOBES: Bright red.
BEAK: Yellow, with dark stripe down upper mandible.
EYES: Reddish bay.
SHANKS AND TOES: Yellow.
PLUMAGE: See description of Columbian plumage color, pages 71, 72 and 73.

SILVER-PENCILED WYANDOTTE MALE

SILVER-PENCILED WYANDOTTE FEMALE

COLUMBIAN WYANDOTTE MALE

COLUMBIAN WYANDOTTE FEMALE

JAVAS

One of the earliest breeds known in the United States is the Java fowl. It is not an American-made breed, but came from the Isle of Java in the East Indies to this country in 1835. Javas were admitted to the Standard in 1883.

ECONOMIC QUALITIES: General purpose fowl for the production of meat and eggs. Color of skin, yellow; color of egg shells, brown.

Disqualifications

(See General Disqualifications and Cutting for Defects.)

STANDARD WEIGHTS

Cock	9½ lbs.	Hen	7½ lbs.
Cockerel	8 lbs.	Pullet	6½ lbs.

SHAPE OF MALE

COMB: Single; rather small, straight and upright; firm on head; lower in front; evenly serrated, having five well-defined points; fine in texture. (See Standard illustration, page 122.)

BEAK: Stout, well-curved.

HEAD: Of medium length and breadth. (See description of Head, page 22, and Standard illustration, page 122.)

EYES: Large, full, prominent.

WATTLES: Of medium length, well rounded at ends, smooth, fine in texture.

EAR-LOBES: Small, oblong.

NECK: Of medium length, arched; hackle, abundant.

WINGS: Rather large, well-folded and carried without drooping; primaries and secondaries, broad, and overlapping in natural order when wing is folded.

BACK: Broad its entire length, long, with a slight decline to a concave sweep near tail; saddle feathers, abundant.

TAIL: Rather long, moderately full and expanded, carried at an angle of fifty-five degrees above the horizontal (see page 28, figures 30 and 31); sickles, long and gracefully curved; maintail feathers, long, broad and overlapping.

BREAST: Broad, full, deep.

BODY AND FLUFF: Body, long, broad, deep; fluff, moderately full.

LEGS AND TOES: Legs, set well apart, straight when viewed from front; lower thighs of medium length, large, well covered with close-fitting feathers; shanks of medium length, stout in bone; toes, of medium length, straight, well-spread.

SHAPE OF FEMALE

COMB: Single, small, straight and upright, lower in front; evenly serrated, having five well-defined points; fine in texture. (See Standard illustration, page 123.)

BEAK: Strong, well-curved.

HEAD: Of medium size. (See Standard illustration, page 123.)

EYES: Of medium size, full, prominent.

WATTLES: Of medium size, well-rounded, smooth, fine in texture.

EAR-LOBES: Small.

NECK: Of medium length, slightly arched.

WINGS: Rather large, well-folded and carried without drooping; primaries and secondaries, broad, and overlapping in natural order when wing is folded.

BACK: Broad its entire length, long, full near tail-coverts.

TAIL: Rather long, full, slightly expanded, carried at an angle of forty-five degrees above the horizontal (see illustrations, page 28, figures 30 and 31); main-tail feathers, broad and overlapping.

BREAST: Broad, full, deep.

BODY AND FLUFF: Body, long, broad, deep; fluff, smooth, moderately full.

LEGS AND TOES: Legs, set well apart, straight when viewed from front; lower thighs of medium length, large, well covered with close-fitting feathers; shanks of medium length, stout in bone; toes of medium length, straight, well-spread.

Note: See Instructions to Judges and paragraph "Quality of Feather," page 53.

BLACK JAVA MALE

BLACK JAVA FEMALE

BLACK JAVAS

Disqualifications

More than one-half inch of positive white in any part of plumage; two or more feathers tipped or edged with positive white; skin or bottoms of feet showing complete absence of yellow. (See General Disqualifications and Cutting for Defects.)

COLOR OF MALE AND FEMALE

COMB, FACE, WATTLES, AND EAR-LOBES: Bright red.

BEAK: Black.

EYES: Dark brown.

SHANKS AND TOES: Shanks, black, or nearly black, with a tendency toward willow, black preferred; toes, same as shanks, except under parts, which must be yellow; bottoms of feet, yellow.

PLUMAGE: See description of Black plumage color, page 63.

MOTTLED JAVAS

Disqualifications

Red or yellow in any part of plumage; skin or bottoms of feet showing complete absence of yellow. (See General Disqualifications and Cutting for Defects.)

COLOR OF MALE AND FEMALE

COMB, FACE, WATTLES, AND EAR-LOBES: Bright red.

BEAK: Horn, shading to yellow at tip.

EYES: Reddish bay.

SHANKS AND TOES: Broken leaden-blue and yellow.

PLUMAGE: Black mottled with white, black predominating.

UNDER-COLOR OF ALL SECTIONS: Slate.

DOMINIQUES

No reliable data of the origin of the American Dominiques are to be found. It is probably a selection from the many hawk-colored or gray fowls kept in the New England States long before any poultry standards existed. The type of the breed indicates composite blood lines, possibly of the Asiatic and Hamburg breeds.

ECONOMIC QUALITIES: Dual purpose, medium weight fowl, for the production of meat and eggs. Color of skin, yellow; color of egg shells, brown.

Disqualifications

Any feather, feathers, or portion of a feather of any color foreign to the breed except black or white. (See General Disqualifications and Cutting for Defects.)

STANDARD WEIGHTS

Cock	7 lbs.	Hen	5 lbs.
Cockerel	6 lbs.	Pullet	4 lbs.

SHAPE OF MALE

COMB: Rose; not so large as to overhang the eyes or beak; firm and straight on head; square in front; uniform on sides; free from hollow center; terminating in a spike at rear, the point of which turns slightly upward; top covered with small points. (See Standard illustration, page 126.)

BEAK: Short, stout, well-curved.

HEAD: Of medium size, carried well up. (See Standard illustration, page 126.)

EYES: Large, full, prominent.

WATTLES: Broad, medium in length, well-rounded, smooth, fine in texture, free from folds or wrinkles.

EAR-LOBES: Oblong, of medium size.

NECK: Of medium length, well-arched, tapering; hackle, abundant.

WINGS: Rather large, well-folded and carried without drooping; wing-bows and points, well covered by breast and saddle feathers; primaries and secondaries, broad, and overlapping in natural order when wing is folded.

BACK: Of medium length, moderately broad, rising with concave sweep to tail.

125

DOMINIQUE MALE

DOMINIQUE FEMALE

TAIL: Long, full, slightly expanded; carried at an angle of forty-five degrees above the horizontal (see illustrations, page 28, figures 30 and 31); sickles, long, well-curved; main-tail feathers, broad and overlapping.

BREAST: Broad, round, and carried well up.

BODY AND FLUFF: Body, broad, full, compact; fluff, moderately full.

LEGS AND TOES: Legs, set well apart, straight when viewed from front; lower thighs, of medium length, well-feathered, smooth; shanks, fine in bone; toes, of medium length, straight, well-spread.

SHAPE OF FEMALE

COMB: Rose; similar to that of male, but much smaller. (See Standard illustration, page 127.)

BEAK: Short, stout, well-curved.

HEAD: Small. (See Standard illustration, page 127.)

EYES: Large, full, prominent.

WATTLES: Rather small, well-rounded, smooth, fine in texture, free from folds and wrinkles.

EAR-LOBES: Of medium size, oblong.

NECK: Medium in length, slightly arched, tapering.

WINGS: Rather large, well-folded; and carried without drooping; primaries and secondaries, broad and overlapping in natural order when wing is folded.

BACK: Of medium length, moderately broad, slightly concave.

TAIL: Full, rather long, slightly expanded, carried at an angle of forty-five degrees above the horizontal (see illustrations, page 28, figures 30 and 31); main-tail feathers, broad and overlapping.

BREAST: Round, full.

BODY AND FLUFF: Body, broad, full, compact; fluff, moderately full.

LEGS AND TOES: Legs, set well apart, straight when viewed from front; lower thighs, of medium length, well-feathered, smooth; shanks, fine in bone; toes of medium length, straight, well-spread.

Note: See Instructions to Judges and paragraph "Quality of Feather," page 53.

COLOR OF MALE AND FEMALE

COMB, FACE, WATTLES, AND EAR-LOBES: Bright red.

BEAK: Yellow.

EYES: Reddish bay.

SHANKS AND TOES: Yellow.

PLUMAGE: Slate; feathers in all sections of fowl crossed throughout their entire length by irregular dark and light bars that stop short of positive black and white; tip of each feather, dark; free from shafting, brownish tinge or metallic sheen; excellence to be determined by distinct contrasts. The male may be one or two shades lighter than the female.

UNDER-COLOR OF ALL SECTIONS: Slate.

RHODE ISLAND REDS

The origin of this breed dates back about eighty years to a fowl bred in that section of New England which is located between Narragansett Bay and Buzzard's Bay. The name Rhode Island Red was given the breed in honor of the state where it originated from crossing the Red Malay Game, Leghorn and Asiatic native stock. In 1904, it was admitted to the American Standard of Perfection as a distinct breed of poultry. This was the single-comb variety. The Rose-Comb Rhode Island Red was admitted to the Standard a year later, although some breeders acclaim it to be the original variety. The earlier Rhode Island Reds sported both single and rose-combs, some even having pea combs, due to their mixed ancestry and the fact of their being bred primarily for market purposes before they became a Standard breed.

RHODE ISLAND WHITES

Rhode Island Whites were admitted to the Standard at Knoxville, Tenn., in 1922. They are said to have originated in Rhode Island, from which state they take their name, and were first offered to the public in 1903. They are the result of crosses of Partridge Cochins, White Wyandottes and Rose-Comb White Leghorns.

The distinctive shape characteristic of both Rhode Island Reds and Rhode Island Whites is the horizontally carried, oblong body. It is a fairly close-feathered fowl, the texture of the feathers being smooth and firm.

ECONOMIC QUALITIES: Rhode Island Reds and Rhode Island Whites are general purpose fowls, bred for the production of meat and eggs. Color of skin, yellow; color of egg shells, brown to dark brown.

Disqualifications

(See General Disqualifications and Cutting for Defects.)

STANDARD WEIGHTS

Cock	8½ lbs.	Hen	6½ lbs.
Cockerel	7½ lbs.	Pullet	5½ lbs.

SHAPE OF MALE

COMB: Single; medium in size, set firmly on head, perfectly straight and upright, with five even and well-defined points, those in front and rear smaller than those in center; of considerable breadth where it joins to head; blade, smooth, inclining slightly downward but not following too closely the shape of head. (See Standard illustration, page 132.)

COMB: Rose; low, firm on head; oval, free from hollow center, surface covered with small rounded points, terminating in a spike at the rear, the spike drooping slightly but not conforming too closely to the shape of head. (See Standard illustration, page 136.)

BEAK: Medium length, slightly curved.

HEAD: Moderate in length, fairly deep, inclined to be flat on top rather than round; face clean-cut, skin fine in texture, free from wrinkles. (See Standard illustrations, page 132 and 136.)

EYES: Large, full, prominent.

WATTLES: Of medium size, uniform, free from folds or wrinkles.

EAR-LOBES: Oblong, well-defined, smooth.

NECK: Of medium length; hackle, abundant, flowing over shoulders, not too closely feathered.

WINGS: Of good size, well-folded, carried horizontally; primaries and secondaries, broad and overlapping in natural order when wing is folded.

BACK: Long, moderately broad its entire length, carried horizontally; saddle, moderately broad, feathers of medium length, moderately abundant, blending into tail.

TAIL: Of medium length, well-spread, carried at an angle of forty degrees above the horizontal (see illustrations, page 28, figures 30 and 31); sickles of medium length, extending slightly beyond main-tail feathers; lesser sickles and tail-coverts, of medium length, well feathered; main-tail feathers, broad and overlapping.

BREAST: Moderately deep, full, well-rounded.

BODY AND FLUFF: Body, long, broad, moderately deep, straight, extending well forward, giving body an oblong appearance; feathers carried close to body; fluff, moderately full.

SINGLE-COMB RHODE ISLAND RED MALE

SINGLE-COMB RHODE ISLAND RED FEMALE

LEGS AND TOES: Legs, set well apart, straight when viewed from front; lower thighs, large, of medium length, and well-feathered, smooth; shanks, of medium length, smooth; toes, of medium length, straight, well-spread.

SHAPE OF FEMALE

COMB: Single; medium in size, set firmly on head, perfectly straight and upright, with five even and well-defined points, those in front and rear smaller than those in center. (See Standard illustration, page 133.)

COMB: Rose; low, free from hollow center, set firmly on head, much smaller than that of male and in proportion to its length, narrower; covered with small points and terminating in a small, short spike at the rear. (See Standard illustration, page 137.)

BEAK: Of medium length, slightly curved.

HEAD: Moderate in length, fairly deep, inclined to be flat on top rather than round; face, clean-cut, skin, fine in texture, free from wrinkles. (See Standard illustration, page 137.)

EYES: Large, full, prominent.

WATTLES: Of medium size, regularly curved.

EAR-LOBES: Oblong, well-defined, smooth.

NECK: Of medium length, moderately full-feathered.

WINGS: Rather large, well-folded; fronts, well covered by breast feathers; flights, carried nearly horizontally; primaries and secondaries, broad and overlapping when wing is folded.

BACK: Long, moderately broad its entire length, carried horizontally, blending into tail.

TAIL: Of medium length, moderately well-spread, carried at an angle of thirty degrees (see illustrations, page 28, figures 30, and 31) above the horizontal; main-tail feathers, broad and overlapping.

BREAST: Moderately deep, full, well-rounded.

BODY AND FLUFF: Body, long, moderately broad, moderately deep, straight, extending well forward, giving the body an oblong appearance; feathers, carried close to body; fluff, moderately full.

LEGS AND TOES: Legs, set well apart, straight when viewed from front; lower thighs, of medium length, well-feathered, smooth; shanks, of medium length, smooth; toes, of medium length, straight, well-spread.

Note: See Instructions to Judges and paragraph "Quality of Feather," page 53.

RHODE ISLAND REDS

Disqualifications

One or more entirely white feathers showing in outer plumage; shanks and feet other than yellow or reddish horn. (See General Disqualifications and Cutting for Defects.)

COLOR OF MALE

COMB, FACE, WATTLES, AND EAR-LOBES: Bright red.

BEAK: Reddish horn.

HEAD: Plumage, brilliant red.

EYES: Reddish bay.

NECK: Rich, brilliant red; plumage on front of neck, rich red.

WINGS: Fronts and bows, rich brilliant red; coverts, red, primaries, upper webs red, lower webs black and narrow edging of red; primary coverts, black edged with red; secondaries, lower webs red, the red extending around end of feathers sufficient to secure a red wing-bay and lacing the upper portion of upper webs, this color growing wider in shorter secondaries; remainder of each secondary black, feathers next to body being red on surface so that wing when folded in natural position shall show one harmonious red color.

BACK AND SADDLE: Rich, brilliant red.

TAIL: Main-tail feathers, black; sickle feathers, rich, lustrous greenish black; coverts, mainly greenish black, red as they approach the saddle.

BREAST: Rich red.

BODY AND FLUFF: Rich red.

LEGS AND TOES: Lower thighs, rich red; shanks and toes, rich yellow tinged with reddish horn. A line of red pigment down the sides of shanks, extending to tip of toes, is desirable.

PLUMAGE: General surface, rich, brilliant red, except where black is specified; not so dark as to appear brown or chocolate nor so light as to appear orange, free from shafting or mealy appear-

135

ROSE-COMB RHODE ISLAND RED MALE

ROSE-COMB RHODE ISLAND RED FEMALE

RHODE ISLAND WHITE MALE

RHODE ISLAND WHITE FEMALE

ance; the less contrast there is between wing-bows, back, hackle, and breast the better. A harmonious blending in all sections is desired. The specimen should be so brilliant in color as to have a glossed appearance. (See definition of "Feather", page 18.)

UNDER-COLOR OF ALL SECTIONS: Red.

COLOR OF FEMALE

COMB, FACE, WATTLES, AND EAR-LOBES: Bright Red.

BEAK: Reddish horn.

HEAD: Plumage, brilliant red.

EYES: Reddish bay.

NECK: Rich red, with slight ticking of black, confined to tips of lower neck feathers; feathers on front of neck, rich red.

WINGS: Fronts and bows, rich red; coverts, red; primaries, upper webs red, lower webs black with narrow edging of red; primary coverts, black edged with red; secondaries, lower webs red, the red extending around the end of the feathers sufficient to secure a red wing-bay and lacing the upper portion of upper webs, this color growing wider in the shorter secondaries; remainder of each secondary, black, feathers next to body being red on surface, so that wing when folded in natural position shall show one harmonious red color.

BACK: Rich red.

TAIL: Main-tail feathers, black; the two top feathers may be edged with red.

BREAST: Rich red.

BODY AND FLUFF: Red.

LEGS AND TOES: Lower thighs, red; shanks and toes, rich yellow tinged with reddish horn.

PLUMAGE: General surface color, rich, even red, except where black is specified, not so dark as to appear brown or chocolate nor so light as to appear chestnut, free from shafting or mealy appearance. (See definition of "Feather", page 18.)

UNDER-COLOR OF ALL SECTIONS: Red.

RHODE ISLAND WHITES

ROSE COMBS

Disqualifications

Shanks and toes shcwing complete absence of yellow. (See General Disqualifications and Cutting for Defects.)

COLOR OF MALE AND FEMALE

COMB, FACE, WATTLES AND EAR-LOBES: Bright red.

BEAK: Yellow.

EYES: Reddish bay.

SHANKS AND TOES: Yellow.

PLUMAGE: See description of White plumage color, page 63.

CHANTECLER

The Chantecler is the first breed of Canadian creation. It was originated at the Oka Agricultural Institute, in the Province of Quebec, and was first presented to the public in 1918 and admitted to the Standard of Perfection in 1921. It is the result of efforts made from 1908 to 1918 to obtain a fowl of vigorous and rustic temperament that could resist the climatic conditions of Canada, a "general purpose fowl," a good winter layer, and especially with comb and wattles reduced to a minimum, qualities intended to give the new breed its typical character.

In the production of this breed two crosses were made in 1908, a Dark Cornish male mated to a White Leghorn female and a Rhode Island Red male mated to a White Wyandotte female. The following season the pullets from the first cross, the Dark Cornish male and the White Leghorn female, were mated to a cockerel from the Rhode Island Red and White Wyandotte cross. Selected pullets from this last mating were then mated with a White Plymouth Rock male and the subsequent matings produced the typical fowl sought for as it is today.

Economic Qualities: General purpose fowl, for egg and meat production. Color of skin, yellow. Color of egg shells, light brown to dark brown.

Disqualifications
(See General Disqualifications and Cutting for Defects.)

STANDARD WEIGHTS

Cock	8½ lbs.	Hen	6½ lbs.
Cockerel	7½ lbs.	Pullet	5½ lbs.

SHAPE OF MALE

Comb: Cushion-shaped; rather small, set firm and low on fore part of head, front, rear and sides nearly straight, surface smooth. (See Standard illustration, page 16.)

Beak: Short, stout, slightly curved.

Head: Moderately small, short, broad; juncture with neck, well-defined. (See Standard illustration, page 144.)

Eyes: Of medium size, nearly round.

Wattles: Very small, well-rounded, smooth.

Ear-Lobes: Small, oval.

NECK: Of medium length, slightly arched; tapering toward the head; hackle abundant, flowing well over shoulders with no apparent break between neck and back.

WINGS: Rather small, well-folded and carried without drooping, the points of primaries well covered by saddle feathers.

BACK: Long, broad its entire length, curving sharply into tail; saddle feathers abundant.

TAIL: Of medium length, moderately well-spread, carried at an angle of thirty degrees above the horizontal (see illustration, page 28, figures 30 and 31); sickles of medium length, slightly extending beyond the main-tail feathers.

BREAST: Broad, deep, well-rounded, carried forward.

BODY AND FLUFF: Body, long, broad, full-feathered with feathers fitting closely to body; fluff, short and full.

LEGS AND TOES: Legs, set well apart, straight when viewed from front; lower thighs of medium length, large, well-feathered and smooth; shanks of medium length; toes, medium in length, straight, well-spread.

SHAPE OF FEMALE

COMB: Cushion-shaped; very small, low on head, front, rear, and sides nearly straight, surface smooth. (See Standard illustration, page 145.)

BEAK: Short, well-curved.

HEAD: Moderately small, short, broad; juncture with neck, well-defined. (See Standard illustration, page 145.)

EYES: Medium in size, round.

WATTLES: Very small.

EAR-LOBE: Very small.

NECK: Of medium length, arched, tapering to the head.

WINGS: Rather small, well-folded, of medium length, carried nearly horizontally, fronts well covered by breast feathers; primaries and secondaries, broad, and overlapping in natural order when wing is folded.

BACK: Long, broad at shoulders, sloping slightly downward to rear, where it curves sharply into tail.

TAIL: Of medium length; moderately well-spread, carried at an angle of thirty degrees above the horizontal (see illustrations, page 28, figures 30, and 31).

BREAST: Broad, full, well-rounded, carried forward.

BODY AND FLUFF: Long, broad, full-feathered with feathers fitting closely to body; fluff, short and full.

CHANTECLER MALE

CHANTECLER FEMALE

LEGS AND TOES: Legs, set well apart, straight when viewed from front; lower thighs of medium length, well-feathered and smooth; shanks of medium length; toes, straight, of medium length, well-spread.

Note: See Instructions to Judges and paragraph "Quality of Feather," page 53.

COLOR OF MALE AND FEMALE

COMB, FACE, WATTLES, AND EAR-LOBES: Bright red.

BEAK: Yellow.

EYES: Reddish bay.

SHANKS AND TOES: Rich yellow.

PLUMAGE: See description of White Plumage color, page 63.

PARTRIDGE CHANTECLER

This variety was originated in Edmonton, Alberta, Canada, and is the result of efforts to provide a variety of utility characteristics for use in cold winter climates, a "general purpose fowl," a good winter layer, with comb and wattles reduced to a minimum. In the production of this variety four crosses were made, Partridge Wyandotte, Partridge Cochin, Dark Cornish and Rose Comb Brown Leghorn. Partridge Chanteclers were admitted into the Standard in 1935.

ECONOMIC QUALITIES: General purpose fowl for meat and egg production. Color of skin, yellow; color of egg shell, light brown to dark brown.

Disqualifications

Positive enamel white covering more than one-fourth of ear-lobe, one or more entirely white feathers in plumage. (See General Disqualifications and Cutting for Defects.)

STANDARD WEIGHTS

Cock ....10 lbs.	Hen ....7½ lbs.
Cockerel .... 8½ lbs.	Pullet ....6½ lbs.

SHAPE OF MALE AND FEMALE

See pages 142, 143 and 146 in Standard.

COLOR OF MALE AND FEMALE

COMB, FACE, WATTLES AND EAR-LOBES: Bright red.

BEAK: Dark horn, shading to yellow at point.

SHANKS AND TOES: Yellow.

PLUMAGE: See description of Partridge plumage color, page 69 in Standard.

JERSEY BLACK GIANTS

This breed originated in New Jersey, sixty or more years ago, by crossing Black Javas, Dark Brahmas and Black Langshans, although Cornish blood was introduced in some strains in more recent years. It was admitted to the Standard in 1922.

As their name implies, Jersey Black Giants are large and very heavy fowls. Being a super-heavy market fowl, due attention should be paid to the Standard weights, in order to maintain the characteristically heavy meat producing qualities.

ECONOMIC QUALITIES: A general purpose fowl for heavy meat and egg production. Color of skin, yellow; color of egg shells, brown to dark brown.

Disqualifications

More than one-half inch of positive white showing on surface or two or more feathers tipped or edged with positive white; bottoms of feet showing complete absence of yellow. (See General Disqualifications and Cutting for Defects.)

STANDARD WEIGHTS

Cock	13 lbs.	Hen	10 lbs.
Cockerel	11 lbs.	Pullet	8 lbs.

SHAPE OF MALE

COMB: Single; rather large, straight and upright, having six well-defined and evenly serrated points, the blade following the shape of the neck. (See Standard illustration, page 154.)

BEAK: Moderately short, stout, well-curved.

HEAD: Rather large, broad. (See Standard illustration, page 154.)

EYES: Large, round and full.

WATTLES: Of medium size, well-rounded at lower ends, fine in texture, free from folds or wrinkles.

EAR-LOBES: Moderately large, extending down one-half the length of the wattles, smooth.

NECK: Moderately long, full, well-arched.

WINGS: Medium size, well-folded, carried at the same angle as the body; primaries and secondaries, broad and overlapping in natural order when wing is folded.

BACK: Rather long, broad, nearly horizontal, with a short sweep to tail.

TAIL: Rather large, full, well-spread, carried at an angle of forty-five degrees above the horizontal (see illustrations, page 28, figures 30 and 31); sickles, of just sufficient length to cover the main-tail feathers; coverts, moderately abundant and medium in length; main-tail feathers, broad and overlapping.

BREAST: Broad, deep, full, carried well forward.

BODY AND FLUFF: Body, long, wide, deep, compact, smooth at sides; keel, long; fluff, smooth, moderately full.

LEGS AND TOES: Legs, set well apart, straight when viewed from front; lower thighs, large, of moderate length, well-feathered; shanks, stout in bone, moderately long; toes of medium length, straight, well-spread.

SHAPE OF FEMALE

COMB: Single; moderately large, having six well-defined and evenly serrated points, conforming to the shape of head. (See Standard illustration, page 151.)

BEAK: Moderately short, stout, well-curved.

HEAD: Of medium size, broad. (See Standard illustration, page 151.)

EYES: Large, round, full.

WATTLES: Medium in size, fine in texture.

EAR-LOBES: Medium in size, smooth.

NECK: Moderately long and full, slightly arched.

WINGS: Of medium size, well-folded, carried at same angle as the body; primaries and secondaries, broad and overlapping in natural order when wing is folded.

BACK: Rather long, broad its entire length, carried nearly horizontal, ending in a short sweep to tail.

JERSEY BLACK GIANT MALE

JERSEY BLACK GIANT FEMALE

TAIL: Moderately long, well-spread, carried at an angle of thirty degrees above the horizontal (see illustrations, figures 30 and 31); main-tail feathers, broad and overlapping.

BREAST: Full, deep, broad, carried well forward.

BODY AND FLUFF: Body, long, wide, deep, compact, smooth at sides; keel, long; fluff, moderately full.

LEGS AND TOES: Legs, set well apart, straight when viewed from front; lower thighs, fairly large, of moderate length, well-feathered; shanks, moderately long; toes, of medium length, straight, well-spread.

Note: See Instructions to Judges and paragraph "Quality of Feather," page 53.

COLOR OF MALE AND FEMALE

COMB, FACE, WATTLES, AND EAR-LOBES: Bright red.

BEAK: Black, shading to yellow toward the tip.

EYES: Dark brown.

SHANKS AND TOES: Black; under-part of feet, yellow.

PLUMAGE: See description of Black plumage, color, page 63.

UNDER-COLOR: Slate, shading gradually to white at the skin.

LAMONAS

This breed is of American origin, having been originated on the United States Government Experiment Station at Beltsville, Maryland, where the first matings were made in 1912. It was produced by crossing the Silver-Gray Dorking, White Plymouth Rock, and White Leghorn.

ECONOMIC QUALITIES: General purpose fowl for meat and egg production. Color of skin, yellow; color of egg shells, white.

Disqualifications

Shanks other than yellow. Fifth toe. Ear-lobes more than one-third white. (See general disqualifications and cutting for defects for further instructions.)

STANDARD WEIGHTS

Cock ....8 lbs.	Hen ....6½ lbs.
Cockerel ....7 lbs.	Pullet ....5½ lbs.

SHAPE OF MALE

COMB: Single; medium large, straight and upright, evenly serrated, having five well defined points, the front and rear points shorter than the others.

BEAK: Of medium length, stout and well curved.

HEAD: Medium large, face smooth.

EYES: Full, prominent.

WATTLES: Medium large, well rounded.

EAR-LOBES: Of medium length in proportion to the wattles.

NECK: Of medium length, arched. Hackle full and abundant, flowing well over the shoulders.

WINGS: Large, well-folded against body; not drooping. Primaries and secondaries broad and overlapping in natural order when wing is folded.

BACK: Long, broad, its entire length straight, declining to tail. Saddle feathers long and abundant.

TAIL: Large, full, well spread, coverts abundant. Main tail feathers broad and overlapping, carried at an angle of forty-five degrees above the horizontal. (See illustrations, page 28, Figures 30 and 31.)

BREAST: Broad, deep, full, well-rounded and carried well forward.

LAMONA MALE

LAMONA FEMALE

BODY AND FLUFF: Body long, broad, deep; keel bone long; fluff smooth in surface, moderately developed.

LEGS AND TOES: Legs, set well apart and straight when viewed from front, lower thighs large, medium short, well-meated. Shanks, medium short, stout, round in bone; toes, four on each foot; moderately long and straight.

SHAPE OF FEMALE

COMB: Single, having five well defined points. The front portion of the comb and the first point to stand erect, the remainder of the comb, drooping gradually to one side, free from folds or wrinkles.

BEAK: Of medium length, stout and well curved.

HEAD: Of medium size; face smooth.

EYES: Full, prominent.

WATTLES: Medium size, uniform, well-rounded.

EAR-LOBES: Medium length and size in proportion to the wattles.

NECK: Medium length, arched; feathers full and abundant, flowing well over the shoulders.

WINGS: Large, well-folded against body, primaries and secondaries medium long, broad and overlapping in natural order.

BACK: Long, broad, straight; declining slightly to tail.

TAIL: Well developed; main tail feathers broad, fairly close together, carried at an angle of forty degrees above the horizontal. (See illustrations, page 28, Figures 30 and 31.)

BREAST: Broad, deep, well-rounded, carried well forward.

BODY AND FLUFF: Body long, broad, deep. Fluff, smooth in surface, moderately developed.

LEGS AND TOES: Legs, set well apart and straight when viewed from front, lower thighs large, medium short, well-meated. Shanks, medium short, stout, round in bone; toes, four on each foot; moderately long and straight.

Note: See Instructions to Judges, paragraph "Quality of Feather."

COLOR OF MALE AND FEMALE

COMB, FACE, WATTLES AND EAR-LOBES: Bright red.

BEAK: Yellow.

EYES: Reddish bay.

SHANKS AND TOES: Rich yellow.

PLUMAGE: See description of White plumage color, page 63.

NEW HAMPSHIRES

This breed has come into being by a gradual process of development over a period of more than thirty years, from a foundation of Rhode Island Reds, first brought into New Hampshire from Rhode Island and Southern Massachusetts. There is no record of any outside blood having been introduced and the breed has been developed by farm poultrymen of New Hampshire by the continual selection of breeding stock for early maturity, large brown eggs, quick feathering, strength and vigor during the long period of its evolution.

They were admitted into the American Standard of Perfection in 1935.

ECONOMIC QUALITIES: General purpose fowl for egg and meat production. Color of skin, yellow; color of egg shell, brown.

Disqualifications

One or more entirely white feathers showing in outer plumage. (See General Disqualifications and Cutting for Defects.)

STANDARD WEIGHTS

Cock ....8½ lbs.	Hen ....6½ lbs.
Cockerel ....7½ lbs.	Pullet ....5½ lbs.

SHAPE OF MALE

COMB: Single, medium size, well developed, set firmly on head, perfectly straight and upright having five well defined points, those in front and rear smaller than those in center; blade smooth, inclining slightly downward, but not following too closely the shape of neck.

BEAK: Strong, medium in length, regularly curved.

HEAD: Medium in length, fairly deep; inclined to be flat on top rather than round. Face smooth, full in front of eyes, skin fine in texture.

EYES: Large, full, prominent, setting moderately high in head.

WATTLES: Moderately large, uniform, free from folds or wrinkles.

EAR-LOBES: Elongated-oval, smooth, setting close to head.

NECK: Medium length, well arched, hackle abundant flowing well over shoulders, moderately close feathered.

WINGS: Moderately large, well folded, carried horizontally and close to body, fronts well covered by breast feathers; primaries and secondaries broad and overlapping in natural order when wing is folded.

BACK: Medium length, broad its entire length, forming a gradual concave sweep to tail.

TAIL: Medium length, well spread; carried at an angle of forty-five degrees above horizontal. (See illustrations, page 28, figures 30 and 31.) Sickles, medium length, extending well beyond main tail; lesser sickles and coverts, medium length, broad; main tail feathers broad and overlapping.

BREAST: Deep, full, broad and well rounded.

BODY AND FLUFF: Body, medium length, relatively broad, deep, well rounded, keel, relatively long, extending well to front at breast. Fluff, moderately full.

LEGS AND TOES: Legs set well apart, straight when viewed from front; lower thighs, large and muscular, of medium length; toes, of medium length, straight, well spread.

PLUMAGE: Feather character of broad, firm structure, overlapping well and fitting tight to body.

SHAPE OF FEMALE

COMB: Single, medium in size, well developed, smooth texture, firm at base, straight and upright, having five well defined points, those in front and rear smaller than those in center; slightly tilted at rear.

BEAK: Medium length, regularly curved.

HEAD: Medium length, fairly deep, inclined to be flat on top rather than round; face, smooth, full in front of eyes; skin, fine in texture.

EYES: Large, full, prominent, setting moderately high in head.

WATTLES: Medium size, well developed, well rounded.

EAR-LOBES: Elongated-oval, smooth, setting close to head.

NECK: Of medium length, slightly arched, tapering from shoulders to head, moderately close feathered.

WINGS: Rather large, well folded; carried nearly horizontal; fronts well covered by breast feathers; primaries and secondaries broad and overlapping, in natural order when wing is folded.

BACK: Medium length, broad its entire length, forming a gradual concave sweep to tail.

TAIL: Medium length, moderately well spread, carried at an angle of thirty-five degrees above horizontal. (See illustrations, page 28, Figures 30 and 31.) Main tail feathers broad and overlapping.

BREAST: Deep, full, well rounded.

BODY AND FLUFF: Body, medium length, relatively broad, deep, well rounded; keel, relatively long extending well to front at breast. Fluff, moderately full.

LEGS AND TOES: Legs set well apart, straight when viewed from front; lower thighs, medium length, closely feathered. smooth; shanks, medium length, smooth; toes, medium length, straight, well spread.

PLUMAGE: Feather character of broad, firm structure, overlapping well and fitting close to body.

COLOR OF MALE

COMB, FACE, WATTLES AND EAR-LOBES: Bright red.

BEAK: Reddish horn.

HEAD: Plumage, brilliant reddish bay.

EYES: Bay.

NECK: Rich, brilliant reddish bay.

WINGS: Fronts, medium chestnut red; bows, brilliant deep chestnut red; coverts, deep chestnut red; primaries, upper web, medium red; lower web, black edged with medium red; primary coverts, black, edged with medium red; secondaries, upper web, medium chestnut red, having broad black stripe extending along shaft to within one inch of tip; lower web, medium chestnut red; shaft, red.

BACK AND SADDLE: Back, brilliant deep chestnut red; saddle, rich brilliant reddish bay, slightly darker than neck color.

TAIL: Main tail feathers, black, sickle feathers, rich, lustrous greenish black; coverts, lustrous greenish black, edged with deep chestnut red; lesser coverts, deep chestnut red.

BREAST: Medium chestnut red.

NEW HAMPSHIRE MALE

NEW HAMPSHIRE FEMALE

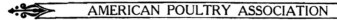

BODY AND FLUFF: Medium chestnut red.

LEGS AND TOES: Lower thighs, medium chestnut red, shanks and toes, rich yellow tinged with reddish horn. A line of pigment down sides of shanks extending to tips of toes is desirable.

COLOR OF FEMALE

COMB, FACE, WATTLES AND EAR-LOBES: Bright red.

BEAK: Reddish horn.

HEAD: Plumage, medium chestnut red.

EYES: Bay.

NECK: Medium chestnut red, each feather edged with brilliant chestnut red, lower neck feathers distinctly tipped with black, feathers in front of neck, medium chestnut red.

WINGS: Fronts, bows and coverts, medium chestnut red; primaries, upper web, medium red; lower web, medium red with a narrow stripe of black extending along the shaft; shaft, medium red; primary coverts, black edged with medium red; secondaries, lower web, medium chestnut red, upper web, medium chestnut red with black marking extending along edge of shaft two-thirds its length.

BACK: Medium chestnut red.

TAIL: Main tail, black edged with medium chestnut red; shaft, medium chestnut red.

BREAST: Medium chestnut red.

BODY AND FLUFF: Medium chestnut red.

LEGS AND TOES: Lower thighs, medium chestnut red, shanks and toes, rich yellow tinged with reddish horn.

ASIATIC

Breeds	*Varieties*
BRAHMAS	Light Dark Buff
COCHINS	Buff Partridge White Black
LANGSHANS	Black White
BRAHMA BANTAMS	Dark Light
COCHIN BANTAMS	Buff Partridge White Black

BRAHMAS AND BRAHMA BANTAMS

An' Asiatic breed of fowls, called Gray Shanghais, came from China in the '40s of the last century, via England, to the United States. It was long after they landed in New England that American poultry fanciers made over and refined the original parent stock into the large, stately and useful Light and Dark Brahma varieties, which were admitted to the first American Standard of Excellence in 1874.

Buff Brahmas, of more recent origin, became a Standard variety in 1924.

The head and crown are most important breed characteristics. Texture of the feathers is also of great importance, for the plumage should be smooth fitting and not loose-feathered and soft as in the Cochin.

ECONOMIC QUALITIES: A general purpose fowl for heavy meat production, and production of brown eggs. Color of skin, yellow; color of egg shells, light to dark brown.

Disqualifications

Vulture-like hocks; shanks not feathered down the outer sides, outer toes not feathered to the last joint; shanks other than yellow or reddish yellow. (See General Disqualifications and Cutting for Defects.)

BRAHMA BANTAMS

Disqualifications

Disqualifications for Brahma Bantams shall be the same as for Brahmas except in hock plumage and weight. (See General Disqualifications and Cutting for Defects.)

STANDARD WEIGHTS

Cock	30 oz.	Hen	26 oz.
Cockerel	26 oz.	Pullet	24 oz.

LIGHT AND DARK BRAHMA BANTAMS

SHAPE AND COLOR OF MALE AND FEMALE

The shape and color of the Brahma Bantam shall conform to the description of the Brahma. Stiff hock plumage is very objectionable.

SHAPE OF MALE

COMB: Pea; small, firm and even on head, lower and narrower in front and rear than at center; each row evenly serrated; points in front and rear smaller than those at center. (See Standard illustration, page 166, and page 16, figure 6.)

BEAK: Stout, well-curved.

HEAD: Of medium length, deep, broad; crown projecting well over eyes. (See Standard illustration, page 166.)

EYES: Large, deep set.

WATTLES: Of medium size, well-rounded.

EAR-LOBES: Large, the lower edges on a level with or slightly below edges of wattles.

NECK: Moderately long, well-arched; hackle abundant, flowing over shoulders and meeting throat, dividing at lower ends of wattles and flowing full at sides.

WINGS: Small, carried rather high, with lower line nearly horizontal; sides, well-rounded; primaries, closely folded under secondaries; primaries and secondaries, broad, and overlapping in natural order when wing is folded.

BACK: Rather long, flat across shoulders, broad, carrying its width well back to tail, rising with slightly concave incline from shoulders to middle of saddle, where it takes a more pronounced concave sweep well up on to tail; saddle, abundant, flowing full over sides, filling well in front of tail and covering wing-points.

TAIL: Of medium size, full, well-spread, carried high enough to continue concave sweep of back, filled underneath with curling feathers; sickles, short, spreading laterally; coverts, plentiful, but not so long as to cover the entire length of lower main-tail feathers; main-tail feathers, broad and overlapping.

BREAST: Broad, deep, full, well-rounded.

BODY AND FLUFF: Body, rather long, deep, well rounded at sides; fluff, abundant, smooth on surface, giving specimen a broad but compact appearance.

LIGHT BRAHMA MALE

LIGHT BRAHMA FEMALE

DARK BRAHMA MALE

DARK BRAHMA FEMALE

LEGS AND TOES: Legs, set well apart, straight when viewed from front; lower thighs, stout, well-feathered and smooth, nicely rounded, free from vulture-like feathering; shanks, large, stout in bone, of sufficient length to balance properly specimen, well covered on outer sides with feathers; toes, straight, stout; outer and middle toes, well feathered.

SHAPE OF FEMALE

COMB: Pea; low, firm and even on head; well-serrated, the middle row higher and more distinctly serrated than the other two. (See Standard illustration, page 167.)

BEAK: Stout, well-curved.

HEAD: Of medium length, deep, broad, crown projecting well over eyes. (See Standard illustration, page 167.)

EYES: Large, deep set.

WATTLES: Small.

EAR-LOBES: Large.

NECK: Of medium length, slightly arched; rather full under throat, hens having dewlap between wattles.

WINGS: Small, carried rather high, with lower line nearly horizontal; sides well rounded; fronts, covered by breast feathers; primaries, closely folded under secondaries; primaries and secondaries, broad, and overlapping in natural order when wing is folded.

BACK: Rather long, flat across shoulders with slightly concave sweep from middle of shoulders to junction with tail; broad, carrying the width well back onto tail.

TAIL: Of medium length, well spread at base, resembling an inverted "U" with wide angle when viewed from rear; carried high enough to continue the sweep of the back; tail-coverts, two rows, covering a greater part of both sides of main tail; main-tail feathers, broad and overlapping.

BREAST: Broad, deep, full, well-rounded.

BODY AND FLUFF: Body, long, deep, well rounded at sides; fluff, abundant, smooth in surface, giving the specimen a broad but compact appearance.

LEGS AND TOES: Legs, set well apart, straight when viewed from front; lower thighs, stout, well-feathered and smooth; shanks, of medium length, stout in bone, well feathered on outer sides; toes, straight, stout; outer and middle toes, well-feathered.

Note: See Instructions to Judges and paragraph "Quality of Feather," page 53.

LIGHT BRAHMAS

Disqualifications

One or more solid black or brown feathers on surface of back; dark spots or mossiness in surface of back or saddle appearing in approximately 15 percent of feathers of this section, except narrow black stripes extending not over half the length of feather in saddle and near tail of male, or dark markings in cape of either sex; red feathers in plumage. (See General and Brahma Disqualifications, and Cutting for Defects.)

STANDARD WEIGHTS

Cock	12 lbs.	Hen	9½ lbs.
Cockerel	10 lbs.	Pullet	8 lbs.

COLOR OF MALE

COMB, FACE, WATTLES, AND EAR-LOBES: Bright red.
BEAK: Yellow, with dark stripe down upper mandible.
EYES: Reddish bay.
SHANKS AND TOES: Shank feathers, white and black; outer toe feathering, white and black, where black, laced with white; shanks and toes, yellow.
PLUMAGE: See description of Columbian male plumage color, page 70 and 72.

COLOR OF FEMALE

COMB, FACE, WATTLES, AND EAR-LOBES: Bright red.
BEAK: Yellow, with dark stripe down the upper mandible.
EYES: Reddish bay.
SHANKS AND TOES: Shank feathers, white; outer toe feathers, white and black, where black, laced with white; shanks and toes, yellow.
PLUMAGE: See description of Columbian female plumage color, pages 71 and 72.

DARK BRAHMAS

Disqualifications

(See General and Brahma Disqualifications, and Cutting for Defects.)

STANDARD WEIGHTS

Cock	11 lbs.	Hen	8½ lbs.
Cockerel	9 lbs.	Pullet	7 lbs.

COLOR OF MALE
COMB, FACE, WATTLES, AND EAR-LOBES: Bright red.
BEAK: Dusky yellow, shading to yellow at point.
EYES: Reddish bay.
SHANKS AND TOES: Shanks, feathers black; shanks and toes, yellow; toe feathers, black.
PLUMAGE: See description of Silver-Penciled male plumage color, pages 64 and 68.

COLOR OF FEMALE
COMB, FACE, WATTLES, AND EAR-LOBES: Bright red.
BEAK: Dusky yellow, shading to yellow at point.
EYES: Reddish bay.
SHANKS AND TOES: Shank feathers, steel gray penciled; toe feathers, steel gray distinctly penciled; shanks and toes, yellow.
PLUMAGE: See description of Silver-Penciled female plumage color, pages 68 and 69.

BUFF BRAHMAS
Disqualifications
One or more solid black, white, or gray feathers on surface of back; black, white, or gray spots or mossiness in surface of back or saddle appearing in approximately 15 per cent of the feathers of this section, except narrow black stripes, extending not over half the length of feather in lower saddle and near tail of male, or dark markings in cape of either sex. (See General and Brahma Disqualifications, and Cutting for Defects.)

STANDARD WEIGHTS
Cock ....11 lbs. Hen ....8½ lbs.
Cockerel .... 9 lbs. Pullet ....7 lbs.

COLOR OF MALE
COMB, FACE, WATTLES, AND EAR-LOBES: Bright red.
BEAK: Yellow, with dark stripe down upper mandible.
HEAD: Plumage, buff.
EYES: Reddish bay.
NECK: Hackle, web, a solid, lustrous greenish black, moderately broad, with a narrow edging of golden buff uniform in width, extending around point of feather; greater portion of shaft, black; plumage on front of neck, buff.

WINGS: Fronts, buff, may be partly black; bows and coverts, rich, lustrous, golden buff; primaries, black with buff edging on lower edge of lower webs; secondaries, lower portion of lower web, buff, sufficient to form a buff wing-bay, the buff extending around the end of feathers and lacing upper portion of upper webs, this color growing wider in the shorter secondaries, sufficient to show buff on surface when wing is folded; remainder of each secondary, black.

BACK AND SADDLE: Surface, lustrous, golden buff, cape, black and buff; saddle, buff, except lower saddle feathers, which should be buff with a very narrow V-shaped black stripe at end of each feather, tapering to a point near its lower extremity, and extending from points of wing to root and sides of tail, this V-shaped stripe increasing in width, length and density as it nears the tail-coverts.

TAIL: Main-tail feathers, black; the curling feathers underneath, black laced with buff; sickles and coverts, lustrous, greenish black; smaller coverts, lustrous, greenish black, edged with golden buff.

BREAST: Surface, golden buff.

BODY AND FLUFF: Body, buff, except under wings, where it may be slate; fluff, buff.

LEGS AND TOES: Lower thighs, buff; shank feathers, buff; outer toe feathering, buff and black, where black, laced with buff; shanks and toes, yellow.

UNDER-COLOR OF ALL SECTIONS: Slate or a light shade of buff, slate preferred.

COLOR OF FEMALE

COMB, FACE, WATTLES, AND EAR-LOBES: Bright red.

BEAK: Yellow, with dark stripe down the upper mandible.

HEAD: Plumage, buff.

EYES: Reddish bay.

NECK: Feathers, beginning at juncture of head, web, a broad, solid, lustrous, greenish black with a narrow lacing of golden buff extending around the outer edge of each feather; greater portion of shafts, black; feathers on front of neck, buff.

WINGS: Fronts, bows and coverts, golden buff; primaries, black with buff edging on lower edge of lower webs; secondaries, lower portion of lower webs buff, sufficient to form a buff wing-bay, the buff extending around the end and lacing upper portion of upper webs, this color growing wider in the shorter secondaries, sufficient to show buff on surface when wing is folded; remainder of each secondary, black.

BACK: Golden buff; cape, black and buff.

TAIL: Main-tail feathers black, except the two top feathers, which are slightly edged with buff; coverts, black with a narrow lacing of buff.

BREAST: Surface, golden buff.

BODY AND FLUFF: Body, golden buff, except under wings, where it may be slate; fluff, golden buff.

LEGS AND TOES: Lower thighs, buff; shank feathers, buff, outer toe feathers, buff and black; where black, laced with buff; shanks and toes, yellow.

UNDER-COLOR OF ALL SECTIONS: Slaty buff.

COCHINS

The Chinese Shanghai fowl came to Great Britain and America in 1845. The name of this Asiatic breed was later changed to Cochin. The earliest Cochins were more or less buff in color. By its striking appearance, due to great size and profuse, soft feathering, which distinguished it from all other known breeds at that early period, Cochins created a sensation in England, resulting in a great boom for the "Cochin China," as it was called in the days of "Cochin craze."

Since then, four varieties have been produced: namely, Buff, White, Black, and Partridge, all being admitted to the Standard in 1874.

Both male and female are massive in appearance, with an extraordinary profusion of long, soft plumage and a great abundance of down fibre in the under-fluff, producing a rather bulky appearance, and conveying the idea of even greater weight than actually exists. Hard or closely-fitting plumage is a very serious defect.

ECONOMIC QUALITIES: Although primarily bred for exhibition, the Cochin is a dual purpose fowl for the production of meat and eggs. Color of skin, yellow; color of egg shells, brown.

Disqualifications

Vulture hocks, shanks not feathered down the outer sides, outer toes not feathered to last joint, bare middle toes, plucked hocks. (See General Disqualifications and Cutting for Defects.)

STANDARD WEIGHTS

Cock	11 lbs.	Hen	8½ lbs.
Cockerel	9 lbs.	Pullet	7 lbs.

COCHIN BANTAMS

Disqualifications

Disqualifications for Cochin Bantams shall be the same as for the Cochins except in hock plumage and weight. (See General Disqualifications and Cutting for Defects.)

STANDARD WEIGHTS

Cock	30 oz.	Hen	26 oz.
Cockerel	26 oz.	Pullet	24 oz.

BUFF, BLACK, WHITE AND PARTRIDGE COCHIN BANTAMS

SHAPE AND COLOR OF MALE AND FEMALE

The shape and color of the Cochin Bantam shall conform to the description of the Cochin. Stiff hock plumage is very objectionable.

SHAPE OF MALE

COMB: Single, of medium size, set firmly on head, stout at base, upright, straight from front to rear, low in front; serrations moderately deep, dividing comb into five regular points, the middle one highest; free from wrinkles, fine in texture. (See Standard illustration, page 178.)

BEAK: Short, stout at base, curving to point.

HEAD: Rather short, broad, deep, prominent over eyes, juncture with neck well-defined; face, smooth, of fine texture. (See Standard illustrations, page 178.)

EYES: Moderately large, mild in expression.

WATTLES: Rather long, well-rounded at lower edges, thin and fine in texture.

EAR-LOBES: Smooth, well-defined, about two-thirds as long as wattles.

NECK: Short, full, well-proportioned, beautifully arched from rear of head to back; hackle, very long and abundant, flowing well over shoulder and cape.

WINGS: Small, carried well up and well folded; fronts, embedded in plumage of breast; tips nicely tucked under saddle plumage; wing-bows, smooth and exceedingly well-rounded; primaries and secondaries, broad, and overlapping in natural order when wing is folded.

BACK: Short in appearance, very broad and well-rounded; shoulders, very broad, flat under hackle; saddle or cushion rising at base of hackle or cape, very broad and round; plumage, very profuse and long; saddle feathers, flowing over tips of wings and mingling with fluff and under-plumage of tail.

TAIL: Main-tail, short, well spread at base, filled underneath with profusion of soft feathers; sickles, short, well-rounded and enveloped by coverts and lesser sickles, showing as little of the stiff feathers as possible; saddle and tail to have soft, round, bulky appearance; main-tail feathers, broad and overlapping.

BREAST: Carried forward, very full, well rounded, of great breadth and depth.

BODY AND FLUFF: Body, of moderate length, broad, deep, well-rounded from point of breast to abdomen, well let down between the legs, broad and well-rounded from breast bone to tail, depending more on length of feathers for fullness than on muscular development; fluff, soft, full, abundant.

LEGS AND TOES: Legs, set well apart, straight when viewed from front; lower thighs, of moderate length; large, straight the more long, soft, outstanding plumage, extending well down the shanks and covering hock joints, the better, having the appearance of two great globes of feathers concealing the legs from view; hocks, covered with flexible feathers, curving inward about the joints; free from vulture-like feathering; shanks, short, stout in bone; plumage, long, beginning just below hocks and covering front and outer sides of shanks, from which it should be outstanding, the upper part growing out from under thigh plumage and continuing into foot feathering. There should be no marked break in the outlines between the plumage of these sections; they should merge naturally into each other and blend together; toes, straight, stout, well-spread; middle and outer toes, heavily feathered to ends.

SHAPE OF FEMALE

COMB: Single, small, straight and upright; nicely rounded to conform to shape of head; divided into five points; free from wrinkles, fine in texture. (See Standard illustration, page 179.)

BEAK: Short, stout at base, curving to point.

HEAD: Neat, fairly full in skull, fashioned after that of male, except finer in form; face smooth, of fine texture.

EYES: Of medium size, mild in expression.

WATTLES: Small, nicely rounded; fine in texture.

EAR-LOBES: Oblong, fairly well defined, fine in texture.

NECK: Short, nicely arched; plumage, very full, flowing well over shoulders and cape.

WINGS: Small, well-folded and carried without drooping; fronts, embedded in plumage of breast; tips, concealed between cushion and thigh plumage; wing-bows, smooth and exceedingly well-rounded; primaries and secondaries, broad, and overlapped in natural order when wing is folded.

BACK: Short in appearance, very broad, well-rounded; shoulders, broad, flat under neck feathers; cushion, rising from cape,

BUFF COCHIN MALE

BUFF COCHIN FEMALE

PARTRIDGE COCHIN MALE

PARTRIDGE COCHIN FEMALE

BLACK COCHIN MALE

BLACK COCHIN FEMALE

large, full and round; plumage, profuse, flowing over tips of wings well into thigh plumage and almost covering tail feathers.

TAIL: Short, broad at base, carried rather low; well filled underneath with profusion of soft feathers and nearly enveloped by tail coverts, which help to form the cushion; main-tail feathers, broad and overlapping.

BREAST: Carried low in front, full, well-rounded, of great breadth and depth.

BODY AND FLUFF: Body of medium length, broad, deep, full and well rounded from point of breast to abdomen, well let down between legs, full and round from breast bone to tail, with great length and fullness of feather; fluff, full, soft, profuse.

LEGS AND TOES: Legs, set well apart, straight when viewed from front; lower thighs, of medium length, moderately large, straight; with great profusion of long, soft, outstanding fluff plumage, completely hiding hocks and covering shanks almost to feet; hocks should be well covered with profusion of soft, flexible feathers, curving inward about joints, free from vulture-like feathers; shanks, short, stout in bone, covered profusely with long plumage; toes, straight, well-spread; middle and outer toes, heavily feathered to ends.

Note: See Instructions to Judges, paragraph "Quality of Feather," page 53.

BUFF COCHINS

Disqualifications

Shanks other than yellow. (See General and Cochin Disqualifications, and Cutting for Defects.)

COLOR OF MALE AND FEMALE

COMB, FACE, WATTLES, AND EAR-LOBES: Bright red.

BEAK: Yellow.

EYES: Reddish bay.

LEGS AND TOES: Shank and toe feathers, rich golden buff; shanks and toes, rich yellow.

PLUMAGE: See description of Buff plumage color, page 64.

PARTRIDGE COCHINS

Disqualifications

Positive white in main-tail feathers, sickles, or secondaries; shanks other than yellow or dusky yellow. (See General and Cochin Disqualifications, and Cutting for Defects.)

COLOR OF MALE

COMB, FACE, WATTLES, AND EAR-LOBES: Bright red.

BEAK: Dark horn, shading to yellow at point.

EYES: Reddish bay.

LEGS AND TOES: Shank and toe feathers, black; shanks and toes, yellow.

PLUMAGE: See description of Partridge male plumage color, page 69.

SHAPE OF FEMALE

COMB, FACE, WATTLES, AND EAR-LOBES: Bright red.

BEAK: Dark horn, shading to yellow at point.

EYES: Reddish bay.

LEGS AND TOES: Shank and toe feathers, deep reddish bay penciled with black; shanks and toes, yellow.

PLUMAGE: See description of Partridge female plumage color, page 70.

WHITE COCHINS

Disqualifications

Shanks other than yellow. (See General and Cochin Disqualifications, and Cutting for Defects.)

COLOR OF MALE AND FEMALE

COMB, FACE, WATTLES, AND EAR-LOBES: Bright red.

BEAK: Yellow.

EYES: Reddish bay.

LEGS AND TOES: Shank and toe feathers, white.

PLUMAGE: See description of White plumage color, page 63.

BLACK COCHINS

Disqualifications

More than one-half inch of positive white in any part of plumage, except less than one inch in under-color of hackles and saddles of cocks; two or more feathers tipped or edged with positive white, except in foot or toe feathers; shanks other than yellow or black gradually shading into yellow; bottoms of feet showing complete absence of yellow. (See General and Cochin Disqualifications, and Cutting for Defects.)

COLOR OF MALE AND FEMALE

COMB, FACE, WATTLES, AND EAR-LOBES: Bright red.

BEAK: Yellow, shaded with black.

EYES: Reddish bay.

LEGS AND TOES: Shank and toe feathers, black; shanks and toes, yellow; bottoms of feet, yellow.

PLUMAGE: See description of Black plumage color, page 64.

LANGSHANS

The Black Langshan originated in China, where it has been bred over a very long period of years. Its prepotent reproductive qualities indicate it to be a pure race of domesticated poultry. Black Langshans were imported from China into England by the late Major Croad, so there is a class of "Croad Langshans" in the English Standard. They became a Standard variety in this country in 1883. White Langshans were admitted to the Standard in 1893.

The general characteristics of Langshans are great proportionate depth of body, round contour of breast and fineness of bone for the size of the fowl. The male develops a large, well-spread tail with feathers of great length, the sickles often attaining a length of sixteen or seventeen inches. The closely-fitting saddle feathers, full-hackled neck and upright carriage give the effect of a short back. The surface plumage throughout is close and smooth. The body in both sexes should be evenly balanced on firm, straight legs, with very little backward bend at the hocks. The height of the Langshan should be gained by depth of body and erectness of carriage, and not from what may be described as stiltiness of legs. Close-standing hocks and narrowness of body are highly objectionable.

ECONOMIC QUALITIES: General purpose fowl for the production of meat and eggs. Color of skin, white; color of egg shells, very dark brown.

Disqualifications

Shanks not feathered down the outer sides, feathers not growing on the outer toes beyond the middle joint; vulture-like hocks; yellow skin; bottoms of feet, yellow in any part. (See General Disqualifications and Cutting for Defects.)

STANDARD WEIGHTS

Cock	9½ lbs.	Hen	7½ lbs.
Cockerel	8 lbs.	Pullet	6½ lbs.

SHAPE OF MALE

COMB: Single; of medium size, straight, upright, having five points, evenly serrated, not conforming closely to neck, fine in texture. (See illustration, page 190.)

BEAK: Stout at base, well curved.

HEAD: Of medium size, rather broad.

EYES: Moderately large, round.

WATTLES: Of moderate length, well-rounded.

EAR-LOBES: Oblong, well-developed.

NECK: Of good length, well-arched; hackle, abundant, flowing well over shoulders.

WINGS: Of medium size, well-folded, carried closely to body without drooping; primaries and secondaries, broad, and overlapping in natural order when wing is folded.

BACK: Short, broad, flat at shoulders, rising from middle of back in a decidedly sharp concave sweep to tail; saddle feathers, abundant, flowing over sides.

TAIL: Long, large, full, well spread at base, carried at an angle of seventy-five degrees above the horizontal (see page 28, figures 30 and 31); sickles, long, extending decidedly beyond the tail; coverts, long—the longer the better; main-tail feathers, broad and overlapping.

BREAST: Broad, round, deep.

BODY AND FLUFF: Body, rather broad and deep in front of thighs; fluff, fairly developed, but not so abundant as to hide profile of hocks.

LEGS AND TOES: Legs set well apart and straight when viewed from front; lower thighs, rather long, strong, well feathered; shanks, rather long, stout in bone, straight, slender; outer toes, feathered to the end; middle toes, free from feathers.

SHAPE OF FEMALE

COMB: Single; smaller than that of male, straight and upright, evenly serrated, having five points, fine in texture. (See Standard illustration, page 191.)

BEAK: Stout at base, well curved.

HEAD: Similar to that of male, but smaller.

EYES: Moderately large, round.

WATTLES: Fairly developed, well-rounded; fine in texture.

EAR-LOBES: Fairly developed, oblong, fine in texture.

NECK: Of good length, full-feathered.

WINGS: Of good size, well-folded, carried close to body without drooping; primaries and secondaries, broad, and overlapping in natural order when wing is folded.

BACK: Of medium length, broad, flat at shoulders, rising from middle of back in a sharp, concave sweep ending well up on tail.

TAIL: Rather long, well spread at base, carried at an angle of seventy degrees above the horizontal (see illustrations, page 28, figures 30 and 31); carried well above and beyond the cushion and furnished with long coverts; main-tail feathers, broad and overlapping.

BREAST: Broad, round, deep.

BODY AND FLUFF: Body, rather short, broad, deep, well-balanced; fluff, well-developed.

LEGS AND TOES: Lower thighs, rather long, strong, well covered with soft feathers; shanks, of good length, small-boned, set well apart, feathered down outer sides; toes, long, straight, slender; outer toes, feathered to ends; middle toes, free from feathers.

Note: See Instructions to Judges, and paragraph "Quality of Feather", page 53.

BLACK LANGSHANS

Disqualifications

More than one-half inch of positive white in any part of the plumage, or two or more feathers tipped or edged with positive white, except in foot or toe feathering; shanks other than black or dark leaden blue. (See General and Langshan Disqualifications, and Cutting for Defects.)

COLOR OF MALE AND FEMALE

COMB, FACE, WATTLES, AND EAR-LOBES: Bright red.

BEAK: Dark horn shading to pinkish tint near lower edge.

EYES: Dark brown.

SKIN ON BODY: Pinkish white.

SHANKS AND TOES: Bluish black, showing pink between scales; web and bottoms of feet, pinkish white.

PLUMAGE: Surface, lustrous, greenish black.

UNDER-COLOR: Dull black.

BLACK LANGSHAN MALE

BLACK LANGSHAN FEMALE

WHITE LANGSHANS

Disqualifications

(See General and Langshan Disqualifications, and Cutting for Defects.)

COLOR OF MALE AND FEMALE

COMB, FACE, WATTLES, AND EAR-LOBES: Bright red.

BEAK: Light slate blue, shading to pinkish white.

EYES: Dark brown.

SHANKS AND TOES: Slaty blue, showing pink between the scales.

PLUMAGE: See description of White plumage color, page 63. (See definition of "Feather.")

MEDITERRANEAN

Breeds	*Varieties*
LEGHORNS	Single-Comb Dark Brown Single-Comb Light Brown Rose-Comb Dark Brown Rose-Comb Light Brown Single-Comb White Rose-Comb White Single-Comb Buff Single-Comb Black Single-Comb Silver Single-Comb Red Single-Comb Black-Tailed Red Single-Comb Columbian
MINORCAS	Single-Comb Black Rose-Comb Black Single-Comb White Rose-Comb White Single-Comb Buff
SPANISH	White-Faced Black
BLUE ANDALUSIANS	
ANCONAS	Single-Comb Rose-Comb
BUTTERCUPS	

LEGHORNS

The original breed came from Italy, but its many sub-varieties originated or were developed in England, Denmark or America. They comprise a group characterized by comparatively small size, great activity, hardiness and prolific egg-laying qualities. The females are non-sitters, very few of them exhibiting a tendency to broodiness. Aside from the manifold points of beauty in type and color found in all varieties of Leghorns as exhibition specimens, their excellent productive qualities are valuable assets of the breed.

Breeders, exhibitors and judges should pay due regard to the Standard weights of Leghorns, in order to maintain the egg products up to required market weight grades.

The different varieties of Leghorns were admitted to the Standard as follows: Single-Comb Browns, Whites and Blacks, 1874; Rose-Comb Browns and Whites, 1886; Single-Comb Buffs, 1894; Single-Comb Columbians, 1929; and Reds and Black-Tailed Reds, 1929.

ECONOMIC QUALITIES: Especially noted for the production of eggs. Color of skin, yellow; color of egg shells, white.

Disqualifications

Red covering more than one-third the surface of ear-lobes in cockerels and pullets, more than one-half in cocks and hens; males more than one and a half pounds under weight; females more than one pound under weight. (See General Disqualifications and Cutting for Defects.)

STANDARD WEIGHTS

Cock	6 lbs.	Hen	4½ lbs.
Cockerel	5 lbs.	Pullet	4 lbs.

SHAPE OF MALE

COMB: Single; fine in texture, of medium size, straight and upright, firm and even on head (see page 212), having five distinct points, deeply serrated and extending well over back of head with no tendency to follow shape of neck; smooth, free from twists, folds or excrescences. (See Standard illustration, page 198.)

COMB: Rose; of medium size, square in front, firm and even on head, tapering evenly from front to rear and terminating in a well-developed spike which extends horizontally well back of head; flat, free from hollow center and covered with small, rounded points. (See page 213.)

BEAK: Medium in length, strong, nicely curved.

HEAD: Moderate in length, fairly deep, inclined to be flat on top rather than round; face clean-cut, skin fine in texture, free from wrinkles. (See description of Head, page 20.)

EYES: Rather large, full, prominent.

WATTLES: Moderately long, uniform, well-rounded, smooth, fine in texture, free from folds or wrinkles.

EAR-LOBES: Oval in shape but rather broad, smooth, of moderate size, fitting closely to head.

NECK: Moderately long, nicely arched, hackle abundant, flowing well over shoulders.

WINGS: Large, well-folded and carried without drooping; primaries and secondaries, broad, and overlapping in natural order when wing is folded.

BACK: Rather long, moderately broad its entire length, slightly rounded at shoulders, slightly sloping downward from shoulders to center of back, then rising in a gradually increasing concave sweep to tail. Saddle feathers long, of good width, abundant, filling well in front of tail.

TAIL: Large, well-spread; main-tail feathers, broad and overlapping, carried at an angle of forty degrees above the horizontal; sickle feathers of good width, well-curved; lesser sickles and tail-coverts, long, of good width, nicely curved and abundant. (See illustrations, page 28, figures 30 and 31.)

BREAST: Full, well-rounded, carried well forward.

BODY AND FLUFF: Body, moderately long, rather deep, showing good heart and body girth (see chapter on "Economic Qualities of Fowls") ; carried nearly horizontal but sloping very slightly from front to rear; fluff, short. Under line to conform generally to top line.

LEGS AND TOES: Legs, set well apart, straight when viewed from front; lower thighs and shanks, moderately long; toes, medium length, straight, well-spread.

SHAPE OF FEMALE

COMB: Single; medium in size (see page 212); deeply serrated, having five distinct points, the front portion of the comb and the first point to stand erect and the remainder of comb drooping gradually to one side; fine in texture; free from folds or wrinkles. (See Standard illustration, page 199.)

COMB: Rose; of medium size, square in front, firm and even on head, tapering evenly from front to rear and terminating in a well-developed spike which extends horizontally back of head; flat, free from hollow center, covered with very small, rounded points. (See Standard illustration, page 213.)

BEAK: Medium in length, strong, nicely curved.

HEAD: Moderate in length, fairly deep, inclined to be flat on top rather than round; face, clean-cut, skin, fine in texture, free from wrinkles.

EYES: Rather large, full, prominent.

WATTLES: Of moderate size, uniform, free from folds or wrinkles, fine in texture, smooth, well-rounded.

EAR-LOBES: Of moderate size, oval in shape, smooth, thin, free from folds or wrinkles, fitting closely to head.

NECK: Moderately long, gracefully arched, tapering to head.

WINGS: Large, well-folded and carried without drooping; primaries and secondaries, broad, and overlapping in natural order when wing is folded.

BACK: Rather long, moderately broad its entire length, slightly rounded, with a slight slope down from shoulders to center of back, and rising from center with a concave sweep to tail, feathers of sufficient length to carry well up to tail.

TAIL: Long, full, well-spread, feathers of good width, carried at an angle of thirty-five degrees above the horizontal; maintail feathers, broad and overlapping (see illustrations, page 28, figures 30 and 31); coverts, broad and abundant, extending well onto main tail.

BREAST: Full, well-rounded, carried well forward.

BODY AND FLUFF: Body, moderately long, rather deep, carried nearly horizontally, but sloping very slightly downward from front to rear; fluff, rather short. Under line to conform generally to top line.

LEGS AND TOES: Legs, set well apart, straight when viewed from front; lower thighs and shanks, moderately long; toes, medium length, straight, well-spread.

Note: See Instructions to Judges, paragraph "Quality of Feather", page 53.

DARK BROWN LEGHORNS
(SINGLE-COMBS)
Disqualifications

Positive white in main-tail feathers, sickles or secondaries; shanks other than yellow. (See General and Leghorn Disqualifications, and Cutting for Defects.)

COLOR OF MALE

COMB, FACE, AND WATTLES: Bright red.

BEAK: Horn.

HEAD: Plumage, dark red.

EYES: Reddish bay.

EAR-LOBES: Enamel white.

NECK: Rich, brilliant red, with a lustrous, greenish black stripe running nearly parallel with edges and extending through the middle of each feather, tapering to a point near its lower extremity; plumage on front of neck, lustrous, greenish black.

WINGS: Fronts, black; bows, rich brilliant red; coverts, lustrous, greenish black, forming well-defined wing-bars when wings are folded; primaries, black, lower webs edged with brown; secondaries, black, edges of lower webs a rich brown of sufficient width to form wing-bay of same color.

BACK AND SADDLE: Rich, brilliant red with a lustrous greenish black stripe running through the middle of each feather, same as in hackle.

TAIL: Main-tail feathers, black; sickles and coverts, lustrous, greenish black.

BREAST: Lustrous black.

BODY AND FLUFF: Black.

LEGS AND TOES: Lower thighs, black; shanks and toes, yellow.

UNDER-COLOR OF ALL SECTIONS: Slate.

SINGLE-COMB DARK BROWN LEGHORN MALE

SINGLE-COMB DARK BROWN LEGHORN FEMALE

199

COLOR OF FEMALE

COMB, FACE, AND WATTLES: Bright red.

BEAK: Horn.

HEAD: Plumage, reddish bay.

EAR-LOBES: Enamel white.

NECK: Reddish bay, with a black stripe running nearly parallel with edges and extending through the middle of each feather, tapering to a point near its lower extremity; plumage on front of neck, same as breast.

WINGS: Fronts, bows, and coverts, same color as described for back; primaries, slaty black, the outer web slightly edged with brown; secondaries, slaty black, the outer web stippled with rich reddish brown.

BACK: Web of feathers on surface, black, coarsely stippled with rich reddish brown, the brown to predominate; free from shafting, purple, and regular penciling; exposed portion of feather to carry a lustrous green sheen; unexposed portion of feather, dull slaty black.

TAIL: Main-tail feathers, greenish black, the two top feathers stippled with rich reddish brown; coverts, same as back.

BREAST: Same color as described for back, except that breast carries a slightly lighter shade, due to the greater predominance of the reddish brown stippling.

BODY AND FLUFF: Body, slaty black, tinged with brown; free from shafting; fluff, slaty black, tinged with brown.

LEGS AND TOES: Lower thighs, slaty black, tinged with brown; shanks and toes, yellow.

UNDER-COLOR OF ALL SECTIONS: Dull slaty black.

DARK BROWN LEGHORNS

(ROSE COMB)

COLOR OF MALE AND FEMALE

See color description for Single Comb Dark Brown Leghorns.

LIGHT BROWN LEGHORNS

(SINGLE-COMBS)

Disqualifications

Same as for Dark Brown Leghorns.

COLOR OF MALE

COMB, FACE AND WATTLES: Bright red.

BEAK: Horn.

HEAD: Plumage, orange red.

EYES: Reddish bay.

EAR-LOBES: Enamel white.

NECK: Hackle, orange red at head, gradually shading to a lighter orange or golden yellow toward shoulders; a dull black stripe, free from shafting extending down the middle of each lower hackle feather and tapering to a point; the black stripe increasing in intensity and brilliance of color to a lustrous, greenish black at the lower extremity. Plumage, on front of neck: black, slightly marked with salmon.

WINGS: Fronts, black; bows, rich, lustrous, deep orange red; coverts, lustrous, greenish black; primaries, dull black, lower web edged with brown; secondaries, dull black, edges of lower webs light brown of sufficient width to form wing-bay of the same color.

BACK AND SADDLE: Lustrous, deep orange red, free from shafting, shading to lustrous, light orange in lower saddle feathers.

TAIL: Main-tail feathers, black; sickle and coverts, lustrous black.

BREAST: Lustrous black.

BODY AND FLUFF: Slate, slightly tinged with brown.

LEGS AND TOES: Lower thighs, slate; shanks and toes, yellow.

UNDER-COLOR OF ALL SECTIONS: Light slate.

201

SINGLE-COMB LIGHT BROWN LEGHORN MALE

SINGLE-COMB LIGHT BROWN LEGHORN FEMALE

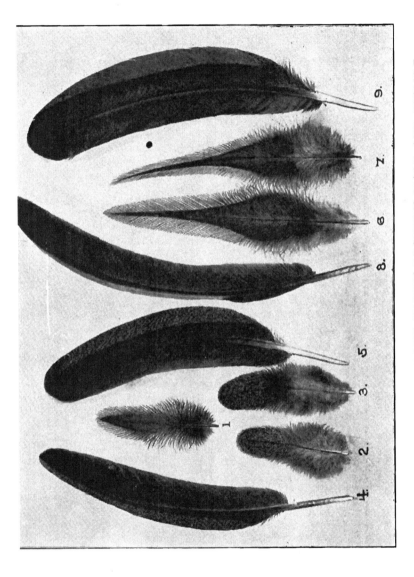

FEATHERS FROM DARK BROWN LEGHORN MALE AND FEMALE

Feathers from female: 1, Neck; 2, Breast; 3, Back; 4, Primary; 5, Secondary.

204

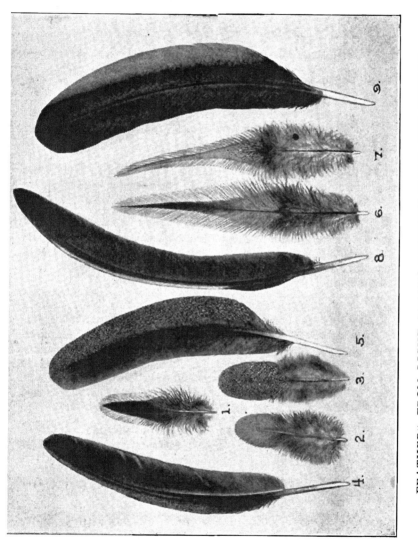

FEATHERS FROM LIGHT BROWN LEGHORN MALE AND FEMALE
Feather from female: 1, Neck; 2, Breast; 3, Back; 4, Primary; 5, Secondary.
Male: 6. Hackle: 7. Saddle: 8. Primary: 9. Secondary.

COLOR OF FEMALE

COMB, FACE AND WATTLES: Bright red.

BEAK: Horn.

HEAD: Plumage, lustrous, deep orange.

EYES: Reddish bay.

EAR-LOBES: Enamel white.

NECK: Light orange, with lustrous black stripe, free from shafting extending down the middle of each feather and tapering to a point near its lower extremity; feathers on front of neck, rich salmon.

WINGS: Fronts, bows and coverts, same color as described for backs; primaries, slaty-brown, the outer webs slightly edged with brown; secondaries, brown, the outer webs finely stippled with lighter brown.

BACK: Web of feathers on surface, dark brown finely stippled with lighter brown, the lighter shade predominating; more importance is attached to fineness, sharp definition of stippling, evenness of color and freedom from shafting than to the particular shade or color, but it is important that the effect produced be that of a soft, even brown that is not suggestive of gray, as one extreme to be avoided, or of red, as the other; the unexposed portion of the feather to be dark brown, shading into slate.

TAIL: Main-tail feathers, dull black, except the two top feathers which are stippled with lighter brown; coverts, same as back.

BREAST: Rich salmon, shading off lighter under body; free from shafting.

BODY AND FLUFF: Body, dark brown stippled with a lighter brown, free from shafting; fluff, slate plentifully tinged with brown.

LEGS AND TOES: Lower thighs, slate plentifully tinged with brown; shanks and toes, yellow.

UNDER-COLOR OF ALL SECTIONS: Slate.

LIGHT BROWN LEGHORNS
(ROSE COMB)
COLOR OF MALE AND FEMALE
See color description for Single Comb Light Brown Leghorns.

WHITE LEGHORNS
(SINGLE AND ROSE-COMBS)
Disqualifications
Shanks other than yellow. (See General and Leghorn Disqualifications, and Cutting for Defects.)

COLOR OF MALE AND FEMALE
COMB, FACE, AND WATTLES: Bright red.
BEAK: Yellow:
EYES: Reddish bay.
EAR-LOBES: Enamel white.
SHANKS AND TOES: Yellow.
PLUMAGE: See description of White plumage color, page 63.

BUFF LEGHORNS
(SINGLE-COMBS)
Disqualifications
Shanks other than yellow. (See General and Leghorn Disqualifications, and Cutting for Defects.)

COLOR OF MALE AND FEMALE
COMB, FACE, AND WATTLES: Bright red.
BEAK: Yellow.
EYES: Reddish bay.
EAR-LOBES: Enamel white.
SHANKS AND TOES: Rich yellow.
PLUMAGE: See description of Buff plumage color, page 64.

SINGLE-COMB WHITE LEGHORN MALE

SINGLE-COMB WHITE LEGHORN FEMALE

ROSE-COMB WHITE LEGHORN MALE

ROSE-COMB WHITE LEGHORN FEMALE

MALE COMBS

(1) Medium.   (2) Large.   (3) Small.

FEMALE COMBS

(1) Medium.   (2) Large.   (3) Small.

RELATIVE SIZE OF LEGHORN COMBS
(Single)

MALE COMBS

(1) Medium.   (2) Large.   (3) Small.

FEMALE COMBS

(1) Medium.   (2) Large.   (3) Small.

RELATIVE SIZE OF LEGHORN COMBS
(Rose)

BLACK LEGHORNS

(SINGLE-COMBS)

Disqualifications

More than one-half inch of positive white in any part of the plumage, except one inch or less in under-color of hackles and saddles of cocks; or two or more feathers tipped or edged with positive white; beak or shanks other than yellow or yellow shaded with black. (See General and Leghorn Disqualifications, and Cutting for Defects.)

COLOR OF MALE AND FEMALE

COMB, FACE, AND WATTLES: Bright red.
BEAK: Yellow.
EYES: Reddish bay.
EAR-LOBES: Enamel white.
SHANKS AND TOES: Yellow.
PLUMAGE: See description of Black plumage color, page 64.
UNDER COLOR OF ALL SECTIONS: Slate.

SILVER LEGHORNS

(SINGLE-COMBS)

Disqualifications

Red feather or feathers in any part of male plumage; shanks other than yellow or dusky yellow. (See General and Leghorn Disqualifications, and Cutting for Defects.)

COLOR OF MALE

COMB, FACE, AND WATTLES: Bright red.
BEAK: Yellow.
HEAD: Plumage, silvery white.
EYES: Reddish bay.
EAR-LOBES: Enamel white.
NECK: Hackle, silvery white with a narrow dull black stripe extending down middle of each lower hackle feather, tapering to a point near its lower extremity; plumage on front of neck, rich, glossy black.

WINGS: Fronts, black; bows, silvery white; coverts, lustrous, greenish black, forming a distinct bar across the wing; primaries, black, except the lower feathers, the outer edges of which should be silvery white; secondaries, part of outer webs of feathers in wing-bay, white, remainder of feathers, black.

BACK: Silvery white; cape, black; saddle, silvery white.

TAIL: Main-tail feathers, black; sickles, lustrous, greenish black; upper coverts, lustrous, greenish black; lower coverts, silvery white.

BREAST: Lustrous black.

BODY AND FLUFF: Black.

LEGS AND TOES: Lower thighs, black; shanks and toes, yellow.

UNDER-COLOR OF ALL SECTIONS: Light slate.

COLOR OF FEMALE

COMB, FACE, AND WATTLES: Bright red.

BEAK: Yellow.

HEAD: Plumage, silvery gray.

EYES: Reddish bay.

EAR-LOBES: Enamel white.

NECK: Silvery gray, with narrow, dull black stripe extending down middle of each feather, tapering to a point near its lower extremity; feathers on front of neck, light salmon.

WINGS: Fronts, bows and coverts, gray, formed of silvery white finely stippled with ashy gray, free from dark marks or bars; primaries and secondaries, upper webs, dark slate, lower webs, slaty gray.

BACK: Gray, formed of silvery white finely stippled with ashy gray.

TAIL: Main-tail feathers black, except the two top feathers which are light gray; coverts, gray.

BREAST: Salmon, shading to gray towards sides.

BODY AND FLUFF: Body, gray, formed of silvery white, finely stippled with ashy gray, free from dark marks or bars; fluff, light, ashy gray.

LEGS AND TOES: Lower thighs, gray, formed of silvery white finely stippled with ashy gray; shanks and toes, yellow.

UNDER-COLOR OF ALL SECTIONS: Slate.

SINGLE-COMB BUFF LEGHORN MALE

SINGLE-COMB BUFF LEGHORN FEMALE

217

RED LEGHORNS

(SINGLE-COMBS)

Disqualifications

One or more white feathers showing in surface color; two or more solid black primaries, two or more solid black secondaries, two or more solid black main-tail feathers, or tail more than one-third black. (See General and Leghorn Disqualifications, and Cutting for Defects.)

COLOR OF MALE AND FEMALE

COMB, FACE, AND WATTLES: Bright red.
BEAK: Yellow tinged with reddish horn.
EYES: Reddish bay.
EAR-LOBES: Enamel white.
SHANKS AND TOES: Yellow.
PLUMAGE: Surface, an even shade of rich, brilliant red in all sections; under-color, red.

BLACK-TAILED RED LEGHORNS

(SINGLE-COMBS)

Disqualifications

One or more white feathers showing in surface color; two or more solid red feathers in primaries, two or more solid red feathers in secondaries, two or more solid red main-tail feathers, or tail more than one-third red. (See General and Leghorn Disqualifications, and Cutting for Defects.)

COLOR OF MALE

COMB, FACE, AND WATTLES: Bright red.
BEAK: Yellow tinged with reddish horn.
HEAD: Plumage, rich, even red.
EYES: Reddish bay.
EAR-LOBES: Enamel white.
NECK: Rich, even red; plumage on front of neck, rich red.
WINGS: Fronts, bows and coverts, rich, even red; primaries, upper webs, red, lower webs black with narrow edging of red;

primary coverts, black edged with red; secondaries, lower webs red, the red extending around end of feathers sufficient to form a red wing-bay and lacing the upper portion of upper webs, this color growing wider in shorter secondaries; remainder of each secondary black, feathers next to body being red on surface so that wing when folded in natural position shall show one harmonious rich, even red color.

BACK AND SADDLE: Rich, even red.

TAIL: Main-tail feathers, black; sickle feathers, rich, lustrous, greenish black; coverts, mainly greenish black, rich red as they approach the saddle.

BREAST: Rich, even red.

BODY AND FLUFF: Rich, even red.

LEGS AND TOES: Lower thighs, rich, even red; shanks and toes, yellow tinged with reddish horn.

UNDER-COLOR OF ALL SECTIONS: Rich, even red.

COLOR OF FEMALE

COMB, FACE, AND WATTLES: Bright red.

BEAK: Yellow tinged with reddish horn.

HEAD: Plumage, rich, even red.

EYES: Reddish bay.

EAR-LOBES: Enamel white.

NECK: Rich, even red, with slight ticking of black on tips of feathers on back of neck permissible; feathers on front of neck, rich, even red.

WINGS: Fronts and bows, rich, even red; coverts, red; primaries, upper webs red, lower webs black with narrow edging of red; primary coverts, black edged with red; secondaries, lower webs, red, the red extending around the end of the feathers sufficient to secure a red wing-bay and lacing the upper portion of upper webs, this color growing wider in the shorter secondaries; remainder of each secondary, black, feathers next to body being red on surface, so that wing when folded in natural position shall show one harmonious rich, even red color.

BACK: Rich, even red.

TAIL: Main-tail feathers, black; the two top feathers may be edged with red.

BREAST: Rich, even red.
BODY AND FLUFF: Rich, even red.
LEGS AND TOES: Lower thighs, rich, even red; shanks and toes, yellow tinged with reddish horn.
UNDER-COLOR OF ALL SECTIONS: Rich, even red.

COLUMBIAN LEGHORNS

(SINGLE-COMBS)

Disqualifications

One or more solid black or brown feathers on surface of back; dark spots or mossiness in surface of back or saddle appearing in approximately 15 per cent of the feathers of this section, except narrow black stripes extending not over half the length of feather in saddle and near tail of male, or dark markings in cape of either sex; red feathers in plumage; shanks and toes other than yellow. (See General and Leghorn Disqualifications, and Cutting for Defects.)

COLOR OF MALE

COMB, FACE, AND WATTLES: Bright red.
BEAK: Yellow.
EYES: Reddish bay.
EAR-LOBES: Enamel white.
SHANKS AND TOES: Yellow.
PLUMAGE: See description of Columbian male plumage color, page 70.

COLOR OF FEMALE

COMB, FACE, AND WATTLES: Bright red.
BEAK: Yellow.
EYES: Reddish bay.
EAR-LOBES: Enamel white.
SHANKS AND TOES: Yellow.
PLUMAGE: See description of Columbian female plumage color, page 71.

MINORCAS

Minorcas, originally called Red-Faced Black Spanish, are the largest and heaviest of Mediterranean breeds of poultry. Long strong bodies, large combs, long wattles, large white ear-lobes, large and full tail, moderately elevated, with firm muscular legs set squarely under the powerful looking body, are the distinct characteristics of the Minorca breed. The plumage should be compact, smooth on surface and fit closely to the body.

Single-Comb Black and Single-Comb White Minorcas were admitted to the Standard in 1888; other varieties came into the Standard as follows: Rose-Comb Blacks, 1904; Single-Comb Buffs, 1913; Rose-Comb Whites, 1914.

Economic Qualities: Dual purpose fowl for the production of meat and large, white eggs. Color of skin, white; color of egg shells, chalk white.

Disqualifications

Red in ear-lobes covering more than one-third of surface. (See General Disqualifications, and Cutting for Defects.)

STANDARD WEIGHTS
(Single-Comb Black)

Cock	9 lbs.	Hen	7½ lbs.
Cockerel	7½ lbs.	Pullet	6½ lbs.

(Single and Rose-Comb Whites, Rose-Comb Black, and Single-Comb Buff)

Cock	8 lbs.	Hen	6½ lbs.
Cockerel	6½ lbs.	Pullet	5½ lbs.

SHAPE OF MALE

Comb: Single; large, straight and upright, firm and even on head, smooth, deeply and evenly serrated, having six regular and distinct points, the middle points the longest and same in length as width of blade; front not to extend beyond point half-way between nostrils and point of beak, but extending well over back of head, with tendency to follow shape of neck. (See Standard illustration, page 224.)

COMB: Rose; moderately large, square in front, not covering nostrils; firm and even on head, tapering evenly from front to rear, terminating in a well-developed spike, which extends well back of head with tendency to follow shape of neck; top, flat, free from hollow center, and covered with small rounded points.

BEAK: Of good length, stout, well-curved.

HEAD: Moderately long, wide, deep; face, full and smooth. (See Standard illustration, page 224.)

EYES: Large, full, prominent.

WATTLES: Long, large, free from folds or wrinkles, smooth, fine in texture.

EAR-LOBES: Large, almond-shaped, smooth, thin, free from folds or wrinkles, fitting closely to head.

NECK: Rather long, slightly arched; hackle, abundant, flowing well over shoulders.

WINGS: Large, well-folded and carried without drooping; primaries and secondaries, broad, and overlapping in natural order when wing is folded.

BACK: Long, flat at shoulders, broad its entire length, and rounded at sides, sloping slightly downward to tail; saddle feathers, long and abundant.

TAIL: Large and full, main-tail feathers carried at an angle of thirty-five degrees above the horizontal (see illustrations, page 28, figures 30 and 31); sickles, large, long, well-curved; coverts, abundant; main-tail feathers, broad and overlapping.

BREAST: Broad, deep, well-rounded and prominent.

BODY AND FLUFF: Body, long, broad, deep, straight from front to rear; fluff, rather short.

LEGS AND TOES: Legs, set well apart, straight when viewed from front; lower thighs of medium length, stout; shanks, rather long, straight; toes, straight, well-spread.

SHAPE OF FEMALE

COMB: Single; large, forming one loop over beak, then drooping down the opposite side of head; deeply and evenly serrated, with six regular and distinct points. (See Standard illustration, page 225.)

COMB: Rose, moderately large, square in front, not covering nostrils, firm and even on head, tapering evenly from front to rear, terminating in a well-developed spike, which extends back of head with tendency to follow shape of neck; top, flat, free from hollow center, and covered with small rounded points.

BEAK: Of good length, stout, well-curved.

HEAD: Moderately long, wide, deep; face, full and smooth. (See Standard illustration, page 225.)

EYES: Large, full, prominent.

WATTLES: Long, large, free from folds or wrinkles, smooth and fine in texture.

EAR-LOBES: Large, almond-shaped, smooth, thin, free from folds or wrinkles, fitting closely to head.

NECK: Rather long, slightly arched.

WINGS: Large, well-folded and carried without drooping; primaries and secondaries, broad, and overlapping in natural order when wing is folded.

BACK: Long, flat at shoulder, broad its entire length, rounded at sides, sloping slightly downward to tail.

TAIL: Long, full, and carried at an angle of thirty-five degrees above the horizontal; main-tail feathers, broad and overlapping. (See illustration, page 225.) and figures 30 and 31, page 28.)

BREAST: Broad, deep, well-rounded, prominent.

BODY AND FLUFF: Body, long, broad, deep, straight from front to rear; fluff, rather short.

LEGS AND TOES: Legs, set well apart, straight when viewed from front; lower thighs of medium length, stout; shanks, rather long, straight; toes, straight, well-spread.

Note: See Instructions to Judges, paragraph "Quality of Feather", page 53.

BLACK MINORCAS

(SINGLE AND ROSE-COMBS)
Disqualifications

More than one-half inch of positive white in any part of plumage, or two or more feathers tipped or edged with positive white;

SINGLE-COMB BLACK MINORCA MALE

SINGLE-COMB BLACK MINORCA FEMALE

shanks other than dark slate or dark leaden blue. (See General and Minorca Disqualifications, and Cutting for Defects.)

COLOR OF MALE AND FEMALE

COMB, FACE, AND WATTLES: Bright red.
BEAK: Black.
EYES: Dark brown.
EAR-LOBES: Enamel white.
SHANKS AND TOES: Dark slate.
PLUMAGE: See description of Black plumage color, page 64.

WHITE MINORCAS
(SINGLE AND ROSE-COMBS)
Disqualifications

Shanks other than white or pinkish white. (See General and Minorca Disqualifications, and Cutting for Defects.)

COLOR OF MALE AND FEMALE

COMB, FACE, AND WATTLES: Bright red.
BEAK: Pinkish white.
EYES: Reddish bay.
EAR-LOBES: Enamel white.
SHANKS AND TOES: Pinkish white.
PLUMAGE: See description of White plumage color, page 63.

BUFF MINORCAS
(SINGLE-COMBS)
Disqualifications

Shanks other than white or pinkish white. (See General and Minorca Disqualifications, and Cutting for Defects.)

COLOR OF MALE AND FEMALE

COMB, FACE, AND WATTLES: Bright red.
BEAK: Pinkish white.
EYES: Reddish bay.
EAR-LOBES: Enamel white.
SHANKS AND TOES: Pinkish white.
PLUMAGE: See description of Buff plumage color, page 64.

WHITE-FACED BLACK SPANISH

This is probably the oldest breed in the Mediterranean Class. The large, smooth, white face and ear-lobes are distinct characteristics of this Spanish breed, but these features should not be subjected to abnormal development. The Standard descriptions for these sections should be adhered to strictly, for extreme development of any one quality is obtained only by subordinating other qualities, such as size, stamina and activity, which must be maintained in this breed as well as in all other Standard breeds of poultry. Therefore, the white face and lobes should be developed to attractive but not grotesque proportions. White-Faced Black Spanish were admitted to the Standard in 1874.

ECONOMIC QUALITIES: A non-sitting fowl noted for the production of large chalk-white eggs. Color of skin, white.

Disqualifications

Positive red in the face, except directly above the eyes; face so puffy as to obstruct the sight; more than one-half inch of positive white in any part of the plumage, or two or more feathers tipped or edged with positive white; shanks other than dark slate or dark leaden blue. (See General Disqualifications and Cutting for Defects.)

STANDARD WEIGHTS

Cock	8 lbs.	Hen	6½ lbs.
Cockerel	6½ lbs.	Pullet	5½ lbs.

SHAPE OF MALE

COMB: Single; of medium size, straight and upright, firm and even on head, rising from the base of beak and extending in an arch form beyond back of head; deeply and evenly serrated, having five points; fine in texture. (See Standard illustration, page 228.)

BEAK: Rather long, stout.

HEAD: Long, broad, deep. (See Standard illustration, page 228.)

FACE: Smooth, deep, free from wrinkles, rising well over eyes

WHITE-FACED BLACK SPANISH MALE

WHITE-FACED BLACK SPANISH FEMALE

in an arched form and not obstructing sight, extending towards back of head and to base of beak, covering cheeks and joining the wattles and ear-lobes.

EYES: Large, oval.

WATTLES: Smooth, long, thin.

EAR-LOBES: Large, free from folds or wrinkles, meeting in front, extending well backward on each side of neck, hanging low and regularly rounded on lower edges; very smooth; extending somewhat below the wattles.

NECK: Long, well-arched; hackle, abundant, flowing well over shoulders.

WINGS: Large, well-folded and carried without drooping; primaries and secondaries, broad and overlapping in natural order when wing is folded.

BACK: Long and broad, sloping downward to tail; saddle feathers, moderately long.

TAIL: Large and full; main-tail feathers, broad and overlapping, carried at an angle of forty-five degrees above the horizontal (see illustrations, page 28, figures 30 and 31); sickles, large, long, well curved; coverts, abundant.

BREAST: Deep, well-rounded.

BODY AND FLUFF: Body, long, deep, moderately wide, width extending well back; fluff, short.

LEGS AND TOES: Legs, set well apart, straight when viewed from front; lower thighs of moderate size, long; shanks, long; toes, straight, well-spread.

SHAPE OF FEMALE

COMB: Single; moderately large, rising from front of head, drooping gently to one side, deeply serrated, having five points, fine in texture. (See Standard illustration, page 229.)

BEAK: Rather long, stout.

HEAD: Long, broad, deep. (See Standard illustration, page 229.)

FACE: Deep, smooth, free from wrinkles, rising well over eyes in an arched form and not obstructing the sight, extending towards back of head and to base of beak, covering the cheeks and joining wattles and ear-lobes.

EYES: Large, oval.

WATTLES: Smooth, long, thin.

EAR-LOBES: Large, free from folds or wrinkles, meeting in front, extending well backward on each side of neck, hanging low and regularly rounded on lower edges; very smooth; extending somewhat below the wattles.

NECK: Long, well-arched.

WINGS: Large, well-folded and carried without drooping; primaries and secondaries, broad, and overlapping in natural order when wing is folded.

BACK: Long, broad, sloping downward to tail.

TAIL: Large, carried at an angle of forty degrees above the horizontal (see illustrations, page 28, figures 30 and 31); the two top main-tail feathers slightly curved, especially in pullets; main-tail feathers, broad and overlapping.

BREAST: Deep, well-rounded.

BODY AND FLUFF: Body, long and deep, moderately wide, width extending well back; fluff, short.

LEGS AND TOES: Legs, set well apart, straight when viewed from front; lower thighs moderately long; shanks, long; toes, straight, well-spread.

Note: See Instructions to Judges, paragraph "Quality of Feather", page 53.

COLOR OF MALE AND FEMALE

COMB: Bright red.

BEAK: Black.

EYES: Dark brown.

FACE: Pure white.

WATTLES: Males, bright red, except inside of upper part, which is white; females, bright red.

EAR-LOBES: Enamel white.

SHANKS AND TOES: Dark slate.

PLUMAGE: See description of Black plumage color, page 64.

BLUE ANDALUSIANS

Blue Andalusians are credited with being natives of Andalusia, a province in Spain. They originated from crossing a black fowl with one of its white sports, these two colors producing a slaty-blue fowl. In Cornwall and Devon, England, similar blue fowls were produced by crossing black and white sports. This was before Andalusians were imported into that country. They resembled the earlier Andalusians in type and color. The modern Andalusian should be very symmetrical, graceful, compact, medium in size, and stately in carriage. The dull and uneven blue colored fowl of the past has been transformed into the attractive, blue-laced breed of today by years of scientific breeding. Andalusians were admitted to the Standard in 1874.

Economic Qualities: A non-sitting fowl, laying large chalk-white eggs; color of skin, white.

Disqualifications.

Red in ear-lobes covering more than one-third of surface; red, yellow or positive white in plumage; shanks other than blue or slaty-blue. (See General Disqualifications and Cutting for Defects.)

STANDARD WEIGHTS

Cock	7 lbs.	Hen	5½ lbs.
Cockerel	6 lbs.	Pullet	4½ lbs.

SHAPE OF MALE

Comb: Single; of medium size, smooth, straight and upright, firm and even on head; evenly and deeply serrated, having five well-defined points, the middle point slightly longer and proportionately broader than the other four; blade following slightly the curve of the neck. (See Standard illustration, page 234.)

Beak: Of moderate length, nicely curved.

Head: Moderately long and deep; face, full and smooth, fine in texture. (See Standard illustration, page 234.)

Eyes: Large, full, prominent.

Wattles: Moderately long, thin, smooth.

EAR-LOBES: Of moderate size, almond-shaped, smooth.

NECK: Rather long, well-arched, with abundant hackle flowing well over shoulders.

WINGS: Large, well-folded, carried without drooping; primaries and secondaries, broad, and overlapping in natural order when wing is folded.

BACK: Rather long, rather broad its entire length, high at shoulders, sloping slightly to tail; saddle feathers, long and abundant.

TAIL: Large, full and well-spread, main-tail feathers broad and overlapping, carried at an angle of forty degrees above the horizontal (see illustrations, page 28, figures 30 and 31); sickles, long, even, well-curved; coverts, abundant.

BREAST: Broad, deep, well-rounded, carried well up and forward.

BODY AND FLUFF: Body, long, deep, well-rounded, slightly broader at front than rear; fluff, short.

LEGS AND TOES: Legs, set well apart, straight when viewed from front; lower thighs, of moderate size, rather long; hock joints showing well below body line; shanks, long; toes, straight, well-spread.

SHAPE OF FEMALE

COMB: Single; medium in size, evenly and deeply serrated, having five distinct points, the front portion of comb and first point to stand erect and the remainder of comb drooping gradually to one side; fine in texture, free from folds or wrinkles. (See Standard illustration, page 235.)

BEAK: Of moderate length, nicely curved.

HEAD: Moderately long, deep, full and smooth. (See Standard illustration, page 235.)

EYES: Large, full, and prominent.

WATTLES: Moderately long, thin, well-rounded.

EAR-LOBES: Of moderate size, almond-shaped, smooth.

NECK: Rather long, gracefully arched.

WINGS: Large, well-folded and carried without drooping; primaries and secondaries, broad, and overlapping in natural order when wing is folded.

BACK: Rather long, rather broad its entire length, and ele-

BLUE ANDALUSIAN MALE

BLUE ANDALUSIAN FEMALE

vated at shoulders, sloping slightly downward at rear, then rising with a short, abrupt curve to tail.

TAIL: Long, full, well-spread, carried at an angle of thirty degrees above horizontal; main-tail feathers, broad and overlapping. (See illustrations, page 28, figures 30 and 31).

BREAST: Broad, deep and well-rounded, carried well up and forward.

BODY AND FLUFF: Body, long, deep, well-rounded, slightly broader at front than rear; fluff, short.

LEGS AND TOES: Legs, set well apart, straight when viewed from front; lower thighs, of moderate size, rather long; hock joints showing well below body line; shanks, long; toes, straight, well-spread.

Note: See Instructions to Judges, paragraph "Quality of Feather", page 53.

COLOR OF MALE

COMB, FACE, AND WATTLES: Bright red.

BEAK: Horn.

EYES: Reddish bay.

EAR-LOBES: Enamel white.

SHANKS AND TOES: Dark slaty blue.

PLUMAGE: See description of Blue male plumage color, page 73.

COLOR OF FEMALE

COMB, FACE, AND WATTLES: Bright red.

BEAK: Horn.

EYES: Reddish bay.

EAR-LOBES: Enamel white.

SHANKS AND TOES: Dark slaty blue.

PLUMAGE: See description of Blue female plumage color, page 74.

ANCONAS

This breed takes its name from the City of Ancona, a port in Italy, from which the first Anconas were shipped to England, where they were first exhibited under this name in the middle of the last century. That Anconas originated from crosses of Italian fowl common in Central Italy is evident by their close resemblance in type and size to the Leghorn breed.

Anconas came to America from England in 1888, the Single-Comb variety was admitted to the Standard in 1898; the Rose-Comb variety gained admission in 1914.

The Standard color description specifies approximately the proportion of white-tipped to solid black feathers in each section for both male and female.

ECONOMIC QUALITIES: Anconas are excellent layers of white eggs; non-sitters and with yellow skin.

Disqualifications.

Red in ear-lobes, covering more than one-third of surface; red in any part of plumage; shanks other than yellow or yellow mottled with black; males more than one and one-half pounds under weight; females more than one pound under weight. (See General Disqualifications and Cutting for Defects.)

STANDARD WEIGHTS

Cock	6 lbs.	Hen	4½ lbs.
Cockerel	5 lbs.	Pullet	4 lbs.

SHAPE OF MALE

COMB: Single; of medium size, straight and upright, firm and even in head; having five distinct points, deeply serrated and extending well over back of head, with no tendency to follow shape of neck; smooth, free from twists, folds, or excrescences. (See Standard illustration, page 238.)

COMB: Rose; medium in size, square in front, firm and even on head, tapering evenly from front to rear and terminating in a well-developed spike which extends horizontally well back of head; flat; free from hollow centers, and covered with small rounded points.

BEAK: Medium in length, strong, nicely curved.

HEAD: Moderate in length, fairly deep, inclined to be flat on top rather than round; face, clean-cut, skin fine in texture, free

SINGLE-COMB ANCONA MALE

SINGLE-COMB ANCONA FEMALE

from wrinkles. (See Standard illustration, page 238.)

EYES: Rather large, full, prominent.

WATTLES: Moderately long, uniform, well-rounded, smooth, fine in texture, free from folds or wrinkles.

EAR-LOBES: A broadened almond-shape, of moderate size, smooth, fitting close to head.

NECK: Moderately long, nicely arched; hackle, abundant, flowing well over shoulders.

WINGS: Large, well-folded, carried without drooping; primaries and secondaries, broad and overlapping in natural order when wing is folded.

BACK: Of good length, rather wide its entire length, somewhat rounded at shoulders, slightly sloping downward from shoulders to saddle then rising with a concave sweep to tail; saddle feathers, long, of good width, abundant, filling well in front of tail.

TAIL: Large, well-spread; main-tail feathers, broad and overlapping, carried at an angle of forty degrees above horizontal (see illustrations, page 28, figures 30 and 31); sickles, long, well-curved; coverts, abundant.

BREAST: Well-rounded, carried well forward.

BODY AND FLUFF: Body, moderately long, fairly deep, full, straight from front to rear; fluff, short.

LEGS AND TOES: Legs, set well apart, straight when viewed from front; lower thighs and shanks, moderately long; toes, straight, well-spread.

SHAPE OF FEMALE

COMB: Single; medium in size, deeply serrated, having five distinct points, the front portion of comb and first point to stand erect, the remainder of comb drooping gradually to one side; fine in texture, free from folds or wrinkles. (See Standard illustration, page 239.)

COMB: Rose; medium in size, square in front, firm and even on head, tapering evenly from front to rear and terminating in a well-developed spike which extends horizontally back of head; flat, free from hollow center, covered with very small rounded points.

BEAK: Medium in length, strong, nicely curved.

HEAD: Moderate in length, fairly deep, inclined to be flat on top rather than round; face clean-cut, skin fine in texture, free from wrinkles. (See Standard illustration, page 239.)

EYES: Rather large, full prominent.

WATTLES: Of moderate size, uniform, well-rounded, smooth, fine in texture, free from folds or wrinkles.

EAR-LOBES: Oval in shape, smooth, thin, free from folds or wrinkles, fitting closely to head.

NECK: Moderately long, slender and gracefully arched.

WINGS: Large and well-folded, carried without drooping; primaries and secondaries, broad, and overlapping in natural order when wing is folded.

BACK: Of good length and rather wide its entire length, somewhat rounded, with a slight slope downward from shoulders to rear, then rising in a concave sweep to tail.

TAIL: Long, full and well-spread, carried at an angle of thirty-five degrees above the horizontal; main-tail feathers, broad and overlapping. (See illustrations, page 28, figures 30 and 31.)

BREAST: Well-rounded, carried well forward.

BODY AND FLUFF: Body, moderately long, fairly deep, full, straight from front to rear; fluff, rather short, more developed than in male.

LEGS AND TOES: Legs, set well apart, straight when viewed from front; lower thighs and shanks, moderately long; toes, straight, well-spread.

Note: See Instructions to Judges, paragraph "Quality of Feather," page 53.

COLOR OF MALE

COMB, FACE, AND WATTLES: Bright red.

BEAK: Yellow, upper mandible shaded with black.

HEAD: Plumage, black, one feather in three tipped with white.

EYES: Reddish bay.

EAR-LOBES: Enamel white.

NECK: Lustrous, greenish black, about one feather in two tipped with white; plumage on front of neck, same as breast.

WINGS: Fronts and bows, lustrous, greenish black, about one feather in three ending with a white tip; coverts, lustrous, greenish black, ending with a small, sharply defined white tip; primaries, black, tipped with white; secondaries, black, ending with white tips.

BACK AND SADDLE: Lustrous, greenish black, one feather in five tipped with white; saddle, lustrous, greenish black, one feather in two ending with white tips.

TAIL: Main-tail feathers, black ending with white tips; sickles and coverts, lustrous, greenish black ending with white tips.

BREAST: Lustrous, greenish black, about one feather in two tipped with white.

BODY AND FLUFF: Body, lustrous, greenish black, about one feather in two tipped with white; fluff, black, slightly tinged with white.

LEGS AND TOES: Lower thighs, black slightly tipped with white; shanks and toes, yellow.

UNDER-COLOR OF ALL SECTIONS: Dark slate.

Note: In all sections, the white tip is to be V-shaped. (See page 67, figure 62.)

COLOR OF FEMALE

COMB, FACE, AND WATTLES: Bright red.

BEAK: Yellow, upper mandible shaded with black.

HEAD: Plumage, black, one feather in three tipped with white.

EYES: Reddish bay.

EAR-LOBES: Enamel white.

NECK: Lustrous, greenish black, about one feather in two tipped with white; feathers on front of neck same as breast.

WINGS: Fronts and bows, lustrous, greenish black, one feather in two ending with a small, sharply defined white tip; coverts, lustrous, greenish black, about one feather in three ending with a white tip; primaries, black tipped with white; secondaries, black, ending with white tips.

BACK: Lustrous, greenish black, about one feather in two ending with a white tip.

TAIL: Main-tail, black, feathers ending with white tips; coverts, black, at least one feather in three ending with a white tip.

BREAST: Lustrous, greenish black, about one feather in two ending with a small, sharply defined, white tip.

BODY AND FLUFF: Body, black, about one feather in two ending with a small, sharply defined white tip; fluff, black, slightly tinged with white.

LEGS AND TOES: Lower thighs, black, slightly tipped with white; shanks and toes, yellow.

UNDER-COLOR OF ALL SECTIONS: Dark slate.

Note: In all sections, the white tip is to be V-shaped. (See page 67, figure 62.)

BUTTERCUPS

The Sicilian Buttercup, as its name implies, originated in Sicily, the first importation from that island coming to America in 1835. The word "Sicilian", however, has been dropped from the American Standard classification. To the cup-shaped comb—its most characteristic feature—and the golden ground color of its plumage, the Buttercup owes its name. It was not until 1892, however, that eggs for hatching were imported into America; from these the present stock descended. Buttercups were admitted to the Standard in 1918.

ECONOMIC QUALITIES: A non-sitting, egg production fowl. Color of skin, white; color of eggs, white.

Disqualifications.

Ear-lobes more than two-thirds red. (See General Disqualifications and Cutting for Defects.)

STANDARD WEIGHTS

Cock	6½ lbs.	Hen	5 lbs.
Cockerel	5½ lbs.	Pullet	4 lbs

SHAPE OF MALE

COMB: A single leader from base of beak to a cup-shaped crown well set on center of skull, and surmounted by a complete circle of medium-sized, regular points. Entire comb smooth, of fine texture, and with deep cavity. (See page 22, figure 24.)

BEAK: Of medium length, strong.

HEAD: Medium in size and length, fairly deep.

EYES: Round, full, prominent.

WATTLES: Of medium length, thin and well-rounded, free from folds.

EAR-LOBES: Almond-shaped, flat and smooth, fitting close to head.

NECK: Rather long, slender and well-arched; hackle, abundant and flowing.

WINGS: Large, well-folded and carried close to body without drooping; primaries and secondaries, broad, and overlapping in natural order when wing is folded.

BACK: Long, broad and straight, sloping downward to saddle, then rising with slight concave sweep to tail.

TAIL: Moderately large, well-spread; main-tail feathers, long, carried at an angle of forty-five degrees above the horizontal; sickles, long and well-curved; coverts, abundant. (See illustrations, page 28, figures 30 and 31.)

BREAST: Broad, full and carried well forward.

BODY AND FLUFF: Body, moderately long, of good depth; fluff, full.

LEGS AND TOES: Legs, set well apart, straight when viewed from front; lower thighs and shanks, of medium size and length; toes, of medium length, straight, well-spread.

SHAPE OF FEMALE

COMB: Small, a single leader from base of beak to a cup-shaped crown, well set on center of skull and surmounted by complete circle of medium-sized, regular points. Entire comb smooth, of fine texture, and with deep cavity. (See page 22, figure 24.)

BEAK: Of medium length, strong.

HEAD: Medium in size and length, fairly deep.

EYES: Round, full, prominent.

WATTLES: Moderately small, thin and well-rounded, free from folds.

EAR-LOBES: Almond-shaped, flat and smooth, fitting close to head.

NECK: Rather long, slender and well-arched.

WINGS: Large, well-folded and carried close to body without drooping; primaries and secondaries, broad and overlapping in natural order when wing is folded.

BACK: Long, moderate in width, sloping downward to middle of back and continuing in a slight concave sweep to tail.

TAIL: Moderately large, well-spread and carried at an angle of forty degrees above the horizontal. (See illustrations, page 28, figures 30 and 31.)

BREAST: Broad, full and carried well forward.

BODY AND FLUFF: Body, long, of good depth; fluff, full.

LEGS AND TOES: Legs, set well apart, straight when viewed

BUTTERCUP FEATHERS

MALE   FEMALE

from front; lower thighs of moderate length; shanks of moderate length; toes, straight, well-spread.

Note: See Instructions to Judges, paragraph "Quality of Feather", page 53.

COLOR OF MALE

COMB, FACE, AND WATTLES: Bright. red.

BEAK: Light horn.

HEAD: Plumage, rich brilliant reddish orange.

EYES: Reddish bay.

EAR-LOBES: White.

NECK: Rich, lustrous reddish orange.

WINGS: Fronts and wing-bows, bright, lustrous, reddish orange; wing-bar and wing-bay, an even shade of reddish bay; primaries, black lower web edged with bay; secondaries outer web bay with black markings, inner web black with bay markings, small feathers on underside of wing having black markings.

BACK AND SADDLE: Bright, lustrous, reddish orange; cape feathers at base of hackle, dark buff with distinct black spangles, covered by hackle; saddle, lustrous reddish orange.

TAIL: Main-tail feathers, black; sickles, lustrous, greenish black; lesser sickles, greenish black, edged with reddish bay, some showing characteristic black markings.

BREAST: Reddish bay.

BODY AND FLUFF: Body, light bay; fluff, rich bay shading to light bay on stern, some feathers on rear body marked with distinct black markings.

LEGS AND TOES: Lower thighs, reddish bay; shanks and toes, willow-green; bottoms of feet, yellow.

UNDER-COLOR OF ALL SECTIONS: Slaty blue gradually changing to light grayish buff at base; quill, buff, becoming lighter at base.

COLOR OF FEMALE

COMB, FACE, AND WATTLES: Bright red.

BEAK: Light horn.

HEAD: Plumage, golden buff.

EYES: Reddish bay.

EAR-LOBES: White.

NECK: Plumage, lustrous, golden buff.

WINGS: Fronts, wing-bow and wing-bar, ground color of golden buff marked with parallel rows of elongated black spangles, each spangle extending slightly diagonally across web; quill and edge of feathers, golden buff; primaries, buff splashed with black; secondaries, golden buff barred with parallel black markings; small feathers on underside of wing having black markings.

BACK: Ground color, golden buff, regularly marked with same pattern of black spangling as in wing-bow, and extending over entire surface.

TAIL: Main-tail feathers, dull black, lower web barred with buff markings; coverts, same as back.

BREAST: Golden buff, lower half marked with characteristic spangles as described in wing-bow.

BODY AND FLUFF: Body, buff marked with black spangles of similar pattern to wing-bows and back; fluff, buff.

LEGS AND TOES: Lower thighs, pale buff marked with black spangles of similar pattern as wing-bow and back; shanks and toes, willow-green; bottoms of feet, yellow.

UNDER-COLOR OF ALL SECTIONS: Slaty blue gradually shading to light grayish buff at base; quill, buff, becoming lighter at base.

ENGLISH

Breeds		*Varieties*

Dorkings .... { White / Silver-Gray / Colored

Redcaps ....

Orpingtons............................... { Buff / Black / White / Blue

Cornish................................. { Dark / White / White-Laced Red

Sussex.................................. { Speckled / Red / Light

Australorps..............................

SCALE OF POINTS

ERRATA

Scale of points on English varieties page 248 is published in error. The universal scale of points on page 76 applies to all English varieties.

Editor

.... 4
.... 4
.... 6
.... 6
.... 4
.... 4
.... 4
Wattles—Shape 2 2
Ear-Lobes—Shape 2, Color 2.................... 4
Neck—Shape 3, Color 5......................... 8
Wings—Shape 4, Color 6........................ 10
Back—Shape 6, Color 6......................... 12
Tail—Shape 4, Color 4......................... 8
Breast—Shape 5, Color 5....................... 10
Body and Fluff—Shape 5, Color 3.............. 8
Legs and Toes—Shape 3, Color 3............... 6

                                          100

DORKINGS

The Dorking is one of the most ancient of all domesticated races of poultry. It was brought to Great Britain by the Romans with Julius Caesar, but it was known and described by the Roman writer Columella long before it became a popular breed in England. He speaks of the hens as being "square-framed, large and broad-breasted, with big heads and small upright combs," adding that "the purest breed are five-clawed."

The Red Dorking is the earliest one known in England, but the Silver-Gray, Colored and White varieties are the only ones recognized by the Standard today.

ECONOMIC QUALITIES: A dual purpose fowl for meat and egg production. Color of skin, white; color of egg shells, white.

Disqualifications.

Shanks other than white or pinkish white. (See General Disqualifications and Cutting for Defects.)

STANDARD WEIGHTS

WHITES

Cock	7½ lbs.	Hen	6 lbs.
Cockerel	6½ lbs.	Pullet	5 lbs.

SILVER-GRAY AND COLORED

Cock	9 lbs.	Hen	7 lbs.
Cockerel	8 lbs.	Pullet	6 lbs.

SHAPE OF MALE

COMB: Silver-Gray and Colored Dorkings, single; rather large, straight and upright, evenly serrated, having six well-defined points, the front and rear points shorter than the other four. (See Standard illustration, page 252.)

COMB: White Dorkings, rose; square in front, firm and even on head, terminating in a well-defined spike; top, comparatively flat and covered with small, rounded points. (See page 16, figure 5.)

BEAK: Of medium length, stout, well-curved.

HEAD: Rather large: face, smooth.

EYES: Medium in size, oval.

WATTLES: Rather large, well-rounded at lower end.

EAR-LOBES: Of medium size, about one-half the length of wattles, smooth.

NECK: Of medium length, arched; hackle, very full and abundant, flowing well over shoulders, making it appear very broad, tapering to head.

WINGS: Large, well-folded against body, carried without drooping; primaries and secondaries, long, broad, and overlapping in natural order when wing is folded.

BACK: Long, broad its entire length, straight, declining to tail; saddle feathers abundant.

TAIL: Large, full, somewhat expanded, main-tail feathers, broad and overlapping; carried at an angle of forty-five degrees above horizontal. (See page 28, figures 30 and 31.)

BREAST: Broad, deep, full, well-rounded, carried forward.

BODY AND FLUFF: Body, long, broad, deep, keel bone long; fluff, smooth in surface, moderately developed.

LEGS AND TOES: Legs, set well apart, straight when viewed from front; lower thighs, large, short, well-meated; shanks, short, stout; toes, five on each foot, front and fifth toes moderately long and smooth, fifth toe well separated from fourth and directly above it, rising on a slight incline from base to point.

SHAPE OF FEMALE

COMB: Silver-Gray and Colored Dorkings, single; similar to that of male but much smaller and falling over to one side. (See Standard illustration, page 253.)

COMB: White Dorkings, rose; similar to that of male, except much smaller.

BEAK: Of medium length, stout, well-curved.

HEAD: Of medium size; face, smooth. (See Standard illustration, page 253.)

EYES: Medium in size, oval.

WATTLES: Rather broad, well-rounded.

EAR-LOBES: Medium size, smooth.

NECK: Rather short, arched; feathers full and abundant, flowing over shoulders, tapering to head.

WINGS: Large, well-folded against body, carried without drooping; primaries and secondaries, long, broad, and overlapping in natural order when wing is folded.

BACK: Long, broad its entire length, straight, declining slightly to tail.

TAIL: Moderately long, main-tail feathers broad, fairly close together, carried at an angle of thirty-five degrees above the horizontal. (See page 28, figures 30 and 31.)

BREAST: Broad, deep, well-rounded, carried forward.

BODY AND FLUFF: Body, long, broad, deep, low-set, keel bone long; fluff, smooth in surface, moderately developed.

LEGS AND TOES: Legs, set well apart, straight when viewed from front; lower thighs, large, short, well-meated; shanks, short, stout; toes, five on each foot, front and fifth toes moderately long, smooth, fifth toe well separated from fourth and directly above it and rising on a slight incline from base to point.

Note: See Instructions to Judges, paragraph "Quality of Feather," page 53.

WHITE DORKINGS

Disqualifications.

(See General and Dorking Disqualifications, and Cutting for Defects.)

COLOR OF MALE AND FEMALE

COMB, FACE, AND WATTLES: Bright red.

BEAK: Pinkish white.

EYES: Reddish bay.

EAR-LOBES: Bright red, showing not more than one-third white.

SHANKS AND TOES: Pinkish white.

PLUMAGE: See description of White plumage color, page 63.

SILVER-GRAY DORKINGS

Disqualifications.

(See General and Dorking Disqualifications, and Cutting for Defects.)

COLOR OF MALE

COMB, FACE, AND WATTLES: Bright red.

BEAK: Pinkish white, streaked with horn.

HEAD: Plumage, silvery white.

EYES: Reddish bay.

SILVER-GRAY DORKING MALE

SILVER-GRAY DORKING FEMALE

EAR-LOBES: Bright red, showing not more than one-third white.

NECK: Hackle, pure silvery white; plumage on front of neck, black.

WINGS: Fronts and bows, silvery white; coverts, lustrous, greenish black, forming a wide bar across wing; primaries, quills black, upper webs black, lower webs white; secondaries, quills black, upper webs black, lower webs white, with black spot at end of each feather.

BACK AND SADDLE: Silvery white; cape, black.

TAIL: Main-tail feathers, black; sickles and coverts, greenish black; smaller coverts next to saddle, greenish black edged with silvery white.

BREAST: Lustrous black.

BODY AND FLUFF: Black.

LEGS AND TOES: Lower thighs, black; shanks and toes, pinkish white.

UNDER-COLOR OF ALL SECTIONS: Slate.

COLOR OF FEMALE

COMB, FACE, AND WATTLES: Bright red.

BEAK: Pinkish white streaked with horn.

HEAD: Plumage, silvery white.

EYES: Reddish bay.

EAR-LOBES: Bright red, showing not more than one-third white.

NECK: Silvery white, with a narrow black stripe, slightly stippled with ashy gray extending down middle of each feather, tapering to a point near its extremity; feathers on front of neck, reddish salmon.

WINGS: Fronts and bows, gray, finely stippled with silvery white, resulting in an ashy gray appearance; coverts, gray, stippled with silvery white, resulting in an ashy gray appearance; primaries and secondaries, upper webs dark slate, lower webs slaty gray.

BACK: Gray, finely stippled with silvery white, resulting in an ashy gray appearance.

TAIL: Main-tail feathers, dull black, stippled with gray on surface; unexposed portion of feathers, dark slate.

BREAST: Reddish salmon, shading to ashy gray at sides.

BODY AND FLUFF: Body, gray finely stippled with ashy gray, free from dark marks across feathers; under part of body, gray; fluff, ashy gray.

LEGS AND TOES: Lower thighs, ashy gray; shanks and toes, pinkish white.

UNDER-COLOR OF ALL SECTIONS: Slate.

COLORED DORKINGS

Disqualifications.

(See General and Dorking Disqualifications, and Cutting for Defects.)

COLOR OF MALE

COMB, FACE, AND WATTLES: Bright red.

BEAK: Dark horn.

HEAD: Plumage, very light gray.

EYES: Reddish bay.

EAR-LOBES: Bright red, showing not more than one-third white.

NECK: Light straw color, with a wide, black stripe extending down middle of each feather and terminating in a point near its lower extremity; plumage on front of neck, black.

WINGS: Fronts, black; bows, light straw; coverts, lustrous greenish black, forming a wide bar across wing; primaries, dark slate; secondaries, upper webs black, lower webs white.

BACK AND SADDLE: Cape, black; back feathers black, laced around end with straw color; saddle feathers, straw with a wide black stripe extending down middle of each feather.

TAIL: Main-tail feathers, black; sickles, greenish black; coverts, lustrous black.

BREAST: Lustrous black.

BODY AND FLUFF: Black.

LEGS AND TOES: Lower thighs, black; shanks and toes, pinkish white.

UNDER-COLOR OF ALL SECTIONS: Slate.

COLOR OF FEMALE

COMB, FACE, AND WATTLES: Bright red.

BEAK: Dark horn.

HEAD: Plumage, black.

EYES: Reddish bay.

EAR-LOBES: Bright red, showing not more than one-third white.

NECK: Black with a narrow edging of straw color; shaft of feather, straw color; feathers on front of neck, dark salmon.

WINGS: Fronts, bows and coverts, black, a slight admixture of dark, brownish gray in center of feathers; shafts of feathers, straw; primaries, slaty brown; secondaries, upper webs black, lower webs black with an admixture of dark gray.

BACK: Lustrous black; shaft of feathers, straw color.

TAIL: Main-tail feathers, dark brown penciled with gray on surface, and black on inside.

BREAST: Dark salmon, feathers marked on lower edges with black; shafts of feathers light bay.

BODY AND FLUFF: Body, black, slightly mixed with gray; fluff, dull black edged with gray.

LEGS AND TOES: Lower thighs, dark gray and brown; shanks and toes, pinkish white.

UNDER-COLOR OF ALL SECTIONS: Dark slate.

REDCAPS

Redcaps originated in Derbyshire, England, probably from Hamburg crossed with other breeds. The very large rose-comb is the most striking characteristic of the breed.

ECONOMIC QUALITIES: A dual purpose fowl for meat and egg production. Color of skin, white; color of egg shells, white.

Disqualifications.

Solid white ear-lobes; foreign colored feathers except white in primaries; mottled breast in male; shanks other than slate or leaden blue in color. (See General Disqualifications and Cutting for Defects.)

STANDARD WEIGHTS

Cock	7½ lbs.	Hen	6 lbs.
Cockerel	6 lbs.	Pullet	5 lbs.

SHAPE OF MALE

COMB: Rose; large, wide, square in front, full on top, uniform on both sides; covered with comparatively long rounded points, flat and set evenly on head, without inclining to either side, terminating at rear in a well-developed and straight spike.

BEAK: Of medium size, stout at base, well-curved.

HEAD: Short, deep.

EYES: Full, round, prominent.

WATTLES: Of medium size, smooth.

EAR-LOBES: Of medium size, smooth.

NECK: Of medium size, rather long, well-arched; with full hackle flowing well over shoulders.

WINGS: Large, folded well against body and carried without drooping; primaries and secondaries, broad and overlapping in natural order when wing is folded.

BACK: Of medium length, fairly broad, sloping straight to tail; saddle feathers, long and sweeping.

TAIL: Full, well-expanded, carried at an angle of fifty degrees above horizontal (see page 28, figures 30 and 31); sickles, long, well-curved; coverts, abundant; main-tail feathers, broad and overlapping.

BREAST: Broad, deep, very prominent.

BODY AND FLUFF: Body, long, rounded, broadest in front and tapering to rear; fluff, rather short.

LEGS AND TOES: Legs, set well apart, straight when viewed from front; lower thighs, of medium length, well-developed; shanks, rather long; toes, straight, well-spread.

SHAPE OF FEMALE

COMB: Similar to that of male, but smaller.

BEAK: Of medium size, stout at base, well-curved.

HEAD: Short, deep.

EYES: Full, round, prominent.

WATTLES: Of medium size, well-rounded, smooth.

EAR-LOBES: Of medium size, smooth.

NECK: Rather long, well-arched, full-feathered.

WINGS: Large, well-folded against body and carried without drooping; primaries and secondaries, broad, and overlapping in natural order when wing is folded.

BACK: Rather long, fairly broad, straight, sloping to tail.

TAIL: Long, full, well-expanded, carried at an angle of forty-five degrees above the horizontal (see page 28, figures 30 and 31); main-tail feathers, broad and overlapping.

BREAST: Broad, prominent.

BODY AND FLUFF: Body, long, rounded, deep; fluff, rather short.

LEGS AND TOES: Legs, set well apart, straight when viewed from front; lower thighs, of medium length, well-developed; shanks, of medium length; toes, straight, well-spread.

Note: See Instructions to Judges, paragraph "Quality of Feather," page 53.

COLOR OF MALE

COMB, FACE, WATTLES AND EAR-LOBES: Bright red.

BEAK: Horn.

HEAD: Plumage, rich, dark red.

EYES: Reddish bay.

NECK: Hackle, blue-black, each feather edged with red, the entire hackle shading off to black at base; plumage on front of neck, black.

WINGS: Fronts, black; bows, mahogany red; coverts, rich deep brown, each feather ending with a black spangle shaped like a half-moon, forming double black bars across wings; primaries, dull black; secondaries, upper web black, lower web black with a broad edging of brown, each feather ending with a bluish black spangle, shaped like a half-moon.

BACK AND SADDLE: Rich red and black; saddle feathers, rich, dark red, with a bluish black stripe extending down middle of each feather.

TAIL: Main-tail black; sickles and coverts, greenish black.

BREAST: Lustrous black.

BODY AND FLUFF: Black.

LEGS AND TOES: Lower thighs, black; shanks and toes, dark leaden blue.

UNDER-COLOR OF ALL SECTIONS: Bluish slate.

COLOR OF FEMALE

COMB, FACE, WATTLES AND EAR-LOBES: Bright red.

BEAK: Horn.

HEAD: Plumage, brown.

EYES: Reddish bay.

NECK: Black, each feather laced with golden bay; feathers on front of neck, same as breast.

WINGS: Fronts, brown; bows, rich brown, each feather ending with a bluish black spangle, shaped like a half-moon; coverts, similar to bows; primaries, dull black, with a narrow edging of brown on lower webs; secondaries, black, lower webs with a broad edging of brown, each feather ending with a bluish black spangle, shaped like a half-moon.

BACK: Rich brown, each feather ending with a bluish black spangle, shaped like a half-moon.

TAIL: Main-tail feathers, black: coverts, brown, each feather ending with a bluish black spangle, shaped like a half-moon.

BREAST: Rich brown, each feather ending with a bluish black spangle, shaped like a half-moon.

BODY AND FLUFF: Body, similar to that of breast, but shading off lighter on under parts; fluff, black, powdered with brown.

LEGS AND TOES: Lower thighs, light brown; shanks and toes, dark leaden blue.

UNDER-COLOR OF ALL SECTIONS: Bluish slate.

ORPINGTONS

The Single-Comb Black Orpington, produced in 1886 at Orpington, County Kent, England, from a Black Langshan-Black Minorca-Black Plymouth Rock cross, is the original Orpington. The Buff and White varieties were produced from crosses other than those which were used to make up the Black Orpington. That Cochin blood was introduced into some of the earlier strains of Orpingtons is evinced by the more loosely feathered specimens bred and exhibited today. The original Black Orpington came to America in 1890, and was first exhibited at the Boston Show the same year. It was in 1895, however, that the originator of Orpingtons made a large exhibit of Black Orpingtons at the Madison Square Garden, New York, and this new breed became popular.

The Single-Comb Black and White Orpingtons were admitted to the Standard in 1905; the Buffs in 1902, and the Blue Orpingtons, produced from crossing the Black and White varieties, in 1923.

The plumage of Orpingtons is all important in order to maintain the ideal type of the breed. The feathers should be broad and smooth fitting on the deep and massive body of the fowl. The appearance of great massiveness, however, should not be secured by developing extreme length of feathers in the plumage. The sides of the body, sometimes erroneously referred to as the "fluff," should be comparatively straight with full but not profusely feathered.

ECONOMIC QUALITIES: A general purpose fowl for heavy meat production and for eggs. Color of skin, white; color of egg shells, light brown to dark brown.

Disqualifications

Positive enamel white in ear-lobes; yellow beak, shanks, feet or skin. (See General Disqualifications and Cutting for Defects.)

STANDARD WEIGHTS

Cock	10 lbs.	Hen	8 lbs.
Cockerel	8½ lbs.	Pullet	7 lbs.

SHAPE OF MALE

COMB: Single; of medium size, set firmly on head, perfectly straight and upright; with five well-defined points, those at front and rear smaller than those in the middle; fine in texture; blade closely following shape of head. (See Standard illustration, page 262.)

BEAK: Short, stout, regularly curved.

HEAD: Medium in length, broad, deep; face, clean-cut and free from coarseness. (See Standard illustration, page 262.)

EYES: Large, round, full.

WATTLES: Of medium size, well-rounded at lower edges.

EAR-LOBES: Of medium size, oblong, smooth.

NECK: Rather short, slightly arched, with abundant hackle.

WINGS: Of medium size, well-folded, carried horizontally; fronts, well covered by breast feathers; points well covered by saddle feathers; primaries and secondaries, broad, and overlapping in natural order when wing is folded.

BACK: Broad, flat at shoulders, rather long, width carried well back to base of tail; rising with a slight concave sweep to tail; saddle feathers, of medium length, abundant.

TAIL: Moderately long, well-spread, carried at an angle of twenty-five degrees above the horizontal (see illustrations, figures 30 and 31, page 28); forming no apparent angle with back where those sections join; sickles of medium length, spreading laterally beyond main-tail feathers; lesser sickles and tail-coverts, of medium length, nicely curved, sufficiently abundant to cover main-tail feathers; main-tail feathers, broad and overlapping.

BREAST: Broad, deep, well-rounded and well-filled in all parts.

BODY AND FLUFF: Body, broad, deep, rather long, straight, extending well forward; lower body feathers, not too profuse; fluff, moderately full.

LEGS AND TOES: Legs, set well apart, straight when viewed from front; lower thighs, large, rather short, well feathered; shanks, rather short, stout, smooth; toes, of medium length, straight, well-spread.

SHAPE OF FEMALE

COMB: Single; of medium size, set firmly on head, perfectly straight and upright; with five well-defined points, those in front and rear smaller than the middle ones; fine in texture. (See Standard illustration, page 263.)

BEAK: Short, stout, regularly curved.

BUFF ORPINGTON MALE

BUFF ORPINGTON FEMALE

HEAD: Rather large, broad, deep; face, clean-cut and free from coarseness. (See Standard illustration, page 263.)

EYES: Large, round, full.

WATTLES: Of medium length, fine in texture, well-rounded.

EAR-LOBES: Of medium size, oblong, smooth.

NECK: Rather short, slightly arched, nicely tapering to head, having moderately full plumage.

WINGS: Of medium size, well-folded, carried horizontally, fronts well covered by breast feathers; primaries and secondaries, broad, and overlapping in natural order when wing is folded.

BACK: Broad, rather long, width carried well back to base of tail; rising with a gradual incline to tail.

TAIL: Moderately long, well-spread, carried at an angle of fifteen degrees above the horizontal (see illustrations, figures 30 and 31, page 28); tail-coverts, abundant; main-tail feathers, broad, and overlapping.

BREAST: Broad, deep, well-rounded; well filled in all parts.

BODY AND FLUFF: Body, long, broad, well filled in all parts, deep, straight, extending well forward; lower body feathers, not too profuse; fluff, moderately full.

LEGS AND TOES: Legs, set well apart, straight when viewed from front; lower thighs, large, rather short, well-feathered; shanks, rather short, stout; toes of medium length, straight, well-spread.

Note: See Instructions to Judges, paragraph "Quality of Feather," page 53.

BUFF ORPINGTONS

Disqualifications

Shanks other than white or pinkish white. (See General and Orpington Disqualifications and Cutting for Defects.)

COLOR OF MALE AND FEMALE

COMB, FACE, WATTLES AND EAR-LOBES: Bright red.

BEAK: Pinkish white.

EYES: Reddish bay.

SHANKS AND TOES: Pinkish white.

PLUMAGE: See description of Buff plumage color, page 64.

BLACK ORPINGTONS

Disqualifications

More than one-half inch of positive white in any part of the plumage, or two or more feathers tipped or edged with positive white; shanks other than dark slate or dark leaden blue. (See General and Orpington Disqualifications, and Cutting for Defects.)

COLOR OF MALE AND FEMALE

COMB, FACE, WATTLES AND EAR-LOBES: Bright red.
BEAK: Black.
EYES: Dark brown.
SHANKS AND TOES: Dark slate; web and bottom of toes, pinkish white.
PLUMAGE: See description of Black plumage color, page 64.

WHITE ORPINGTONS

Disqualifications

Shanks other than white or pinkish white. (See General and Orpington Disqualifications, and Cutting for Defects.)

COLOR OF MALE AND FEMALE

COMB, FACE, WATTLES AND EAR-LOBES: Bright red.
BEAK: Pinkish white.
EYES: Reddish bay.
SHANKS AND TOES: Pinkish white.
PLUMAGE: See description of White plumage color, page 63.

BLUE ORPINGTONS

Disqualifications

Red, yellow or positive white in plumage. (See General and Orpington Disqualifications, and Cutting for Defects.)

WHITE ORPINGTON MALE

WHITE ORPINGTON FEMALE

COLOR OF MALE

COMB, FACE, WATTLES AND EAR-LOBES: Bright red.

BEAK: Horn.

EYES: Dark Brown.

SHANKS AND TOES: Leaden blue.

PLUMAGE: See description of Blue male plumage color, page 73.

COLOR OF FEMALE

COMB, FACE, WATTLES AND EAR-LOBES: Bright red.

BEAK: Horn.

EYES: Dark Brown.

SHANKS AND TOES: Leaden blue.

PLUMAGE: See description of Blue female plumage color, page 74.

CORNISH

The Cornish fowl originated in Cornwall, England. This was the Dark Cornish, the parent breed generally known abroad as "Indian Game," albeit the name Cornish is the more correct one. It is a composite of several different blood lines—Asell (or Asil), Black-Red Old English, and Malay. A distinguishing characteristic of the Cornish is that the body of both male and female is of the same conformation. The texture of the feathers is another strong characteristic in the breed. The body plumage should be close fitting, the feathers short, hard and quite narrow, the well-knitted webs giving brilliancy to the color pigments. A humped or decidedly roach back is a serious defect. Dark Cornish were admitted to the Standard in 1893.

White Cornish were produced from White Malay-Dark Cornish crosses in 1890, and were admitted to the Standard in 1898.

White-Laced Red Cornish were produced in America in 1898, from a Shamo Japanese-Dark Cornish cross, and became a Standard variety in 1909.

ECONOMIC QUALITIES: A super-heavy meat producing fowl, valuable also for crossing on other breeds for the production of market poultry. Color of skin, yellow; color of egg-shells, brown.

STANDARD WEIGHTS
Dark, White, White-Laced Red and Buff

Cock	10½ lbs.	Hen	8 lbs.
Cockerel	8½ lbs.	Pullet	6½ lbs.

CORNISH BANTAMS

Disqualifications

Same as for the Dark Cornish, except weight. (See General Disqualifications and Cutting for Defects.)

STANDARD WEIGHTS

Cock	36 oz.	Hen	30 oz.
Cockerel	30 oz.	Pullet	24 oz.

SHAPE AND COLOR OF MALE AND FEMALE

The general shape and color of Dark Cornish Bantams shall conform to the description of the Dark Cornish.

SHAPE OF MALE

COMB: Pea; small, firmly and closely set upon head. (See Standard illustration, page 272.)

BEAK: Short, very stout, well-curved.

HEAD: Large, short, deep and broad, indicating great vigor and strong constitution; the crown flat, broader at front than rear, projecting forward over eyes; face, round and full; general features of head and eyes giving a bold expression. (See Standard illustration, page 272.)

EYES: Large, full.

WATTLES: Small, even, smooth in texture.

EAR-LOBES: Small, smooth in texture.

NECK: Medium in length, carried erect, arched; hackle feathers short, just covering base of neck; throat full, dotted with small feathers.

WINGS: Short and muscular, closely folded; fronts rounding out prominently from body and shoulders; points, slightly curved at extreme ends when folded, the surface of wing when folded to have a convex appearance, closely tucked at ends and held on a line with lower tail-coverts; primaries and secondaries broad, and overlapping in natural order.

BACK: Medium in length, top line of back slightly convex, sloping downward from base of neck to tail, and sloping slightly from each side of backbone, well filled in and broad at base of neck; hip bones very wide apart; very broad across shoulders, carrying its width well back to a line with thighs, showing good width between wings and then narrowing to tail.

TAIL: Short and closely folded, carried slightly below the horizontal; sickles and coverts, short, fitting closely, nearly covering main-tail. (See illustrations, figures 30 and 31, page 28.)

BREAST: Very broad and deep, prominent, well rounded at sides, projecting beyond wing-fronts.

BODY AND FLUFF: Body, compact, well rounded at sides and deep, carried higher in front than at rear, the greatest depth of body near front of breast bone, not lower than level with vent; fluff, short, well tucked up.

LEGS AND TOES: Legs, set very widely apart, straight when viewed from front; upper thighs, medium in length, large and well rounded on outer sides; lower thighs, muscular; of medium length; shanks, round, moderately short, stout; toes, long, straight, well-spread, scales smooth.

PLUMAGE: Short, narrow, fitting closely in all sections.

SHAPE OF FEMALE

COMB: Pea; small and closely set on head. (See Standard illustration, page 273.)

BEAK: Short, well-curved, stout.

HEAD: Large, short, deep and broad, indicating great vigor and strong constitution; the crown flat, broader at front than rear, projecting forward over eyes; face, round and full; general features of head and eyes giving a bold expression. (See Standard illustration, page 273.)

EYES: Large, full.

WATTLES: Small, even, smooth in texture.

EAR-LOBES: Small, smooth in texture.

NECK: Medium in length, carried erect, arched; hackle feathers short, just covering base of neck; throat full, dotted with small feathers.

WINGS: Short and muscular, closely folded; fronts rounding out prominently from body and shoulders; points, slightly curved at extreme ends when folded, the surface of wing when folded to have a convex appearance, closely tucked at ends and held on a line with lower tail-coverts; primaries and secondaries, broad and overlapping in natural order.

BACK: Medium in length, top line of back slightly convex, sloping downward from base of neck to tail, and sloping slightly from each side of backbone, well filled in and broad at base of neck; hip bones very wide apart; very broad across shoulders, carrying its width well back to a line with thighs, showing good width between wings and then narrowing to tail.

TAIL: Short and closely folded, carried slightly below the horizontal; coverts, fitting closely. (See page 28, figures 30 and 31.)

BREAST: Very broad and deep, prominent, well rounded at sides, projecting beyond wing-fronts.

BODY AND FLUFF: Body, compact, well rounded at sides and deep, carried higher in front than at rear, the greatest depth of body near front of breast bone, not lower than level with vent; fluff, short, well tucked up.

LEGS AND TOES: Legs, set very widely apart, straight when viewed from front; upper thighs, medium in length, large and well rounded on outer sides; lower thighs, muscular, of medium length; shanks, round, moderately short and stout; toes, long, straight, well-spread, scales smooth.

PLUMAGE: Short, narrow and fitting closely in all sections.

Note: See Instructions to Judges, paragraph "Quality of Feather," page 53.

DARK CORNISH MALE

DARK CORNISH FEMALE

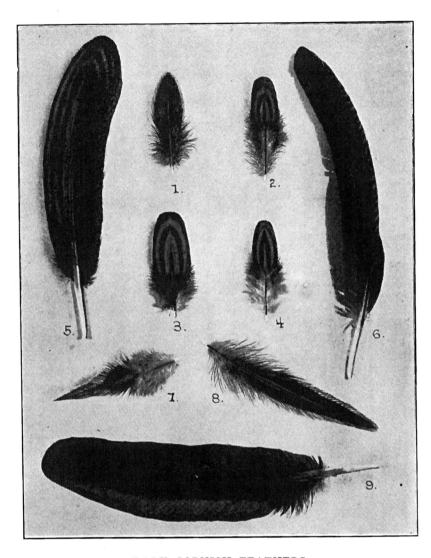

DARK CORNISH FEATHERS

Female Plumage:
(1) Neck Feather.
(2) Breast Feather.

(3) Back Feather.
(4) From Lower Thigh.
(5) Secondary.
(6) Primary.

Male Plumage:
(7) Saddle Feather
(8) Hackle Feather.
(9) Secondary.

274

DARK CORNISH

Disqualifications

Shanks other than yellow. (See General Disqualifications and Cutting for Defects.)

COLOR OF MALE

COMB, FACE, WATTLES AND EAR-LOBES: Bright red.

BEAK: Yellow.

HEAD: Greenish black.

EYES: Pearl.

NECK: Hackle, lustrous, greenish black; shafts, red; plumage, other than hackle, lustrous, greenish black.

WINGS: Fronts, greenish black; bows, lustrous, greenish black and dark red intermixed, the black greatly predominating; coverts, forming wing-bars, lustrous, greenish black; primaries, black except a narrow edging of bay on outer webs; secondaries, upper web black, lower web one-third black next to shaft, the remainder bay, slightly edged with black; short upper secondaries, black, shaft of primaries and secondaries, black.

BACK AND SADDLE: Lustrous, greenish black, with irregular dark red centers, the black greatly predominating; saddle feather, like back in color, but with a somewhat larger proportion of dark red centers.

TAIL: Main-tail feathers black; sickles and coverts, lustrous, greenish black.

BREAST: Lustrous, greenish black.

BODY AND FLUFF: Lustrous, greenish black on surface; fluff, black.

LEGS AND TOES: Lower thighs, greenish black; shanks and toes, yellow.

UNDER-COLOR OF ALL SECTIONS: Dark slate.

COLOR OF FEMALE

COMB, FACE, WATTLES AND EAR-LOBES: Bright red.

BEAK: Yellow.

HEAD: Plumage, greenish black.

EYES: Pearl.

NECK: Lustrous, greenish black, with bay shaft in each feather; feathers on front of neck, bay, approaching mahogany, each feather evenly edged with a narrow lacing of lustrous greenish black, the bay being subdivided by one similar crescentic penciling of black.

WINGS: Fronts and bows, bay, approaching mahogany, each feather evenly laced with a narrow, lustrous, greenish black lacing, the bay being subdivided by one similar crescentic penciling of black; coverts, like bows in color, but with the innermost bay of each feather expanding in width to admit within its center a short stripe of black, covering part of the shaft; primaries, black, except a narrow edging of irregularly penciled bay on outer part of webs; secondaries, upper webs black, except slight penciling of bay near tips, the short upper feathers completely penciled; lower webs, bay, laced on edge and subdivided by pencilings of greenish black running lengthwise of feather; shaft of primaries and secondaries, black.

BACK: Bay, approaching mahogany, each feather edged with a narrow lacing of lustrous, greenish black, the bay being subdivided by one similar crescentic penciling of black; cape, like other sections of body in color and lacing.

TAIL: Main-tail feathers, black, except the two upper feathers, which are irregularly penciled with bay; coverts, bay, approaching mahogany, each feather evenly edged with a narrow lacing of lustrous, greenish black, the bay being subdivided by one similar crescentic penciling of black, and in the largest feathers, a short stripe of black covering part of the shaft.

BREAST: Bay, approaching mahogany, each feather evenly edged with a narrow lacing of lustrous, greenish black, the bay being subdivided by one similar crescentic penciling of black, and in the largest feathers on the lower breast, a short stripe of black covering part of the shaft.

BODY AND FLUFF: Body, bay, approaching mahogany, each feather evenly edged with a narrow lacing of lustrous, greenish black, the bay being subdivided by one similar crescentic penciling of black, and in the largest feathers, a short stripe of black covering part of shaft; fluff, black tinged with reddish bay.

LEGS AND TOES: Lower thighs, greenish black, more or less penciled with bay; shanks and toes, yellow.

UNDER-COLOR OF ALL SECTIONS: Moderately dark slate.

WHITE CORNISH

Disqualifications

Shanks other than yellow. (See General Disqualifications and Cutting for Defects.)

COLOR OF MALE AND FEMALE

COMB, FACE, WATTLES AND EAR-LOBES: Bright red.
BEAK: Yellow.
EYES: Pearl.
SHANKS AND TOES: Yellow.
PLUMAGE: See description of White plumage color, page 63.

WHITE-LACED RED CORNISH

Disqualifications

Shanks other than yellow. (See General Disqualifications and Cutting for Defects.)

COLOR OF MALE

COMB, FACE, WATTLES AND EAR-LOBES: Bright red.
BEAK: Yellow.
HEAD: Plumage, rich red, each feather tipped with white.
EYES: Pearl.
NECK: Hackle, lustrous, rich red, each feather laced with silvery white; plumage on front of neck, same as breast.
WINGS: Fronts, and bows, lustrous, rich red, each feather regularly laced with a narrow lacing of silvery white; coverts, lustrous, rich red, forming wing-bars, regularly laced with white; primaries, rich red, with well-defined, regular lacings of white; secondaries, rich red, with well-defined, regular lacings of white; flight coverts, red, laced with white.
BACK AND SADDLE: Lustrous, rich red, each feather ending with a silvery white V-shaped lacing; saddle feathers, each feather laced with silvery white, the texture of the feather giving a radiant appearance.
TAIL: Main-tail feathers, white with shaft and extreme center red; sickles and coverts, white, with red shaft and center.
BREAST: Lustrous, rich red, each feather laced with a narrow, regular lacing of white, following shape of web to fluff.
BODY AND FLUFF: Rich red, each feather regularly laced with a narrow lacing of white.

277

WHITE-LACED RED CORNISH MALE

WHITE-LACED RED CORNISH FEMALE

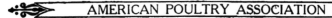

LEGS AND TOES: Lower thighs, rich red, each feather regularly laced with white; shanks and toes, rich yellow.

UNDER-COLOR OF ALL SECTIONS: White.

COLOR OF FEMALE

COMB, FACE, WATTLES AND EAR-LOBES: Bright red.

BEAK: Yellow.

HEAD: Plumage, rich red, each feather laced with white.

EYES: Pearl.

NECK: Rich red, each feather regularly laced with white; feathers on front of neck, same as breast.

WINGS: Fronts, bows, and wing-bars, rich red, regularly laced with a narrow lacing of white; primaries, rich red, ending with white and well up on lower edge; secondaries, rich red, with well-defined, regular lacings of white.

BACK: Rich red, with each feather, from cape to tail, regularly laced with a narrow white lacing conforming to shape of feather.

TAIL: Main-tail feathers, red, each feather laced with white, the white being wider at extremity of feather.

BREAST: Rich red, with each feather regularly laced with a narrow lacing of white, conforming to shape of feather.

BODY AND FLUFF: Rich red, each feather regularly laced with white.

LEGS AND TOES: Lower thighs, red, each feather regularly laced with white; shanks and toes, rich yellow.

UNDER-COLOR OF ALL SECTIONS: White.

BUFF CORNISH

Disqualifications

Shanks other than yellow. (See General Disqualifications.)

COLOR OF MALE AND FEMALE

COMB, FACE, WATTLES AND EAR LOBES: Bright red.

BEAK: Yellow.

EYES: Pearl.

SHANKS AND TOES: Yellow.

PLUMAGE: See description of Buff Plumage color, page 64.

SUSSEX

This is a very old English breed, which originated in the County of Sussex over a century ago. It was primarily bred for market purposes, Sussex being famed for its production of table fowls. The size and shape of the breed make it desirable for fattening and this quality with the white flesh and legs appeals to the English poulterers. Length of body is important when size and weight are to be considered.

Speckled and Red Sussex were admitted to the Standard in 1914; Light Sussex in 1929.

ECONOMIC QUALITIES: A dual purpose fowl for production of meat and eggs. Color of skin, white; color of egg shells, brown.

Disqualifications

Yellow skin, shanks or feet. (See General Disqualifications and Cutting for Defects.)

STANDARD WEIGHTS

Cock	9 lbs.	Hen	7 lbs.
Cockerel	7½ lbs.	Pullet	6 lbs.

SHAPE OF MALE

COMB: Single; medium in size, set firmly on head, perfectly straight and upright, having five well-defined points, those at front and rear being smaller than those in the middle; fine in texture, blade following curve of neck. (See Standard illustration, page 284.)

BEAK: Stout, rather short, slightly curved.

HEAD: Moderately large, broad, medium in length. (See Standard illustration, page 284.)

EYES: Large, full, prominent.

WATTLES: Of medium size, equal in length, well-rounded at lower edges.

EAR-LOBES: Medium in size, oval, smooth.

NECK: Of medium length, slightly arched, having abundant hackle, flowing well over shoulders.

WINGS: Rather long, well-folded, carried closely to body without drooping; points well covered with saddle feathers; primaries and secondaries, broad, and overlapping in natural order when wing is folded.

BACK: Long, flat, and broad its entire length, sloping slightly to tail; saddle feathers, of medium length, abundant and filling well in front of tail.

TAIL: Of medium length, well-spread, main-tail feathers, broad and overlapping, carried at an angle of forty-five degrees above the horizontal (see page 28, figures 30 and 31); sickles of medium length, well-curved, extending slightly beyond main-tail feathers; lesser sickles and tail-coverts of medium length.

BREAST: Broad, deep, rounding nicely into body.

BODY AND FLUFF: Body, long, broad, deep; fluff, moderately full, fitting closely to body.

LEGS AND TOES: Legs, set well apart, and straight when viewed from front; lower thighs, stout, of medium length; shanks, medium length, rather stout; toes, straight, of medium length, well-spread.

SHAPE OF FEMALE

COMB: Single, rather small in size, set firmly on head, perfectly straight and upright, having five well-defined points, those at front and rear being smaller than those in the middle; fine in texture. (See Standard illustration, page 285.)

BEAK: Stout, rather short, slightly curved.

HEAD: Moderately large, broad, medium in length; face, smooth. (See Standard illustration, page 285.)

EYES: Large, full, prominent.

WATTLES: Small, equal in length, well rounded at lower edges.

EAR-LOBES: Medium in size, oval, smooth.

NECK: Of medium length, nicely curved and tapering; neck feathers, moderately full, flowing well over shoulders with no apparent break at juncture of neck and back.

WINGS: Medium in length, well-folded, carried close to body, without drooping; primaries and secondaries, broad, and overlapping in natural order when wing is folded.

BACK: Long, flat, and broad its entire length, sloping slightly to tail.

TAIL: Of medium length, fairly well-spread, carried at an angle of thirty-five degrees above the horizontal (see illustrations, figures 30 and 31, page 28) ; tail-coverts, well-developed; main-tail feathers, broad and overlapping.

BREAST: Broad, deep, rounding nicely into body.

BODY AND FLUFF: Body, long, broad, deep; fluff, moderately full, fitting closely to body.

LEGS AND TOES: Legs, set well apart, and straight when viewed from front; lower thighs, stout, of medium length, shanks, medium length; toes, straight, of medium length, well-spread.

Note: See Instructions to Judges, paragraph "Quality of Feather," page 53.

SPECKLED SUSSEX

Disqualifications

(See General and Sussex Disqualifications, and Cutting for Defects.)

COLOR OF MALE

COMB, FACE, WATTLES AND EAR-LOBES: Bright red.

BEAK: Horn.

HEAD: Plumage, lustrous mahogany bay, each feather tipped with white, a narrow black bar dividing the white from balance of feather.

EYES: Reddish bay.

NECK: Hackle, lustrous mahogany bay, each feather having a narrow black stripe in lower half of web, the black stripe decreasing in width near end of feather and then branching off to outer edge at each side of shaft near point. Point of feather distinctly marked with diamond-shaped white spangle. (See page 67, figure 61.)

WINGS: Fronts and bows, lustrous mahogany bay, each feather tipped with white, a narrow elongated V-shaped black bar dividing white from balance of feather; coverts, mahogany bay, each feather tipped with a large white spangle, a black bar dividing the white from balance of feather; primaries, black and white; secondaries, outer web bay edged with white, inner web black edged with white, each feather ending with a white spangle.

BACK AND SADDLE: Lustrous mahogany bay, each feather having a narrow black stripe in lower half of web, the black stripe decreasing in width near end of feather and then branching off to outer edge at each side of shaft near point. Point of feather

SPECKLED SUSSEX MALE

SPECKLED SUSSEX FEMALE

distinctly marked with diamond-shaped white spangle. (See page 67, figure 61.)

TAIL: Main-tail feathers, black and white; sickles, coverts and smaller coverts, glossy, greenish black, tipped with white.

BREAST: Mahogany bay, each feather tipped with white, a black bar dividing the white from balance of feather.

BODY AND FLUFF: Body, mahogany bay, each feather tipped with white, a black bar dividing the white from balance of the feather; fluff, slaty brown.

LEGS AND TOES: Lower thighs, mahogany bay, each feather tipped with white, a narrow black bar dividing the white from balance of feather; shanks and toes, pinkish white.

UNDER-COLOR OF ALL SECTIONS: Slate, shading to salmon, the salmon shading to light gray at base.

COLOR OF FEMALE

COMB, FACE, WATTLES AND EAR-LOBES: Bright red.

BEAK: Horn.

HEAD: Plumage, mahogany bay, each feather tipped with a white spangle, a narrow, black bar dividing the white from balance of feather.

EYES: Reddish bay.

NECK: Mahogany bay, each feather tipped with a white spangle, a narrow, crescentic black bar dividing the white from balance of feather; feathers on front of neck, same as breast.

WINGS: Fronts, bows and coverts, mahogany bay, each feather tipped with a small white spangle, a narrow crescentic black bar dividing the white from balance of feather; primaries, black and white; secondaries, outer web, bay edged with white, inner web, black edged with white, each feather ending with a white spangle.

BACK: Mahogany bay, each feather tipped with a small white spangle, a narrow, crescentic black bar dividing white from balance of feather. (See page 67, figure 58.)

TAIL: Main-tail black mottled with brown, each feather tipped with white; coverts, mahogany bay, each feather marked with a crescentic black bar, near lower extremity, and tipped with white.

BREAST: Mahogany bay, each feather tipped with white, a narrow crescentic black bar dividing the white from balance of feather. (See page 67, figure 58.)

BODY AND FLUFF: Body mahogany bay, each feather tipped

with white, a narrow crescentic black bar dividing the white from balance of feather; fluff, slaty brown.

LEGS AND TOES: Lower thighs, mahogany bay, each feather tipped with a white spangle, a narrow crescentic black bar dividing the white from balance of feather; shanks and toes, pinkish white.

UNDER-COLOR OF ALL SECTIONS: Slate, shading to salmon, the salmon shading to light gray at base.

RED SUSSEX

Disqualifications

One or more white feathers showing in outer plumage. (See General and Sussex Disqualifications, and Cutting for Defects.)

COLOR OF MALE

COMB, FACE, WATTLES AND EAR-LOBES: Bright red.

BEAK: Horn.

HEAD: Plumage, lustrous mahogany red.

EYES: Reddish bay.

NECK: Lustrous mahogany red, plumage on front of hackle, rich mahogany red.

WINGS: Fronts, bows and coverts, lustrous mahogany red; primaries, upper web mahogany red, lower web black with a narrow edging of mahogany red; primary coverts, black; secondaries, lower web mahogany red, sufficient to give a mahogany red wing-bay; the remainder of each feather black.

BACK AND SADDLE: Lustrous, mahogany red.

TAIL: Main-tail feathers, black; sickle feathers, greenish black; lesser sickles, mainly greenish black, becoming mahogany red as saddle is approached.

BREAST: Rich mahogany red.

BODY AND FLUFF: Rich mahogany red.

LEGS AND TOES: Lower thighs, rich mahogany red; shanks and toes, pinkish white.

UNDER-COLOR OF ALL SECTIONS: Red, with a slight bar of slate.

COLOR OF FEMALE

COMB, FACE, WATTLES AND EAR-LOBES: Bright red.
BEAK: Horn.
HEAD: Plumage, mahogany red.
EYES: Reddish bay.
NECK: Rich mahogany red.
WINGS: Fronts, bows and coverts, rich mahogany red; primaries, upper webs mahogany red, lower webs black with a narrow edging of mahogany red; secondaries, lower web, mahogany red, the remainder of each feather black, forming a mahogany red bay.
BACK: Rich mahogany red.
TAIL: Main-tail feathers, black, except two top feathers, which may be edged with mahogany red.
BREAST: Rich mahogany red.
BODY AND FLUFF: Rich mahogany red.
LEGS AND TOES: Lower thighs, rich mahogany red; shanks and toes, pinkish white.
UNDER-COLOR OF ALL SECTIONS: Red, with slight bar of slate.

LIGHT SUSSEX

Disqualifications

Red or brown in any part of plumage, or any color foreign to variety; shanks other than white or pinkish white. (See General and Sussex Disqualifications, and Cutting for Defects.)

COLOR OF MALE

COMB, FACE, WATTLES AND EAR-LOBES: Bright red.
BEAK: White, shaded with horn.
HEAD: Plumage, white.
EYES: Reddish bay.
NECK: Hackle, web of feather, solid, lustrous, greenish black, moderately broad, with a narrow edging of silvery white, uniform in width, extending around point of feather; greater portion of shaft, black; plumage on front of neck, white.
WINGS: Fronts, bows, and coverts, white; primaries, black with white edging on lower edge of lower webs; secondaries, lower portion of lower webs, white, sufficient to secure a white

wing-bay, the white extending around ends of feathers and lacing upper portion of upper webs, this color growing wider in the shorter secondaries, sufficient to show white on surface when wing is folded; remainder of each secondary, black.

BACK AND SADDLE: Surface, cape, and saddle, white.

TAIL: Main-tail, lustrous greenish black, the curling feathers underneath, black laced with white; sickles and coverts, lustrous greenish black; lesser coverts, lustrous greenish black edged with silvery white.

BREAST: White.

BODY AND FLUFF: White.

LEGS AND TOES: Lower thighs, white; shanks and toes, pink-ish white.

UNDER-COLOR OF ALL SECTIONS: White.

COLOR OF FEMALE

COMB, FACE, WATTLES AND EAR-LOBES: Bright red.

BEAK: White shaded with horn.

HEAD: Plumage, white.

EYES: Reddish bay.

NECK: Feathers beginning at juncture of head, web, a broad, solid lustrous greenish black, with a narrow lacing of silvery white extending around the outer edge of each feather; greater portion of shaft, black; feathers on front of neck, white.

WINGS: Fronts, bows and coverts, white; primaries, black, with white edging on lower edge of lower webs; secondaries, lower portion of lower webs, white, sufficient to secure a white wing-bay, the white extending around the ends and lacing upper portions of upper webs, this color growing wider in the shorter secondaries, sufficient to show white on surface when wing is folded; remainder of each secondary, black.

BACK: White; cape, white.

TAIL: Black; coverts, black edged with white.

BREAST: White.

BODY AND FLUFF: White.

LEGS AND TOES: Lower thighs, white; shanks and toes, pinkish white.

UNDER-COLOR OF ALL SECTIONS: White.

AUSTRALORPS

The Australorp is a derivative of the Orpington and illustrates nicely the effect on size and type which breeding for one object has on poultry.

The breed was developed in Australia where for twenty-five years it has been bred principally for egg production rather than meat and eggs as has been the case with its progenitor, the Orpington.

It is a medium weight, active bird laying a tinted egg and is a valuable fowl for those who desire an abundance of eggs without sacrificing too much value in meat quality.

It was admitted to the Standard of Perfection in 1929.

Disqualifications

More than one-half inch of positive white in any part of surface plumage, or two or more feathers tipped or edged with positive white; shanks other than dark slate. (See General Disqualifications and Cutting for Defects.)

STANDARD WEIGHTS

Cock	8½ lbs.	Hen	6½ lbs.
Cockerel	7½ lbs.	Pullet	5½ lbs.

SHAPE OF MALE

COMB: Single; of medium size, proportionate to size of specimen; set firmly on head; perfectly straight and upright; free from indentations; evenly serrated, with five distinct points, the one in front being shorter than the other four; fine, even texture; blade slightly following shape of head.

BEAK: Of medium length, fairly stout.

HEAD: Of medium size, broad, rather deep, neatly curved.

EYES: Large, round, somewhat prominent.

WATTLES: Of medium size, proportionate to size of comb; smooth; free from folds or wrinkles; nicely rounded; fine in texture.

EAR-LOBES: Of medium size, oblong, smooth.

NECK: Rather long, moderately well-arched, having abundant hackle flowing well over shoulders.

WINGS: Of medium size, well-folded and carried without drooping; front, well covered by breast feathers and points well covered by saddle feathers; primaries and secondaries, broad and overlapping in natural order when wing is folded.

BACK: Rather long, broad its entire length, slightly sloping downward from shoulders to center of back, then rising in a gradually increasing concave sweep to tail. Saddle feathers, long, of good width, abundant.

TAIL: Moderately large, well spread; main-tail feathers, broad and overlapping, carried at an angle of forty degrees above the horizontal; sickle feathers of good width, well-curved; lesser sickles and tail-coverts long, of good width, nicely curved and abundant. (See illustration, figures 30 and 31, page 28.)

BREAST: Full, well-rounded, carried well forward.

BODY AND FLUFF: Body, moderately long and rather deep; carried nearly horizontal but sloping very slightly from front to rear; fluff of good proportions. Under-line to conform generally to top-line.

LEGS AND TOES: Legs, set well apart and straight when viewed from front; lower thighs and shanks, moderately long; toes, medium length, straight, well-spread.

SHAPE OF FEMALE

COMB: Single, of medium size, set firmly on head, perfectly straight and upright, with five even and well-defined points, the one in front smaller than the other four.

BEAK: Of medium length, neatly curved.

HEAD: Of medium size, broad; face, smooth.

EYES: Large, round, somewhat prominent.

WATTLES: Small, well-rounded, fine in texture, conforming to size and shape of head.

EAR-LOBES: Oblong in shape, smooth.

NECK: Medium in length, nicely curved and tapering to head, where it is comparatively small; neck feathers moderately abundant, flowing well over shoulders with no apparent break at juncture of neck and back.

WINGS: Of medium size, well-folded and carried without drooping; fronts, well covered by breast feathers and points well covered by back feathers; primaries and secondaries, broad and overlapping in natural order when wing is folded.

BACK: Rather long, broad its entire length, with a slight slope down from shoulders to center of back, and rising from center with a concave sweep to tail, feathers of sufficient length to carry well up to tail.

AUSTRALORP MALE

AUSTRALORP FEMALE

TAIL: Medium length, well-spread, carried at an angle of about forty degrees above the horizontal (see illustration, page 28, figures 30 and 31) ; main-tail feathers, broad and overlapping.

BREAST: Moderately deep, full, well-rounded.

BODY AND FLUFF: Body, long, broad, moderately deep, full, extending well forward, giving the body a moderately oblong appearance; feathers carried close to body; fluff, moderately full.

LEGS AND TOES: Legs, set well apart, straight when viewed from the front; lower thighs, of medium length, well-feathered, smooth; shanks, of medium length, well-rounded, smooth; toes, of medium length, strong, straight, well-spread.

Note: See Instructions to Judges, paragraph "Quality of Feather," page 53.

COLOR OF MALE AND FEMALE

COMB, FACE, WATTLES AND EAR-LOBES: Bright red.

BEAK: Black.

EYES: Dark brown.

SHANKS AND TOES: Dark slate; bottoms of feet and toes, pinkish white.

PLUMAGE: See description of Black plumage color, page 64.

POLISH AND POLISH BANTAMS

Breed	*Varieties*
POLISH	White-Crested Black Non-Bearded Golden Non-Bearded Silver Non-Bearded White Non-Bearded Buff Laced Bearded Golden Bearded Silver Bearded White Bearded Buff Laced

The above varieties of Polish are duplicated in miniature in the Polish Bantams.

SCALE OF POINTS
Polish and Polish Bantams

	White and White Cr. Black		Parti Color	
	Shape	Color	Shape	Color
Symmetry	4		4	
Size	4		4	
Condition and Vigor	10		10	
*Crest	6	4	6	4
Beard	3	1	3	1
Comb	1		1	
Beak	2	1	2	1
Head	1	1	1	1
Eyes	2	2	2	2
Wattles	2		2	
Earlobe	2	2	2	2
Neck	3	3	1	5
Wings	5	3	3	5
Back	4	4	3	5
Tail	5	4	3	6
Breast	5	4	3	6
Body and Fluff	3	3	2	4
Legs and Toes	4	2	4	2
	66	34	56	44

*Omit beard in the non-bearded varieties and give the four points to crest, three for shape and one for color.

POLISH BANTAMS

Disqualifications

Same as disqualifications in Polish. (See General Disqualifications and Cutting for Defects.)

STANDARD WEIGHTS

Cock ....26 oz. Hen ....22 oz.
Cockerel ....22 oz. Pullet ....20 oz.

SHAPE AND COLOR OF MALE AND FEMALE

The shape and color of the Polish Bantams shall conform to the description of the Polish.

POLISH

The Crested Dutch, or Polish, of early writers were imported from eastern Europe, and upon landing in England, these were called "Poland Fowls." On the Continent of Europe the name "Padoue" is applied to crested breeds. Charles Darwin classifies all the races of fowl with top-knots as "Crested or Polish" but does not give any data regarding their origin.

Polish is a long established race of domesticated poultry. It was mentioned as a pure breed as early as the sixteenth century. It is among the most ornamental and beautiful breeds of poultry, highly prized for exhibition and the production of white-shelled eggs. The most striking characteristic of the Polish fowl is the crest.

All five varieties of Polish were admitted to the Standard in 1874.

ECONOMIC QUALITIES: A highly ornamental fowl laying a medium sized white egg; a non-sitter; color of skin, white.

SHAPE OF MALE

COMB: V-shaped; of small size, the smaller the better; set evenly on head, retreating into crest; natural absence of comb is preferred. (See Standard illustration, page 298.)

CREST: Very large, profuse, rising well in front so as not to obstruct the sight, and falling over on both sides and to rear in a regular, even mass, composed of feathers similar in shape and texture to those of hackle.

BEAK: Of medium length, slightly curved.

HEAD: Large with a pronounced protuberance on top of skull. (See description of Head, page 16, figure 7.)

NOSTRILS: Large, with crown elevated above the ordinary curved line of beak.

EYES: Large, full.

BEARD (in bearded varieties): Thick and full, running back of eyes in a graceful curve.

WATTLES: Uniform, thin, well rounded on lower edges.

EAR-LOBES: Small, smooth.

NECK: Of medium length, slightly arched, with abundant hackle flowing well over shoulders.

WHITE-CRESTED BLACK POLISH MALE

WHITE-CRESTED BLACK POLISH FEMALE

WINGS: Large, well-folded; carried without drooping; primaries and secondaries, broad and overlapping in natural order when wing is folded.

BACK: Straight, wide across the shoulders, tapering to tail; saddle feathers, abundant, with slight concave sweep near base of tail.

TAIL: Large, well-expanded, carried at an angle of forty-five degrees above the horizontal (see illustrations, page 28, figures 30 and 31); sickles and coverts, abundant and covering main-tail feathers; main-tail feathers, broad and overlapping.

BREAST: Full, prominent.

BODY AND FLUFF: Body, of medium length, moderately full, tapering from front to rear; fluff, rather short.

LEGS AND TOES: Legs set well apart, straight when viewed from front; lower thighs, of medium length; shanks, of medium length; toes, straight, well-spread.

SHAPE OF FEMALE

COMB, HEAD, BEAK, NOSTRILS, EYES, WATTLES, AND EAR-LOBES: Similar to those of male, but smaller.

CREST: Large, compact, profuse, globular, rising well in front, regular and unbroken.

BEARD (in bearded varieties): Same as male.

NECK: Medium length, full at base, tapering to head.

WINGS: Large, well-folded and carried without drooping; primaries and secondaries, broad and overlapping in natural order when wing is folded.

BACK: Straight, broadest at shoulders, tapering, with concave sweep near base of tail.

TAIL: Large, broad, well-expanded, carried at an angle of forty degrees above the horizontal; main-tail feathers, broad and overlapping. (See illustrations, page 28, figures 30 and 31.)

BREAST: Full, round, prominent.

BODY AND FLUFF: Body, medium in length, moderately full; fluff, short.

LEGS AND TOES: Legs, set well apart, straight when viewed from front; lower thighs, of medium length; shanks, of medium length; toes, straight, well-spread.

Note: See Instructions to Judges, paragraph "Quality of Feather," page 53.

NON-BEARDED POLISH

WHITE-CRESTED BLACK POLISH

Disqualifications

More than one-half inch of positive white in any part of plu
mage, or two or more feathers tipped or edged with positiv
white, except in crest; shanks other than dark slate or leade
blue. (See General Disqualifications and Cutting for Defects.

COLOR OF MALE AND FEMALE

COMB AND CREST: Comb, bright red. Crest, white, a narro
band of black feathers at base of crest in front is allowable, bu
the narrower the better.

BEAK: Bluish black.

HEAD: Face, bright red.

EYES: Reddish bay.

WATTLES: Bright red.

EAR-LOBES: White.

SHANKS AND TOES: Dark slate.

PLUMAGE (except Crest): See description of Black plumag
color, page 64.

UNDER-COLOR OF ALL SECTIONS EXCEPT CREST: Slate.

GOLDEN, SILVER, WHITE AND BUFF LACED NON-BEARDED POLISH

For color description, see that of corresponding bearded vari
eties, except for beard only.

BEARDED GOLDEN POLISH

Disqualifications

Shanks other than blue or slaty blue. (See General Disqualifi
cations and Cutting for Defects.)

COLOR OF MALE

COMB AND CREST: Comb, bright red. Crest, in cockerels, blac
laced with golden bay, which after first moult should be golde
bay laced with lustrous black.

BEAK: Dark horn.

HEAD: Face, bright red.

EYES: Reddish bay.

WATTLES: Bright red.

EAR-LOBES: White.

BEARD: Golden bay, laced with lustrous black.

NECK: Golden bay, each feather laced with lustrous black; plumage on front of neck, same as breast.

WINGS: Fronts and bows, golden bay, each feather laced with lustrous black; coverts, golden bay, each feather laced with lustrous black, lacing widest at end, forming two well-defined wing-bars; primaries, golden bay, each feather ending with black, the black tapering to a point on lower edge; secondaries, golden bay, with well-defined black lacings.

BACK AND SADDLE: Golden bay, each feather laced with lustrous black; saddle feathers, golden bay, each feather laced with lustrous black.

TAIL: Main-tail feathers, golden bay, each feather laced with lustrous black, lacing widest at end; sickles and coverts, golden bay, each feather laced with lustrous black, lacing widest at end.

BREAST: Golden bay, each feather laced with lustrous black, the lacing being proportionate to size of feather.

BODY AND FLUFF: Body, golden bay, each feather laced with lustrous black; fluff, bay tinged with black.

LEGS AND TOES: Lower thighs, bay, each feather laced with lustrous black; shanks and toes, slaty blue.

UNDER-COLOR OF ALL SECTIONS: Slate.

COLOR OF FEMALE

COMB AND CREST: Comb, bright red; crest, in pullets, black laced with bay, which after first moult should be golden bay laced with lustrous black.

BEAK: Dark horn.

HEAD: Face, bright red.

EYES: Reddish bay.

WATTLES: Bright red.

EAR-LOBES: White.

BEARD: Golden bay, heavily laced with lustrous black.

NECK: Golden bay, each feather laced with lustrous black; feathers on front of neck, same as breast.

WINGS: Fronts and bows, golden bay, each feather laced with lustrous black; coverts, golden bay, each feather laced with lustrous black, the black growing wider at the extremity, forming two distinctly laced bars across wings; primaries, golden bay, each feather ending with lustrous black, the black tapering to a point on lower edge; secondaries, golden bay with well-defined, lustrous black lacings.

BACK: Golden bay, each feather laced with lustrous black.

TAIL: Main-tail feathers, golden bay, each feather laced with lustrous black, the black being wider at outer end of feather.

BREAST: Golden bay, each feather laced with lustrous black.

BODY AND FLUFF: Body, golden bay, each feather laced with lustrous black; fluff, a lighter shade of bay, tinged with black.

LEGS AND TOES: Lower thighs, bay, each feather laced with lustrous black; shanks and toes, slaty blue.

UNDER-COLOR OF ALL SECTIONS: Slate.

BEARDED SILVER POLISH

Disqualifications

Shanks other than blue or slaty blue. (See General Disqualifications and Cutting for Defects.)

COLOR OF MALE

COMB AND CREST: Comb, bright red. Crest, in cockerels, black laced with white, which after first moult should be white laced with lustrous black.

BEAK: Dark horn.

HEAD: Face, bright red.

EYES: Reddish bay.

WATTLES: Bright red.

EAR-LOBES: White.

BEARD: White, laced with lustrous black.

NECK: White, each feather laced with lustrous black; plumage on front of neck, same as breast.

WINGS: Fronts and bows, white, each feather laced with lustrous black; coverts, white, each feather laced with lustrous black, lacing widest at end, forming two well-defined wing-bars; primaries, white, each feather ending with lustrous black, the black tapering to a point on lower edges; secondaries, white, with well-defined black lacings.

BEARDED SILVER POLISH MALE

BEARDED SILVER POLISH FEMALE

BACK AND SADDLE: White, each feather laced with lustrous black; saddle feathers, white, each feather laced with lustrous black.

TAIL: Main-tail feathers, white, each feather laced with lustrous black, lacing widest at end; sickles and coverts, white, each feather laced with lustrous black, lacing widest at end.

BREAST: White, each feather laced with lustrous black, the lacing being proportionate to size of feather.

BODY AND FLUFF: Body, white, each feather laced with lustrous black; fluff, white tinged with black.

LEGS AND TOES: Lower thighs, white, each feather laced with lustrous black; shanks and toes, slaty blue.

UNDER-COLOR OF ALL SECTIONS: Slate.

COLOR OF FEMALE

COMB AND CREST: Comb, bright red. Crest, in pullets, black laced with white, which after first moult should be white laced with lustrous black.

BEAK: Dark horn.

HEAD: Face, bright red.

EYES: Reddish bay.

WATTLES: Bright red.

EAR-LOBES: White.

BEARD: White heavily laced with lustrous black.

NECK: White, each feather laced with lustrous black; feathers on front of neck, same as breast.

WINGS: Fronts and bows, white, each feather laced with lustrous black; coverts, white, each feather laced with lustrous black, the black growing wider at the extremity, forming two distinctly laced bars across wings; primaries, white, each feather ending with lustrous black, the black tapering to a point on lower edge; secondaries, white with well-defined, lustrous black lacings.

BACK: White, each feather laced with lustrous black.

TAIL: Main-tail feathers, white, each feather laced with lustrous black, the black wider at outer end of feather.

BREAST: White, each feather laced with lustrous black.

BODY AND FLUFF: Body, white, each feather laced with lustrous black; fluff, white, tinged with black.

LEGS AND TOES: Lower thighs, white, each feather laced with lustrous black; shanks and toes, slaty blue.

UNDER-COLOR OF ALL SECTIONS: Slate.

BEARDED WHITE POLISH

Disqualifications

Shanks other than blue or slaty blue. (See General Disqualification and Cutting for Defects.)

COLOR OF MALE AND FEMALE

COMB, FACE, AND WATTLES: Bright red.
BEAK: Dark horn.
EYES: Reddish bay.
EAR-LOBES: White.
SHANKS AND TOES: Slaty blue.
PLUMAGE: See description of White plumage color, page 63.

BEARDED BUFF-LACED POLISH

Disqualifications

Shanks other than blue or slaty blue. (See General Disqualifications and Cutting for Defects.)

COLOR OF MALE

COMB AND CREST: Comb, bright red. Crest, in cockerels, creamy white laced with rich golden buff which, after first moult, should be rich golden buff laced with creamy white.

BEAK: Slaty blue.

HEAD: Face, bright red; plumage, rich golden buff ticked with creamy white.

EYES: Reddish bay.

WATTLES: Bright red.

EAR-LOBES: White.

BEARD: Rich golden buff, each feather laced with creamy white.

NECK: Rich golden buff, each feather laced with creamy white; plumage on front of neck, same as breast.

WINGS: Fronts and bows, rich golden buff laced with creamy white; coverts, rich golden buff, each feather laced with creamy white, lacing widest at ends, forming two well-defined wing-bars; primaries, golden buff, the outer end having an edging of creamy white; secondaries, rich golden buff, with a well-defined lacing of creamy white.

BACK AND SADDLE: Rich golden buff, each feather laced with

creamy white; saddle, rich golden buff, each feather laced with creamy white.

TAIL: Main-tail feathers, golden buff; sickles and coverts, golden buff, each feather laced with creamy white.

BREAST: Rich golden buff, each feather laced with creamy white.

BODY AND FLUFF: Body, rich golden buff, each feather laced with creamy white; fluff, light buff.

LEGS AND TOES: Lower thighs, golden buff laced with creamy white; shanks and toes, slaty blue.

UNDER-COLOR OF ALL SECTIONS: Creamy white.

COLOR OF FEMALE

COMB AND CREST: Comb, bright red. Crest, in pullets, creamy white laced with rich golden buff, which after first moult should be rich golden buff laced with creamy white.

BEAK: Slaty blue.

HEAD: Face, bright red; plumage, rich golden buff ticked with creamy white.

EYES: Reddish bay.

WATTLES: Bright red.

EAR-LOBES: White.

BEARD: Golden buff, each feather laced with creamy white.

NECK: Golden buff, each feather laced with creamy white; feathers on front of neck, same as breast.

WINGS: Fronts and bows, golden buff, each feather laced with creamy white; coverts, golden buff laced with creamy white, creamy white growing wider at extremity, forming two well-defined wing-bars; primaries, golden buff; secondaries, golden buff, with a well-defined lacing of creamy white.

BACK: Golden buff, each feather laced with creamy white.

TAIL: Main-tail feathers; golden buff, each feather laced with creamy white, the creamy white being wider at outer edge of feather.

BREAST: Golden buff, each feather laced with creamy white.

BODY AND FLUFF: Body, golden buff, each feather laced with creamy white; fluff, light buff.

LEGS AND TOES: Lower thighs, golden buff, each feather laced with creamy white; shanks and toes, slaty blue.

UNDER-COLOR OF ALL SECTIONS: Creamy white.

HAMBURGS

Breed   *Varieties*

HAMBURGS..⎧ Golden-Spangled
                                                                                 ⎪ Silver-Spangled
                                                                                 ⎨ Golden-Penciled
                                                                                 ⎪ Silver-Penciled
                                                                                 ⎪ White
                                                                                 ⎩ Black

HAMBURGS

The Hamburg is a very old race of domesticated poultry. The name of the breed is German, but the origin is Dutch. The American Standard of Perfection originally classified Hamburgs among the Continental breeds, albeit they owe their present shape and color qualities to the English fanciers, who, over seventy years ago, began the work of refining the "pheasant fowls" of that period into the modern Hamburgs. The Black and Spangled varieties were evolved in England; the Penciled varieties came from Holland via Hamburg, Germany. All of the six Standard varieties were admitted in 1874.

The symmetrical body, graceful carriage and attractive color patterns of Hamburgs have made them popular exhibition varieties, but Hamburgs are also prolific producers of eggs; in fact, in England, in the years gone by, they were referred to commonly as the "Dutch Everyday Layer." Typical shape and carriage should be the same in all varieties, although the Blacks and Spangles are greater in size than the White and Penciled varieties.

ECONOMIC QUALITIES: An ornamental non-sitting fowl; good layers of white eggs; color of skin, white.

Disqualifications

Red in ear-lobes covering more than one-third of the surface; shanks other than leaden blue. (See General Disqualifications and Cutting for Defects.)

SHAPE OF MALE

COMB: Rose; medium in size, not so large as to overhang the eyes or beak; square in front; firm and even on head; even on sides; top even, covered with small points; fine in texture; terminating at rear in a spike which inclines upward very slightly. (See Standard illustration, page 316.)

BEAK: Of medium length; well-curved.

HEAD: Short, medium in size. (See Standard illustration, page 316.)

EYES: Rather large, round, full.

WATTLES: Medium in size, thin, well-rounded, smooth, free from wrinkles.

EAR-LOBES: Rather large, flat, round, smooth, even, fitting closely to the head.

NECK: Medium length, nicely arched, tapering, with full hackle flowing well over shoulders.

WINGS: Large, well-folded, carried rather low; without drooping; primaries and secondaries, broad, and overlapping in natural order when wing is folded.

BACK: Of medium length, fairly wide, flat at shoulders, straight, gradually sloping to rear of saddle.

TAIL: Moderately long, full, well-expanded, carried at an angle of forty degrees above the horizontal (see illustrations, page 28, figures 30 and 31); sickles, broad and well-curved; coverts, abundant; main-tail feathers, broad and overlapping.

BREAST: Round, prominent, carried well forward.

BODY AND FLUFF: Body, fairly deep, round, smooth; fluff, rather short.

LEGS AND TOES: Legs, set well apart, straight when viewed from front; lower thighs, of medium size and length; shanks of medium length; toes, straight, well-spread.

SHAPE OF FEMALE

COMB: Rose; similar to that of male, but smaller. (See Standard illustration, page 317.)

BEAK: Of medium length; well-curved.

HEAD: Short, medium in size. (See Standard illustration, page 317.)

EYES: Rather large, round, full.

WATTLES: Small, thin, well-rounded, smooth.

EAR-LOBES: Medium in size, flat, round, smooth, even, fitting closely to head.

NECK: Full at base, tapering to head, slightly arched.

WINGS: Large, carried rather low, but without drooping; primaries and secondaries, broad, and overlapping in natural order when wing is folded.

BACK: Of medium length, fairly wide, moderately full, with slight concave sweep to tail.

TAIL: Full, somewhat expanded, carried at an angle of thirty-five degrees above the horizontal; main-tail feathers, broad and overlapping. (See illustrations, figures 30 and 31, page 28.)

BREAST: Round, prominent, carried well forward.

BODY AND FLUFF: Body, fairly deep, round, smooth; fluff, rather short.

LEGS AND TOES: Legs, set well apart, straight when viewed from front; lower thighs, of medium size and length; shanks, of medium length; toes, straight, well-spread.

Note: See Instructions to Judges, paragraph "Quality of Feather," page 53.

GOLDEN-SPANGLED HAMBURGS

Disqualifications

Absence of distinct bars across the wings; markings wholly crescentic. (See General and Hamburg Disqualifications, and Cutting for Defects.)

COLOR OF MALE

COMB, FACE, AND WATTLES: Bright red.

BEAK: Dark horn.

HEAD: Plumage, rich golden bay.

EYES: Reddish bay.

EAR-LOBES: Enamel white.

NECK: Golden bay with a lustrous greenish black stripe extending down middle of each feather, terminating in a point near its lower extremity; Feathers on front of neck, same as breast.

WINGS: Fronts and bows, golden bay, distinctly spangled with lustrous, greenish black; coverts, golden bay, each feather ending with a large, lustrous, greenish black spangle, forming two distinct parallel bars across wings; primaries, upper web black, lower web, golden bay; secondaries, golden bay, each feather ending with a lustrous, greenish black, crescent-shaped spangle, gradually increasing into a V-shaped spangle as it approaches the back.

BACK: Lustrous golden bay, spangled with greenish black, the texture of the feathers giving the spangles a rayed appearance.

SADDLE FEATHERS: A golden bay, having a V-shaped, lustrous greenish black stripe, tapering to a point near the lower extremity; this V-shaped stripe increasing in length, width and density as it nears the tail coverts.

TAIL: Lustrous, greenish black; Sickles: Lustrous, greenish black; Coverts: Lustrous, greenish black.

BREAST: Clear, golden bay, each feather ending with a moderately large, lustrous, greenish black spangle, the spangle being proportionate to size of feather.

BODY AND FLUFF: Body, golden bay, each feather ending with a moderately large, lustrous, greenish black spangle, the spangle being proportionate to size of feather; fluff, slate tinged with bay.

LEGS AND TOES: Lower thighs, golden bay, each feather ending with a large black spangle; shanks and toes, leaden blue. Bottoms of feet, pinkish white.

UNDER-COLOR OF ALL SECTIONS: Slate.

COLOR OF FEMALE

COMB, FACE, AND WATTLES: Bright red.

BEAK: Dark horn.

HEAD: Plumage, rich, golden bay, marked with black.

EYES: Reddish bay.

EAR-LOBES: Enamel white.

NECK: Clear, golden bay, each feather ending with an elongated, small, black spangle; feathers on front of neck, same as breast.

WINGS: Bows golden bay, distinctly spangled with a lustrous, greenish black; Coverts: Clear, reddish bay, free from lacing, each feather ending with a large, lustrous, greenish black spangle, forming two distinct parallel bars across wings. Primaries: Upper webs black, lower webs bay. Secondaries: Golden bay, each feather ending with a lustrous, greenish black, crescent shaped spangle, gradually increasing into V-shaped spangle as it approaches the back.

BACK: Golden bay, each feather ending with a moderately large, lustrous, greenish black spangle.

TAIL: Main-tail feathers, greenish black; coverts, golden bay, each feather ending with a large, lustrous, greenish black spangle.

BREAST: Clear, golden bay, each feather ending with a moderately large, lustrous, greenish black spangle, the spangle being proportionate to size of feather.

BODY AND FLUFF: Body, golden bay, each feather ending with a moderately large, lustrous, greenish black spangle, the spangle being proportionate to size of feather; fluff, slate tinged with gray.

LEGS AND TOES: Lower thighs, golden bay, each feather ending with a large black spangle; shanks and toes, leaden blue. Bottoms of feet, pinkish white.

UNDER-COLOR OF ALL SECTIONS: Slate.

Note: In all sections where the word "Spangle" appears, when shape is not otherwise described, read "edges of spangle following web of feather and meeting at shaft."

SILVER-SPANGLED HAMBURGS

Disqualifications

Absence of distinct bars across wings; markings wholly crescentic. (See General and Hamburg Disqualifications, and Cutting for Defects.)

COLOR OF MALE

COMB, FACE, AND WATTLES: Bright red.

BEAK: Dark horn.

HEAD: Plumage, white.

EYES: Reddish bay.

EAR-LOBES: Enamel white.

NECK: Clear, silvery white, each feather ending with an elongated black spangle, the spangle being proportionate to size of feather; plumage on front of neck, same as breast.

WINGS: Fronts and bows, silvery white, distinctly spangled with lustrous, greenish black; coverts, silvery white, each feather ending with a large, lustrous, greenish black spangle, forming two distinct parallel bars across wings; primaries, white, each feather edged with black at end; secondaries, white, each feather ending with a lustrous, greenish black, crescent-shaped spangle, gradually increasing into a V-shaped spangle as it approaches the back.

BACK AND SADDLE: Clear, silvery white, each feather ending with an elongated, lustrous, greenish black spangle, the texture of feathers giving spangles a rayed appearance; saddle, clear, silvery white, each feather ending with an elongated, lustrous, greenish black spangle, the spangle being proportionate to size of feather.

TAIL: Main-tail feathers, white, each feather ending with a large black spangle; sickles, pure white, ending with medium sized, lustrous, greenish black spangles; coverts, pure white, ending with large, lustrous, greenish black spangles.

BREAST: Clear, silvery white, each feather ending with a moderately large, lustrous, greenish black spangle, the spangle being proportionate to size of feather.

BODY AND FLUFF: Body, silvery white, each feather ending with a moderately large, lustrous, greenish black spangle, the spangle being proportionate to size of feather; fluff, slate tinged with white.

LEGS AND TOES: Lower thighs, white, each feather ending with a large, black spangle; shanks and toes, leaden blue. Bottoms of feet, pinkish white.

UNDER-COLOR OF ALL SECTIONS: Slate.

COLOR OF FEMALE

COMB, FACE, AND WATTLES: Bright red.

BEAK: Dark horn.

HEAD: Plumage, white, marked with black.

EYES: Reddish bay.

EAR-LOBES: Enamel white.

NECK: Clear, silvery white, each feather ending with an elongated, small, black spangle; feathers on front of neck, same as breast.

WINGS: Fronts, and bows, silvery white, distinctly spangled with lustrous, greenish black; coverts, silvery white, each feather ending with a large, lustrous, greenish black spangle, forming two distinct parallel bars across wings; primaries, white, each feather ending with black; secondaries, white, each feather ending with a lustrous, greenish black, crescent-shaped spangle, gradually increasing into a V-shaped spangle as it approaches the back.

BACK: Silvery white, each feather ending with a moderately large, lustrous, greenish black spangle.

TAIL: Main-tail feathers, white, each feather ending with a

SILVER-SPANGLED HAMBURG MALE

SILVER-SPANGLED HAMBURG FEMALE

large, lustrous, greenish black spangle, the spangle being proportionate to size of feather; coverts, white, each feather ending with a large, lustrous, greenish black spangle.

BREAST: Clear, silvery white, each feather ending with a moderately large, lustrous, greenish black spangle, the spangle being proportionate to size of feather.

BODY AND FLUFF: Body, silvery white, each feather ending with a moderately large, lustrous, greenish black spangle, the spangle being proportionate to size of feather; fluff, slate tinged with white.

LEGS AND TOES: Lower thighs, white, each feather ending with a large, black spangle; shanks and toes, leaden blue. Bottoms of feet, pinkish white.

UNDER-COLOR OF ALL SECTIONS: Slate.

Note: In all sections where the word "spangle" appears when shape is not otherwise described, read "edges of spangle following the web of feather and meeting at shaft."

GOLDEN-PENCILED HAMBURGS

Disqualifications

Breast of female not penciled. (See General and Hamburg Disqualifications, and Cutting for Defects.)

COLOR OF MALE

COMB, FACE, AND WATTLES: Bright red.

BEAK: Dark horn.

HEAD: Plumage, rich, bright bay.

EYES: Reddish bay.

EAR-LOBES: Enamel white.

NECK: Rich, bright reddish bay; plumage on front of neck, same as breast.

WINGS: Fronts and bows, bright reddish bay; coverts, reddish bay, upper web slightly penciled across with black bars; primaries, upper webs black, lower webs, bay; secondaries, upper webs, reddish bay, penciled across with black bars, lower webs reddish bay, except on end where penciling from upper web is carried across.

BACK AND SADDLE: Bright, rich, reddish bay; saddle feathers, bright, rich, reddish bay.

TAIL: Main-tail feathers, black; sickles and coverts, greenish black with a distinct edging of rich reddish bay, the narrower and more uniform the better.

BREAST: Rich reddish bay.

BODY AND FLUFF: Body, lustrous, reddish bay, the sides below wings penciled across with indistinct black bars; fluff, black.

LEGS AND TOES: Lower thighs, reddish bay; shanks and toes, leaden blue. Bottoms of feet, pinkish white.

UNDER-COLOR OF ALL SECTIONS: Slate.

COLOR OF FEMALE

COMB, FACE, AND WATTLES: Bright red.

BEAK: Dark horn.

HEAD: Plumage, bright reddish bay.

EYES: Reddish bay.

EAR-LOBES: Enamel white.

NECK: Bright bay; feathers on front of neck, same as breast.

WINGS: Fronts and bows, clear bay, finely and distinctly penciled across with greenish black; primaries, bay; secondaries and coverts, bay, penciled across with greenish black.

BACK: Bay, each feather finely and distinctly penciled across with narrow, parallel bars of greenish black.

TAIL: Main-tail feathers, bay, penciled across with greenish black; coverts, bay, penciled across with greenish black.

BREAST: Bright bay, each feather finely and distinctly penciled across with parallel bars of greenish black.

BODY AND FLUFF: Body, bay, each feather finely and distinctly penciled across with parallel bars of greenish black, the bars forming, as nearly as possible, narrow, parallel lines across specimen; fluff, bay, penciled with black.

LEGS AND TOES: Lower thighs, bay, penciled across with greenish black; shanks and toes, leaden blue. Bottoms of feet, pinkish white.

UNDER-COLOR OF ALL SECTIONS: Slate.

SILVER-PENCILED HAMBURGS

Disqualifications

Breast of female not penciled. (See General and Hamburg Disqualifications, and Cutting for Defects.)

COLOR OF MALE

COMB, FACE, AND WATTLES: Bright red.

BEAK: Dark horn.

HEAD: Plumage, white.

EYES: Reddish bay.

EAR-LOBES: Enamel white.

NECK: Clear white; plumage on front of neck, same as breast.

WINGS: Fronts and bows, white; coverts, white, upper webs penciled across with black bars; primaries, white, upper webs, dull black; secondaries, upper webs, black with a narrow border of white or gray on edges; lower webs, white, with a narrow stripe of black next to shaft of feathers.

BACK AND SADDLE: Silvery white; saddle feathers, silvery white.

TAIL: Main-tail feathers, black; sickles and coverts, black, with a distinct edging of white, the narrower and more uniform the better.

BREAST: White.

BODY AND FLUFF: Body, white, the sides below wings penciled across with indistinct black bars; fluff, slaty white.

LEGS AND TOES: Lower thighs, silvery white; shanks and toes. leaden blue. Bottoms of feet, pinkish white.

UNDER-COLOR OF ALL SECTIONS: Slate.

COLOR OF FEMALE

COMB, FACE, AND WATTLES: Bright red.

BEAK: Dark horn.

HEAD: Plumage white.

EYES: Reddish bay.

EAR-LOBES: Enamel white.

NECK: White, except at base, which should be penciled across with narrow bars of greenish black; feathers on front of neck, same as breast.

WINGS: Fronts and bows, white, finely and distinctly penciled across with greenish black; primaries, white; secondaries and coverts, white, penciled across with greenish black.

BACK: White, each feather finely and distinctly penciled across with narrow parallel bars of greenish black.

TAIL: Main-tain feathers, white, penciled across with greenish black; coverts, silvery white, penciled across with greenish black.

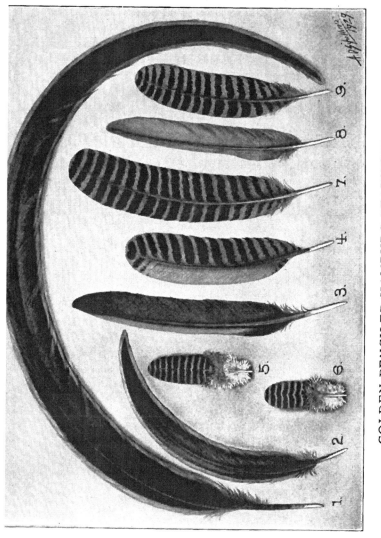

GOLDEN PENCILED HAMBURG FEATHERS

MALE PLUMAGE	FEMALE PLUMAGE
(1). Main Sickle	(5). Back Feather
(2). Lesser Sickle	(6). Breast Feather

BREAST: White, each feather finely and distinctly penciled across with narrow, parallel bars of greenish black.

BODY AND FLUFF: Body, white, each feather finely and distinctly penciled across with parallel bars of greenish black, the bars forming, as nearly as possible, narrow, parallel lines across specimen; fluff, white, penciled with black.

LEGS AND TOES: Lower thighs, white, penciled across with greenish black; shanks and toes, leaden blue. Bottoms of feet, pinkish white.

UNDER-COLOR OF ALL SECTIONS: Slate.

WHITE HAMBURGS

Disqualifications

(See General and Hamburg Disqualifications, and Cutting for Defects.)

COLOR OF MALE AND FEMALE

COMB, FACE, AND WATTLES: Bright red.
BEAK: Leaden blue.
EYES: Reddish bay.
EAR-LOBES: Enamel white.
SHANKS AND TOES: Leaden blue. Bottoms of feet, pinkish white.
PLUMAGE: See description of White plumage color, page 63.

BLACK HAMBURGS

Disqualifications

More than one-half inch of positive white in any part of the plumage, or two or more feathers tipped or edged with positive white; white in the face of cockerels or pullets; shanks other than black or dark leaden blue. (See General and Hamburg Disqualifications, and Cutting for Defects.)

COLOR OF MALE AND FEMALE

COMB, FACE, AND WATTLES: Bright red.
BEAK: Black.
EYES: Reddish bay.
EAR-LOBES: Enamel white.
SHANKS AND TOES: Black; bottoms of feet, pinkish white.
PLUMAGE: See description of Black plumage color, page 64.

FRENCH

Breeds	Varieties
HOUDANS	{ Mottled White
CREVECOEURS	Black
LAFLECHE	Black
FAVEROLLES	Salmon

HOUDANS

This old French breed was known as the Normandy fowl when first imported into England in 1850. It takes its present name from the town of Houdan, located in a section of France where large numbers of Houdans were bred and raised in past years for the Paris and London markets.

In shape, the Houdan resembles the Dorking, to which it probably owes its fifth toe. Crevecoeurs and Polish may also have been used in the original crosses. The Houdan is esteemed highly in France for its fine meat qualities and its large white eggs.

The Mottled Houdan came to America in 1865 and was admitted to the Standard in 1874. The White Houdan originated in America, the result of crossing White Polish with Mottled Houdans, and became a Standard variety in 1914.

ECONOMIC QUALITIES: A general purpose, non-sitting fowl for the production of meat and eggs. Color of skin, white; color of egg shells, white.

Disqualifications

Absence of crest or beard. (See General Disqualifications and Cutting for Defects.)

STANDARD WEIGHTS

Cock	7½ lbs.	Hen	6½ lbs.
Cockerel	6½ lbs.	Pullet	5½ lbs.

SHAPE OF MALE

COMB: V-shaped; of small size, resting against front of crest. (See Standard illustration, page 326.)

CREST: Large, well-fitted on crown of head, falling backward on neck, and composed of feathers similar in shape and texture to those of hackle.

BEAK: Of moderate length, well-curved.

HEAD: Of medium size, carried well up. (See Standard illustration, page 326.)

NOSTRILS: Wide, cavernous.

EYES: Large, full, prominent.

BEARD: Full, well-developed, curving around to back of eyes, nearly hiding face.

WATTLES: Of uniform length, small, well-rounded, nearly concealed by beard.

EAR-LOBES: Entirely concealed by crest and beard.

NECK: Of medium length, well-arched; with abundant hackle flowing well down on shoulders.

WINGS: Moderately large, well-folded, carried without drooping; fronts concealed by breast feathers and points by saddle feathers; primaries and secondaries, broad, and overlapping in natural order when wing is folded.

BACK: Long, broad, slightly sloping toward base of tail; saddle feathers, abundant.

TAIL: Full, expanded, carried at an angle of fifty degrees above the horizontal (see illustrations, page 28, figures 30 and 31); sickles, coverts, abundant and well-curved; main-tail feathers, broad and overlapping.

BREAST: Broad, deep, full and well-rounded.

BODY AND FLUFF: Body, long, compact, well-proportioned; fluff, rather short.

LEGS AND TOES: Legs, set well apart, straight when viewed from front; lower thighs, of medium length, large; shanks, of medium length; toes, five on each foot, straight except fifth, which should be distinct from the others and curve upwards.

SHAPE OF FEMALE

COMB: V-shaped, similar to that of male.

CREST: Large, compact, globular.

BEAK: Of moderate length, well-curved.

HEAD: Of medium size. (See Standard illustration, page 327.)

NOSTRILS: Wide, cavernous.

EYES: Large, full, prominent.

BEARD: Full, well-developed, curving around to back of eyes, nearly hiding face.

WATTLES: Of uniform length, small, well-rounded, nearly concealed by beard.

EAR-LOBES: Entirely concealed by crest and beard.

NECK: Of medium length, well-arched.

WINGS: Moderately large, well-folded, carried without drooping; primaries and secondaries, broad, and overlapping in natural order when wing is folded.

MOTTLED HOUDAN MALE

MOTTLED HOUDAN FEMALE

BACK: Long, broad, slightly sloping toward base of tail.

TAIL: Of medium length, rather compact; carried at an angle of thirty-five degrees above the horizontal (see illustrations, page 28, figures 30 and 31.)

BREAST: Broad, deep, full, well-rounded.

BODY AND FLUFF: Body, long, compact, well-proportioned; fluff, rather short.

LEGS AND TOES: Legs, set well apart, straight when viewed from front; lower thighs, short, strong; shanks, of medium length; toes, five on each foot, straight except fifth, which should be distinct from the others and curve upward.

Note: See Instructions to Judges, paragraph "Quality of Feather," page 53.

MOTTLED HOUDANS

Disqualifications

Any color other than black or white in any part of plumage. (See General and Houdan Disqualifications, and Cutting for Defects.)

COLOR OF MALE

COMB, FACE, AND WATTLES: Bright red.

BEAK: Dark horn.

HEAD: Plumage, black, one feather in three tipped with white.

EYES: Reddish bay.

EAR-LOBES: White.

CREST AND BEARD: Black and white, black predominating.

NECK: Black, about one feather in two tipped with positive white.

WINGS: Fronts, bows, and coverts, black, about one feather in three tipped with positive white; primaries, black and white, colors pure within themselves, black predominating; secondaries, black.

BACK AND SADDLE: Black, about one feather in ten tipped with positive white.

TAIL: Main-tail feathers, black, ends of feathers, in proportion of about one in four, tipped with positive white; sickle feathers, black, which may be edged with white; coverts, black, about one feather in five tipped with positive white.

BREAST: Black, about one feather in three tipped with positive white.

BODY AND FLUFF: Body, black, about one feather in two tipped with positive white; fluff, black, slightly tinged with gray.

LEGS AND TOES: Lower thighs, black, about one feather in two tipped with positive white; shanks and toes, pinkish white, mottled with black.

UNDER-COLOR OF ALL SECTIONS: Dull black.

COLOR OF FEMALE

COMB, FACE, AND WATTLES: Bright red.

BEAK: Dark horn.

HEAD: Plumage, black, one feather in three tipped with white.

EYES: Reddish bay.

EAR-LOBES: White.

CREST AND BEARD: Black and white, black predominating.

NECK: Black, about one feather in two tipped with positive white.

WINGS: Fronts, bows, and coverts, black, about one feather in two tipped with positive white; primaries, black and white, colors pure within themselves, black predominating; secondaries, black.

BACK: Black, about one feather in two tipped with positive white.

TAIL: Main-tail feathers, black, ends of feathers, in proportion of about one to four, tipped with positive white; coverts, black, about one feather in three tipped with positive white.

BREAST: Black, about one feather in two tipped with positive white.

BODY AND FLUFF: Body, black, about one feather in two tipped with positive white; fluff, black tipped with gray.

LEGS AND TOES: Lower thighs, black, about one feather in two tipped with positive white; shanks and toes, pinkish white, mottled with black.

UNDER-COLOR OF ALL SECTIONS: Dull black.

WHITE HOUDANS

Disqualifications

(See General and Houdan Disqualifications, and Cutting for Defects.)

COLOR OF MALE AND FEMALE

COMB, FACE, WATTLES, AND EAR-LOBES: Bright red.

BEAK: Pinkish white.

EYES: Reddish bay.

SHANKS AND TOES: Pinkish white.

PLUMAGE: See description of White plumage color, page 63.

CREVECOEURS

Little is known of the origin of this breed. Darwin classifies Crevecoeurs with Houdans as sub-varieties of the Polish. They originated in Normandy and took their name from a village in that country.

Crevecoeurs are large, handsome and useful fowls, similar in type and utility to the Houdan. They were admitted to the Standard in 1874.

ECONOMIC QUALITIES: A general purpose fowl for the production of meat and eggs. Color of skin, white; color of egg shells, white.

Disqualifications

More than one inch of positive white in any part of plumage, or two or more feathers tipped or edged with positive white, except in crest; shanks other than black or dark leaden blue. (See General Disqualifications and Cutting for Defects.)

STANDARD WEIGHTS

Cock	8 lbs.	Hen	7 lbs.
Cockerel	7 lbs.	Pullet	6 lbs.

SHAPE OF MALE

COMB: Like the letter V in shape, of medium size, resting against front of crest.

CREST: Large, well fitted on crown of head, regular, inclining backward, composed of feathers similar in shape and texture to those of hackle.

BEAK: Strong, well curved.

HEAD: Large, with a pronounced protuberance on top of skull.

FACE: Almost wholly concealed by crest and beard.

NOSTRILS: Broad, highly arched.

EYES: Full, oval.

BEARD: Full, thick, extending around to back of eyes, nearly hiding face.

WATTLES: Of uniform length, small, well-rounded, nearly concealed by beard.

EAR-LOBES: Small, nearly concealed by crest and beard.

NECK: Of medium length, well arched, with abundant hackle, flowing well down on shoulders.

WINGS: Of medium size, well-folded, carried without drooping; primaries and secondaries, broad, and overlapping in natural order when wing is folded.

BACK: Broad, straight; saddle feathers, abundant.

TAIL: Rather long, full, expanded, carried at an angle of forty-five degrees above the horizontal; sickles, well-curved; coverts, abundant; main-tail feathers, broad and overlapping. (See page 28, figures 30 and 31.)

BREAST: Broad, full, rounding well to shoulders.

BODY AND FLUFF: Body, compact, well-proportioned; fluff, rather short.

LEGS AND TOES: Legs, set well apart, straight when viewed from front; lower thighs, short; shanks, rather short, fine in bone; toes, four on each foot; straight, well-spread.

SHAPE OF FEMALE

COMB: Like letter V in shape, small and as nearly as possible concealed by crest.

CREST: Large, compact, even, globular.

BEAK: Strong, well-curved.

HEAD: Large, with a pronounced protuberance on top of skull.

FACE: Almost wholly concealed by crest and beard.

NOSTRILS: Broad, highly arched.

EYES: Full, oval.

BEARD: Full, thick, extending around to back of eyes, nearly hiding face.

WATTLES: Of uniform length, small, well-rounded, nearly concealed by beard.

EAR-LOBES: Small, entirely concealed by crest and beard.

NECK: Of medium length, thick, well-arched.

WINGS: Of medium size, well-folded, carried without drooping; primaries and secondaries, broad, and overlapping in natural order when wing is folded.

BACK: Broad, straight.

TAIL: Rather long, moderately expanded at base, converging to tip, carried at an angle of forty-five degrees above the horizontal; main-tail feathers, broad and overlapping. (See page 28, figures 30 and 31.)

BREAST: Broad, full, rounding well to shoulders.

BODY AND FLUFF: Body, compact, well-proportioned; fluff, rather short.

LEGS AND TOES: Legs, set well apart, straight when viewed from front; lower thighs, short; shanks, rather short, fine in bone; toes, four on each foot, straight, well-spread.

Note: See Instructions to Judges, paragraph "Quality of Feather," page 53.

COLOR OF MALE AND FEMALE

COMB, FACE, WATTLES AND EAR-LOBES: Bright red.

BEAK: Black, shading into horn at tip.

EYES: Reddish bay.

SHANKS AND TOES: Dark leaden blue.

PLUMAGE: See description of Black plumage color, page 64.

LA FLECHE

La Fleche have been bred for many years in the Valley of La Sarthe, where the town of La Fleche is located. That this breed originated from crossing of Black Spanish-Crevecoeur-DuMans blood lines is evident by its high carriage, activity, large white lobes, V-shaped comb, and the trace of crest on head, which crops out on specimens of the French breeds.

The remarkable whiteness and quality of its flesh, however, is attributed to the rich pastures of La Sarthe, upon which La Fleche have been bred for generations, and to the system of feeding adopted by the French.

The breed was admitted to the Standard in 1874.

ECONOMIC QUALITIES: General purpose fowl for the production of meat and eggs. Color of skin, white; color of eggs, white.

Disqualifications

More than one-half inch of positive white in any part of the plumage or two or more feathers tipped or edged with positive white. Shanks other than black or slate in color. (See General Disqualifications and Cutting for Defects.)

STANDARD WEIGHTS

Cock	8½ lbs.	Hen	7½ lbs.
Cockerel	7½ lbs.	Pullet	6½ lbs.

SHAPE OF MALE

COMB: V-shaped; rather large.

BEAK: Rather long, strong, well-curved.

HEAD: Of medium size, long.

NOSTRILS: Wide, cavernous.

EYES: Large, oval.

WATTLES: Uniform, long, well-rounded, pendulous.

EAR-LOBES: Large.

NECK: Long, erect, with abundant hackle flowing well down on shoulders.

WINGS: Long, powerful, well-folded, carried without drooping; primaries and secondaries, broad, and overlapping in natural order when wing is folded.

BACK: Broad, very long, sloping to tail; saddle feathers, abundant.

TAIL: Very long, full, carried at an angle of forty-five degrees above the horizontal; sickles, well-curved; coverts, abundant; main-tail feathers, broad and overlapping. (See illustrations, page 28, figures 30 and 31.)

BREAST: Broad, full, very prominent.

BODY AND FLUFF: Body, large, powerful, tapering slightly to tail, with close plumage; fluff, rather short.

LEGS AND TOES: Legs, set well apart, straight when viewed from front; lower thighs, long, stout; shanks, long, medium in bone; toes, straight, well-spread.

SHAPE OF FEMALE

COMB: V-shaped, moderately large.

BEAK: Rather long, strong, well-curved.

HEAD: Of medium size, long.

NOSTRILS: Wide, cavernous.

EYES: Large, oval.

WATTLES: Uniform, small, well-rounded.

EAR-LOBES: Small.

NECK: Long, carried upright, with full plumage.

WINGS: Long, powerful, well-folded, carried without drooping; primaries and secondaries, broad, and overlapping in natural order when wing is folded.

BACK: Broad, long, sloping to tail.

TAIL: Long, well-expanded, carried at an angle of forty degrees above the horizontal; main-tail feathers, broad and overlapping. (See page 28, figures 30 and 31.)

BREAST: Broad, full, prominent.

BODY AND FLUFF: Body, large, deep, tapering slightly to tail; fluff, rather short.

LEGS AND TOES: Legs, set well apart, straight when viewed from front; lower thighs, long, stout; shanks, long, medium in bone; toes, straight, well-spread.

Note: See Instructions to Judges, paragraph "Quality of Feather," page 53.

COLOR OF MALE AND FEMALE

COMB, FACE, AND WATTLES: Bright red.

BEAK: Black, with a small protuberance of bright red flesh at juncture of beak and nostrils.

EYES: Bright red.

EAR-LOBES: White.

SHANKS AND TOES: Dark slate.

PLUMAGE: See description of Black plumage color, page 64.

FAVEROLLES

The Faverolle is a composite breed originating from crosses of Houdans, Dorkings and Asiatics in the village of Faverolle, France, where they were bred primarily for utility. The production of heavy table poultry and winter eggs was the main object of the French poultry keepers in establishing this breed. Unlike other French breeds of poultry, Faverolles lay tinted instead of white eggs. Faverolles were admitted to the Standard in 1914.

ECONOMIC QUALITIES: A general purpose fowl for the production of meat and eggs. Color of skin, white; color of egg shells, light brown.

Disqualifications

(See General Disqualifications and Cutting for Defects.)

STANDARD WEIGHTS

Cock	8 lbs.	Hen	6½ lbs.
Cockerel	7 lbs.	Pullet	5½ lbs.

SHAPE OF MALE

COMB: Single; of moderate size, straight and upright, evenly serrated, having five well-defined points, the front and rear shorter than the other three, fine in texture.

BEAK: Short, stout, well-curved.

HEAD: Broad, flat, short, free from crest.

EYES: Large, full.

BEARD AND MUFFS: Full, wide, short.

WATTLES: Small, well-rounded, fine in texture.

EAR-LOBES: Oblong, concealed by beard.

NECK: Short, thick, well-arched.

WINGS: Moderately small, prominent in front, carried closely folded to body, without drooping; primaries and secondaries, broad, and overlapping in natural order when wing is folded.

BACK: Broad, flat, almost square.

TAIL: Of moderate length, carried at an angle of fifty degrees above the horizontal (see page 28, figures 30 and 31); sickles and coverts, of medium length and well-curved; main-tail feathers, broad, and overlapping.

BREAST: Broad, deep, carried well forward.

BODY AND FLUFF: Body, deep, compact; fluff, rather short.

LEGS AND TOES: Legs set well apart, straight when viewed from front; lower thighs, of moderate length, stout; toes, five on each foot, the fifth toe distinct from the others and curved upward; shanks and outer toes, slightly feathered.

SHAPE OF FEMALE

COMB: Single, of moderate size, straight and upright, evenly serrated, having five well-defined points, the front and rear shorter than the other three; fine in texture.

BEAK: Short, stout, well-curved.

HEAD: Rather broad, flat, short, free from crest.

EYES: Large, full.

BEARD AND MUFFS: Full, wide, short.

WATTLES: Small, well-rounded, fine in texture.

EAR-LOBES: Oblong, concealed by beard.

NECK: Short, thick, fairly well-arched.

WINGS: Moderately small, carried closely folded to body without drooping; primaries and secondaries, broad, and overlapping in natural order when wing is folded.

BACK: Broad, flat, longer than wide.

TAIL: Full, of moderate length, carried at an angle of fifty degrees above the horizontal; main-tail feathers, broad and overlapping. (See page 28, figures 30 and 31.)

BREAST: Broad, deep, prominent.

BODY AND FLUFF: Body, very deep, long; fluff, rather short.

LEGS AND TOES: Legs, set well apart, straight when viewed from front; lower thighs, of moderate length, rather stout; toes, five on each foot, the fifth toe distinct from the others and curved upward; shanks and outer toes, slightly feathered.

Note: See Instructions to Judges, paragraph "Quality of Feather," page 53.

SALMON FAVEROLLES

COLOR OF MALE

COMB, FACE, WATTLES, AND EAR-LOBES: Bright red.

BEAK: Horn.

HEAD: Plumage, straw.

EYES: Reddish bay.

BEARD AND MUFFS: Black.

NECK: Hackle, straw; plumage on front of neck, same as breast.

WINGS: Fronts, black; bows, straw tinged with reddish brown; primaries, black, lower edge white; secondaries, black, lower one-third of outer web white.

BACK AND SADDLE: Web, the outer portion reddish brown, edged with a lighter shade of brown, portion nearest to under-color black; saddle, straw.

TAIL: Main-tail, black; sickles, lesser sickles and coverts, greenish black.

BREAST: Black.

BODY AND FLUFF: Black.

LEGS AND TOES: Lower thighs, black; shanks and toes, pinkish white; toe feathering, black.

UNDER-COLOR OF ALL SECTIONS: Slate.

COLOR OF FEMALE

COMB, FACE, WATTLES, AND EAR-LOBES: Bright red.

BEAK: Horn.

HEAD: Plumage, salmon-brown.

EYES: Reddish bay.

BEARD AND MUFFS: Creamy white.

NECK: Rich salmon-brown; feathers on front of neck, same as breast.

WINGS: Fronts, bows, and coverts, rich salmon-brown; primaries, black, the lower web slightly edged with salmon-brown, upper web slightly stippled with salmon-brown; secondaries, lower half of outer web, salmon-brown, upper half, black; inner web, black.

BACK: Salmon-brown.

TAIL: Main-tail and coverts, salmon-brown.

BREAST: Cream.

BODY AND FLUFF: Cream.

LEGS AND TOES: Lower thighs, cream; shanks and toes, pinkish white; toe feathering, cream.

UNDER-COLOR OF ALL SECTIONS: Slate.

CONTINENTAL

Breeds	*Varieties*
Campines..	{ Silver { Golden

CAMPINES

The Campine fowl originated in Belgium, where it has been bred for several centuries, so it justly can claim purity of race over a very long period. The name is derived from the Campine country, where these fowls are bred largely for the production of white-shelled eggs. The two Belgian breeds, Braekel and Campine, are practically the same in all points except size, the Braekel being the larger fowl.

The English, or Standard, Campine of today is a composite of the two Belgian varieties; the plumage of the Campine male and female is identical in color pattern.

Campines carry more weight than their appearance indicates, due to the fact that the plumage is close-fitting. The two varieties, Silver and Golden Campines, were admitted to the Standard in 1914.

ECONOMIC QUALITIES: Primarily bred for egg production, classed as a non-sitting, utility fowl, but sprightly carriage and attractive color markings have made Campines popular for exhibition purposes as well. Color of skin, white; color of egg shells, white.

Disqualifications

Red covering more than one-half of the ear-lobes; white in the face of cockerels; shanks other than leaden-blue. Characteristic male feathers appearing in the back, saddle or wing-bows of the male shall disqualify, Campines being hen-feathered in both sexes. (See General Disqualifications and Cutting for Defects.)

STANDARD WEIGHTS

Cock	6 lbs.	Hen	4 lbs.
Cockerel	5 lbs.	Pullet	3½ lbs.

SHAPE OF MALE

COMB: Single, medium size, straight, upright, firm and even on head, having five distinct points, deeply serrated; extending well over back of head; blade carried slightly below the horizontal; smooth, free from twists, folds and excrescences. (See Standard illustration, page 342.)

BEAK: Medium in length, nicely curved.

HEAD: Medium in length, fairly deep; face, smooth, fine in texture. (See Standard illustration, page 342.)

341

SILVER CAMPINE MALE

SILVER CAMPINE FEMALE

EYES: Large, nearly round, prominent.

WATTLES: Of medium size, even in length; well-rounded; smooth in texture; free from folds or wrinkles.

EAR-LOBES: Oval in shape but rather broad, smooth, of moderate size, fitting closely to head.

NECK: Medium length, nicely arched, and well furnished with hackle feathers.

WINGS: Large, well-folded and tucked up; primaries and secondaries, broad, and overlapping in natural order when wing is folded.

BACK: Rather long, slightly sloping to tail, moderately broad at shoulders and narrowing very slightly toward tail; back feathers, abundant, long, wide, ending with well-rounded tips.

TAIL: Well-expanded, main-tail feathers broad and overlapping, carried at an angle of forty-five degrees above the horizontal; sickles of good width, well-curved and extending beyond main-tail feathers; lesser sickles and coverts, of good width, the more abundant the better. (See page 28, figures 30 and 31.)

BREAST: Deep, well-rounded and carried well forward.

BODY AND FLUFF: Body of moderate length, and fairly deep; not narrow in appearance from rear; fluff, moderately short.

LEGS AND TOES: Legs, set well apart, straight when viewed from front; lower thighs and shanks, rather long; shanks, round; toes, rather long, straight, and well-spread.

SHAPE OF FEMALE

COMB: Single; medium in size, deeply serrated, having five distinct points; the front portion of comb and first point to stand erect, and the remainder of comb drooping gradually to one side; fine in texture, free from folds or wrinkles. (See Standard illustration, page 343.)

BEAK: Medium in length, nicely curved.

HEAD: Medium in length, fairly deep, well-rounded; face, smooth, fine in texture. (See Standard illustration, page 343.)

EYES: Large, nearly round, prominent.

WATTLES: Of medium size, well-rounded, fine texture.

EAR-LOBES: Oval in shape, smooth, thin, fitting closely to the head.

NECK: Of medium length, slender, slightly arched.

WINGS: Large, well-folded and tucked up; primaries and secondaries, broad, and overlapping in natural order when wing is folded.

BACK: Rather long, sloping slightly toward tail, moderately broad at shoulders and narrowing very slightly toward tail, somewhat rounded across cape.

TAIL: Long, full, moderately well-spread, carried at an angle of forty degrees above the horizontal; main-tail feathers, broad and overlapping. (See page 28, figures 30 and 31.)

BREAST: Deep, well-rounded, and carried well forward.

BODY AND FLUFF: Body of moderate length, fairly deep, not narrow in appearance from rear; fluff, moderately short.

LEGS AND TOES: Legs, set well apart, straight when viewed from front; lower thighs and shanks rather long; shanks, round; toes, rather long, straight, and well-spread.

Note: See Instructions to Judges, paragraph "Quality of Feather," page 53.

SILVER CAMPINES

COLOR OF MALE

COMB, FACE, AND WATTLES: Bright red.

BEAK: Horn.

HEAD: Plumage, white.

EYES: Dark brown.

EAR-LOBES: Enamel white.

NECK: Hackle, white; slight black markings at extreme base not a serious defect; plumage on front of neck, same as breast.

WINGS: Fronts and bows, lustrous, greenish black, distinctly barred with white, the black being at least three times the width of the white bar, which is slightly V-shaped; primaries, black, barred straight across with white; secondaries and coverts, lustrous, greenish black, barred straight across with white.

BACK AND SADDLE: Lustrous, greenish black, distinctly barred with white, the black being at least three times the width of the white bar, which is slightly V-shaped.

TAIL: Main-tail feathers, greenish black, barred straight across with white; sickles and coverts, lustrous, greenish black, distinctly barred with white, the black being four times the width of the white bar, which is slightly V-shaped.

BREAST: Lustrous, greenish black, barred straight across with white, the black being at least twice the width of the white bar.

BODY AND FLUFF: Lustrous, greenish black, barred straight across with white, the black being at least three times the width of the white bar.

LEGS AND TOES: Lower thighs, lustrous, greenish black, barred straight across with white, the black being at least twice the width of the white bar; shanks and toes, leaden blue.

UNDER-COLOR OF ALL SECTIONS: Slate.

COLOR OF FEMALE

COMB, FACE AND WATTLES: Bright red, some blue at base of comb not a serious defect.

BEAK: Horn.

HEAD: Plumage, white.

EYES: Dark brown.

EAR-LOBES: Enamel white.

NECK: White, slight black markings at extreme base not a serious defect; feathers on front of neck, same as breast.

WINGS: Fronts and bows, lustrous, greenish black, distinctly barred with white, the black being at least three times the width of the white bar, which is slightly V-shaped; primaries, black, barred straight across with white; secondaries and coverts, lustrous, greenish black barred straight across with white.

BACK: Lustrous, greenish black, distinctly barred with white, the black being at least three times the width of the white bar, which is slightly V-shaped.

TAIL: Main-tail feathers, greenish black, distinctly barred straight across with white, the black being four times the width of the white bar.

BREAST: Lustrous, greenish black, distinctly barred with white, the black being equal in width to the white bar at the throat and increasing to at least twice the width of the white bar at the body, the barring running straight across the feathers.

BODY AND FLUFF: Lustrous, greenish black, distinctly barred with white, the black being at least three times the width of the white bar and running straight across the feathers.

LEGS AND TOES: Lower thighs, lustrous, greenish black, barred straight across with white, the black being at least twice the width of the white bar; shanks and toes, leaden blue.

UNDER-COLOR OF ALL SECTIONS: Slate.

GOLDEN CAMPINES

COLOR OF MALE

COMB, FACE, AND WATTLES: Bright red.

BEAK: Horn.

HEAD: Plumage, golden bay

EYES: Dark brown.

EAR-LOBES: Enamel white.

NECK: Hackle, golden bay; slight black markings at extreme base not a serious defect; plumage on front of neck, same as breast.

WINGS: Fronts and bows, lustrous, greenish black, distinctly barred with golden bay, the black being at least three times the width of the golden bay bar, which is slightly V-shaped; primaries, black barred straight across with golden bay; secondaries and coverts, lustrous, greenish black, barred straight across with golden bay.

BACK AND SADDLE: Lustrous, greenish black, distinctly barred with golden bay, the black being at least three times the width of the golden bay bar, which is slightly V-shaped.

TAIL: Main-tail feathers, greenish black, barred straight across with golden bay; sickles and coverts, lustrous, greenish black, distinctly barred with golden bay, the black being four times the width of the golden bay bar, which is slightly V-shaped.

BREAST: Lustrous, greenish black, barred straight across with golden bay, the black being at least twice the width of the golden bay bar.

BODY AND FLUFF: Lustrous, greenish black, barred straight across with golden bay, the black being at least three times the width of the golden bay bar.

LEGS AND TOES: Lower thighs, lustrous, greenish black, barred straight across with golden bay, the black being at least twice the width of the golden bay bar; shanks and toes, leaden blue.

UNDER-COLOR OF ALL SECTIONS: Slate.

COLOR OF FEMALE

COMB, FACE, AND WATTLES: Bright red, some blue at base of comb not a serious defect.

BEAK: Horn.

HEAD: Plumage, golden bay.

EAR-LOBES: Enamel white.

NECK: Golden bay, slight black markings at extreme base not a serious defect; feathers on front of neck, same as breast.

WINGS: Fronts and bows, lustrous, greenish black, distinctly barred with golden bay, the black being at least three times the width of the golden bay bar which is slightly V-shaped; primaries, black, barred straight across with golden bay; secondaries and coverts, lustrous, greenish black barred straight across with golden bay.

BACK: Lustrous, greenish black, distinctly barred with golden bay, the black being at least three times the width of the golden bay bar, which is slightly V-shaped.

TAIL: Main-tail feathers, greenish black, distinctly barred straight across with golden bay, the black being four times the width of the golden bay bar.

BREAST: Lustrous, greenish black, distinctly barred with golden bay, the black being equal in width to the golden bay bar at the throat and increasing to twice the width of the golden bay bar at the body, the barring running straight across the feathers.

BODY AND FLUFF: Lustrous, greenish black, distinctly barred with golden bay, the black being at least three times the width of the golden bay bar and running straight across the feathers.

LEGS AND TOES: Lower thighs, lustrous, greenish black, barred straight across the golden bay, the black being twice the width of the golden bay bar; shanks and toes, leaden blue.

UNDER-COLOR OF ALL SECTIONS: Slate.

GAMES AND GAME BANTAMS

Breeds	*Varieties*
GAMES	Modern Black-Breasted Red Modern Brown-Red Modern Golden Duckwing Modern Silver Duckwing Modern Birchen Modern Red Pyle Modern White Modern Black
GAME BANTAMS	Modern Black-Breasted Red Modern Brown-Red Modern Golden Duckwing Modern Silver Duckwing Modern Birchen Modern Red Pyle Modern White Modern Black
GAMES	Old English Black-Breasted Red Old English Brown-Red Old English Golden Duckwing Old English Silver Duckwing Old English Red Pyle Old English White Old English Black Old English Spangled
GAME BANTAMS	Old English Black-Breasted Red Old English Golden Duckwing Old English Silver Duckwing Old English White Old English Black Old English Spangled

SCALE OF POINTS FOR
MODERN AND MALAY GAMES, GAME BANTAMS AND JAPANESE BANTAMS

(Scale of Points for Old English, See Scale of Points No. 1)

Station	10
Weight and Size	2
Condition and Vigor	6
Comb	2
Beak	4
Head—Shape 4, Color 1	5
Eyes—Shape 1, Color 1	2
Wattles—Shape 1	1
Ear-Lobes—Shape 1	1
Neck—Shape 5, Color 3	8
Wings—Shape 4, Color 6	10
Back—Shape 4, Color 3	7
Tail—Shape 5, Color 3	8
Breast—Shape 4, Color 3	7
Body and Stern—Shape 4, Color 3	7
Legs and Toes—Shape 10, Color 4	14
Hardness of Feather	6
	100

FOR JAPANESE BANTAMS

For Station 10 points substitute	
Symmetry	4
Add to Condition and Vigor	4
Add to Comb	2
For Hardness of Feather 6 points substitute	
Add to shape of breast	3
Add to shape of tail	3

MODERN GAMES AND GAME BANTAMS

The Modern Exhibition Game is strictly a fancier's creation. In type it is far removed from the Old English or Pit Game bred in the days when cock fighting was the vogue of Great Britain. The ideals of breeders of Pit Games were replaced by the ideals of exhibition Game fanciers. A high-stationed Game fowl with a style and carriage peculiar to itself is the result. Modern Games were at the height of their popularity in the closing years of the last century.

Station in Modern Games and Modern Game Bantams is of great importance, and shortness and hardness of feathers are of equal importance. Loose-feathered specimens invariably fail in shape of neck. The comb and wattles of the cock should be dubbed in order to have the head and lower mandible smooth and free from ridges. Exceptionally large specimens are undesirable, as overgrowth tends to coarseness at the expense of form and style of carriage, which are essential characteristics of the Modern Game, and even to a greater degree in the Modern Game Bantam.

Nine varieties of Games were admitted to the American Standard of Excellence in 1874. This number has been reduced to eight in the present Standard.

Color of skin, white; color of egg shells, tinted.

Disqualifications
Cocks not dubbed; artificial coloring; trimming or plucking of feathers. (See General Disqualifications and Cutting for Defects.)

SHAPE OF MALE
COMB: Cock, neatly and smoothly dubbed; cockerel, if undubbed, single, small, straight, thin, erect, evenly serrated. (See Standard illustration, page 354.)
BEAK: Long, tapering, slightly curved.
HEAD: Long, lean, bony.
FACE: Lean, thin, with fine skin.

EYES: Large, full.

WATTLES: Cock, neatly and smoothly dubbed; cockerel, if undubbed, small, thin, round, smooth.

EAR-LOBES: Cocks, neatly and smoothly dubbed; cockerel, if undubbed, small, thin, round, smooth.

NECK: Long, very slightly arched, carried erect, tapering neatly and gradually from body to head, thin and clean-cut at throat, giving a distinct outline to head; hackle, short, close.

WINGS: Large, powerful, the front standing out from body at shoulders, the feathers folded closely together, the points not extending beyond body; carried without drooping, but not carried over the back.

BACK: Flat, rather short, straight on top from hackle to tail, broad at shoulders, narrowing and sloping to stern.

TAIL: Rather short, compact, closely folded, carried nearly horizontal; sickle feathers, narrow, short, tapering; coverts, narrow, fine, short.

BREAST: Broad, rounded at sides.

BODY AND STERN: Body, fine and close on under part; not deep; stern, well tucked up underneath.

LEGS AND TOES: Legs, set well apart, straight when viewed from front; lower thighs, long, muscular, standing out from body, but slightly sloping to hocks; shanks, long, smooth, bony, standing well apart; toes, long, straight, well-spread.

PLUMAGE: Short, close, hard and firm.

STATION: Erect.

SIZE: Exceptionally large birds are undesirable.

Note: Cockerels shown after November first should be dubbed.

SHAPE OF FEMALE

COMB: Single; small, straight, thin, erect, evenly serrated. (See Standard illustration, page 355.)

BEAK: Long, tapering, slightly curved.

HEAD: Long, lean, bony.

FACE: Lean, thin with fine skin.

EYES: Large, full.

WATTLES: Small, thin, round.

EAR-LOBES: Small.

NECK: Long, very slightly arched, carried erect, tapering neatly and gradually from body to head, thin and clean-cut at throat, giving a distinct outline to head; neck feathers, lower portion short, close.

WINGS: Large, powerful, the front standing out from body at shoulders, the feathers folded closely together, the points not extending beyond body; carried without drooping, but not carried over back.

BACK: Flat, rather short, straight on top from base of neck to tail, broad at shoulders, narrowing and sloping to stern.

TAIL: Rather short, compact, closely folded, carried nearly horizontal.

BREAST: Broad, rounded at sides.

BODY AND STERN: Body, fine and close up on under part; not deep; stern, well tucked up underneath.

LEGS AND TOES: Legs, set well apart, straight when viewed from front; lower thighs, long, muscular, standing out from body, but slightly sloping to hocks; shanks, long, smooth, bony, standing well apart; toes, long, straight, well-spread.

PLUMAGE: Short, close, hard and firm.

STATION: Erect.

SIZE: Exceptionally large birds are undesirable.

Note: See Instructions to ·Judges, paragraph "Quality of Feather," page 53.

BLACK-BREASTED RED GAME

Disqualifications

(See General and Game Disqualifications, and Cutting for Defects.)

COLOR OF MALE

COMB, FACE, WATTLES AND EAR-LOBES: Bright red.

BEAK: Horn.

HEAD: Plumage, light orange.

EYES: Red.

NECK: Hackle, light golden; plumage on front of neck, black.

WINGS: Shoulders, black; fronts, black; bows, red; coverts, lustrous black, forming a distinct bar across wing; primaries, black except lower feather, the outer web of which should be bay; secondaries, part of outer webs forming wing-bay, bay; remainder of secondary feathers, black.

BLACK-BREASTED RED GAME MALE

BLACK-BREASTED RED GAME **FEMALE**

355

BACK AND SADDLE: Bright red; saddle, light golden.

TAIL: Main-tail, black; sickle feathers and tail-coverts, lustrous black.

BREAST: Black.

BODY AND STERN: Black.

LEGS AND TOES: Lower thighs, black; shanks and toes, willow-green.

COLOR OF FEMALE

COMB, FACE, WATTLES AND EAR-LOBES: Bright red.

BEAK: Horn.

HEAD: Plumage, golden.

EYES: Red.

NECK: Light golden, with black stripe through middle of each feather, terminating in a point near its lower extremity; feathers on front of neck, reddish salmon.

WINGS: Shoulders, fronts, bows, coverts and secondaries, grayish brown stippled with golden brown; primaries, black.

BACK: Grayish brown, stippled with golden brown.

TAIL: Main-tail feathers, black, except the two top feathers, which, with the coverts, should be stippled with brown.

BREAST: Light salmon, shading off to ashy brown toward thighs.

BODY AND STERN: Ashy brown.

LEGS AND TOES: Lower thighs, ashy brown; shanks and toes, willow-green.

BROWN-RED GAMES

Disqualifications

(See General and Game Disqualifications, and Cutting for Defects.)

COLOR OF MALE

COMB, FACE, WATTLES, AND EAR-LOBES: Dark purple.

BEAK: Black.

HEAD: Plumage, orange.

EYES: Black.

NECK: Hackle, lemon, with a narrow, dark stripe through the middle of each feather, terminating in a point near its lower extremity; plumage on front of neck, black laced with brown.

WINGS: Shoulders, black; fronts, black; bows, lemon; coverts, lustrous black; primaries and secondaries, black.

BACK AND SADDLE: Back, lemon; saddle, lemon, with a narrow lark stripe through the middle of each feather, terminating in a point near its lower extremity.

TAIL: Main-tail feathers, black; sickle feathers and tail-coverts, lustrous black.

BREAST: Black, the feathers laced with lemon.

BODY AND STERN: Black.

LEGS AND TOES: Lower thighs, black; shanks and toes, black.

COLOR OF FEMALE

COMB, FACE, WATTLES, AND EAR-LOBES: Dark purple.

BEAK: Black.

HEAD: Plumage, lemon.

EYES: Black.

NECK: Lemon, with a narrow, dark stripe through the middle of each feather, terminating in a point near its lower extremity; plumage on front of neck, black, each feather laced with lemon.

WINGS: Black.

BACK: Black.

TAIL: Black.

BREAST: Black, each feather laced with lemon.

BODY AND STERN: Black.

LEGS AND TOES: Lower thighs, black; shanks and toes, black.

GOLDEN DUCKWING GAMES

Disqualifications

(See General and Game Disqualifications, and Cutting for Defects.)

COLOR OF MALE

COMB, FACE, WATTLES AND EAR-LOBES: Bright red.

BEAK: Horn.

HEAD: Plumage, creamy white.

EYES: Red.

NECK: Hackle, creamy white, free from striping; plumage on front of neck, black.

WINGS: Shoulders, black; fronts, black; bows, golden; greater

SILVER DUCKWING GAME MALE

SILVER DUCKWING GAME FEMALE

and smaller coverts, lustrous blue-black, forming a distinct bar across wing; primaries, black, except lower feathers, outer web of which should be creamy white; secondaries, part of outer webs forming wing-bay, creamy-white, remainder of secondaries, black.

BACK AND SADDLE: Golden; saddle, light golden, free from black striping.

TAIL: Main-tail, black; sickle feathers and tail-coverts, lustrous blue-black; smaller coverts, light golden.

BREAST: Lustrous black.

BODY AND STERN: Black.

LEGS AND TOES: Lower thighs, black; shanks and toes, willow.

COLOR OF FEMALE

COMB, FACE, WATTLES AND EAR-LOBES: Bright red.

BEAK: Horn.

HEAD: Plumage, silvery gray.

EYES: Red.

NECK: Silvery gray, with narrow, dark stripe through middle of each feather, terminating in a point near its lower extremity; plumage on front of neck, reddish brown.

WINGS: Shoulders, fronts, bows, coverts, and secondaries, dark gray stippled with lighter gray; primaries, dark brown.

BACK: Dark gray stippled with lighter gray.

TAIL: Main-tail feathers, black, except the two top feathers, which shall be dark gray stippled with lighter gray.

BREAST: Rich salmon.

BODY AND STERN: Ashy gray.

LEGS AND TOES: Lower thighs, ashy gray; shanks and toes, willow.

SILVER DUCKWING GAMES

Disqualifications

(See General and Game Disqualifications, and Cutting for Defects.)

COLOR OF MALE

COMB, FACE, WATTLES AND EAR-LOBES: Bright red.

BEAK: Horn.

HEAD: Plumage, white.

EYES: Red.

NECK: Hackle, silvery white, free from striping; plumage on front of neck, black.

WINGS: Shoulders, lustrous black; fronts, lustrous black; bows, silvery white; coverts, lustrous blue-black, forming a distinct bar across wings; primaries, black except lower feathers, outer web of which should be white; secondaries, part of outer webs forming wing-bays, white, remainder of secondaries, black.

BACK AND SADDLE: Silvery white; saddle, silvery white, free from black striping.

TAIL: Main-tail feathers, black; sickle feathers and coverts, lustrous blue-black; smaller coverts, white.

BREAST: Lustrous black.

BODY AND STERN: Black.

LEGS AND TOES: Lower thighs, black; shanks and toes, willow.

COLOR OF FEMALE

COMB, FACE, WATTLES AND EAR-LOBES: Bright red.

BEAK: Horn.

HEAD: Plumage, silvery-gray.

EYES: Red.

NECK: Silvery gray, with a narrow black stripe through middle of each feather, terminating in a point near its lower extremity; feathers on front of neck, dark salmon.

WINGS: Shoulders, fronts, bows, coverts and secondaries, dark gray finely stippled with lighter gray; primaries, black.

BACK: Dark gray, finely stippled with lighter gray.

TAIL: Main-tail feathers, black, except the two top feathers, which should be dark gray, stippled with lighter gray.

BREAST: Light salmon.

BODY AND STERN: Ashy gray.

LEGS AND TOES: Lower thighs, ashy gray; shanks and toes, willow.

BIRCHEN GAMES

(See General and Game Disqualifications, and Cutting for Defects.)

COLOR OF MALE

COMB, FACE, WATTLES, AND EAR-LOBES: Dark purple.

BEAK: Black.
HEAD: Plumage, white.
EYES: Black.
NECK: Hackle, white, with narrow, dark stripes through middle of each feather, terminating in a point near its lower extremity; plumage on front of neck, black, laced with white.
WINGS: Shoulders, black; fronts, black; bows, white; coverts, glossy black; primaries and secondaries, black.
BACK AND SADDLE: White; saddle, white, with narrow, black stripe through middle of each feather.
TAIL: Main-tail feathers, black; sickles and coverts, lustrous black.
BREAST: Ground color, black, the feathers laced with white.
BODY AND STERN: Black.
LEGS AND TOES: Lower thighs, black; shanks and toes, black.

COLOR OF FEMALE
COMB, FACE, WATTLES, AND EAR-LOBES: Dark purple.
BEAK: Black.
HEAD: Plumage, white.
EYES: Black.
NECK: White, with narrow, dark stripe through middle of each feather, terminating in a point near its extremity; feathers on front of neck, black, laced with white.
WINGS: Black.
BACK: Black.
TAIL: Black.
BREAST: Black, feathers laced with white.
BODY AND STERN: Black.
LEGS AND TOES: Lower thighs, black; shanks and toes, black.

RED PYLE GAMES

Disqualifications
(See General and Game Disqualifications, and Cutting for Defects.)

COLOR OF MALE
COMB, FACE, WATTLES, AND EAR-LOBES: Bright red.
BEAK: Yellow.

HEAD: Plumage, bright orange.

EYES: Red.

NECK: Light orange; plumage on front of neck, white, which may be tinged with bright yellow.

WINGS: Shoulders, white; fronts, white; bows, red; coverts, white, forming a distinct bar across wings; primaries, white, except lower feathers, outer webs of which are bay; secondaries, part of outer web forming the wing-bays, red, remainder of secondaries, white.

BACK AND SADDLE: Red; saddle, light orange.

TAIL: Main-tail, sickles and coverts, white.

BREAST: White.

BODY AND STERN: White.

LEGS AND TOES: Lower thighs, white; shanks and toes, yellow.

COLOR OF FEMALE

COMB, FACE, WATTLES, AND EAR-LOBES: Bright red.

BEAK: Yellow.

HEAD: Plumage, golden.

EYES: Red.

NECK: White, the feathers edged with gold; feathers on front of neck, white tinged with salmon.

WINGS: White.

BACK: White.

TAIL: White.

BREAST: Salmon.

BODY AND STERN: White.

LEGS AND TOES: Lower thighs, white; shanks and toes, yellow.

WHITE GAMES

Disqualifications

(See General and Game Disqualifications, and Cutting for Defects.)

COLOR OF MALE AND FEMALE

COMB, FACE, WATTLES, AND EAR-LOBES: Bright red.

SHANKS AND TOES: Yellow.

PLUMAGE: See description of White plumage color, page 63.

RED PYLE GAME MALE

RED PYLE GAME FEMALE

BLACK GAMES

Disqualifications

(See General and Game Disqualifications, and Cutting for Defects.)

COLOR OF MALE AND FEMALE

COMB, FACE, WATTLES, AND EAR-LOBES: Bright red.

BEAK: Black.

EYES: Brown.

SHANKS AND TOES: Black.

PLUMAGE: See description of Black plumage color, page 64.

GAME BANTAMS

Disqualifications

Cocks not dubbed; artificial coloring; trimming or plucking of feathers; duck-foot. (See General Disqualifications and Cutting for Defects.)

STANDARD WEIGHTS

Cock	22 oz.	Hen	20 oz.
Cockerel	20 oz.	Pullet	18 oz.

SHAPE AND COLOR OF MALE AND FEMALE

The shape and color of Game Bantams shall be the same as the corresponding varieties of Games.

OLD ENGLISH GAMES AND OLD ENGLISH GAME BANTAMS

The intriguing history of the Old English Game fowl leads us right back to the misty beginning of the human race. From time immemorial, the Game fowl has stood for courage and a symbol of indomitable spirit.

Blood of the Game fowl has been used in many of our most useful breeds of poultry. For hardiness, vigor and longevity no breed of fowl excels the Game. They are good layers, excellent setters and mothers; as a table fowl the Game is excellent and as a cross for broilers, there is no better breed.

The Old English Game is recommended as a fowl for the family flock, for the farm and for the fancier who appreciates beauty of form and feather and the artistic angle of poultry keeping.

The Old English Game Bantams are among the most satisfactory of all bantam breeds to the fancier; hardy, vigorous little fellows, they are easy to raise and are very good layers and breeders.

In the variety of colors in which they are bred one may suit his own particular fancy and taste.

Disqualifications

Cocks not dubbed; artificial coloring; trimming or plucking of feathers; wry tail. (See General Disqualifications and Cutting for Defects.)

STANDARD WEIGHTS OLD ENGLISH GAMES

Cock	5 lbs.	Hen	4 lbs.
Cockerel	4 lbs.	Pullet	3½ lbs.

STANDARD WEIGHTS OLD ENGLISH GAME BANTAMS

Cock	24 oz.	Hen	22 oz.
Cockerel	22 oz.	Pullet	20 oz.

SHAPE OF MALE

COMB: Cock, neatly and smoothly dubbed, not too close to skull; cockerel, if undubbed, single, straight, small, thin, erect, evenly serrated, and of fine texture.

BEAK: Large, strong at base, well curved.

HEAD: Moderately small, strong, medium length.

FACE: Smooth, of fine texture, flexible.

EYES: Large, bright, prominent, giving a fearless expression.

WATTLES: Cocks, neatly and smoothly dubbed; cockerels, if undubbed, small, thin, smooth, of fine texture.

EAR-LOBES: Cocks, neatly and smoothly dubbed; cockerels, if undubbed, small, thin, smooth, of fine texture.

NECK: Long and very strong at junction with body; hackle, wiry, long, covering the shoulders. Throat-skin, flexible and loose.

WINGS: Large, full and round, inclining to meet under the tail, with strong, prominent points, feathers to be broad and furnished with hard, strong quills, the primaries not to be too long and to be nicely rounded at the ends and to project past the body as little as possible; wings held up tightly to body.

BACK: Short, flat, broad across the shoulders, tapering and sloping well to tail.

TAIL: Carried at an angle of forty-five degrees; feathers broad and strong, well furnished with lesser sickles and coverts; sickles well curved and of good length. Tail, well-spread.

BREAST: Full, broad, rounded.

BODY AND STERN: Keel bone straight, of medium length, tapering well upward behind, giving a small, rounded and compact abdomen.

LEGS AND TOES: Legs, set well apart, straight when viewed from front; lower thighs, short, thick, muscular, sloping slightly to hock; shanks of medium length, with good round bone; toes, long, clean, evenly and well-spread; the back toe carried well backward and flat on the ground. Spurs, set low on shank.

PLUMAGE: Hard, glossy, firm.

CARRIAGE: Bold, alert, quick and graceful in movement.

SHAPE OF FEMALE

COMB: Single; straight, small, thin, erect, evenly serrated, and of fine texture.

BEAK: Large, strong at base, well-curved.
HEAD: Small, strong, of medium length.
FACE: Smooth, of fine texture, flexible.
EYES: Large, bright, prominent, giving a fearless expression.
WATTLES: Small, thin, smooth, of fine texture.
EAR-LOBES: Small, fine in texture.
NECK: Long and very strong at junction with body. Throat-skin, flexible and loose.

WINGS: Large, full and round, inclined to meet under the tail, with strong, prominent points, feathers to be broad and furnished with hard, strong quills, the primaries not to be too long and to be nicely rounded at the ends, and to project past the body as little as possible; wings held up tightly to body.

BACK: Short, flat, broad across the shoulders, tapering and sloping well to the tail.

TAIL: Of good length, carried at an angle of forty-five degrees and fairly well-spread.

BREAST: Full, broad, rounded.

BODY AND STERN: Keel bone straight, of medium depth, tapering well upward behind, giving a small, rounded and compact abdomen.

LEGS AND TOES: Legs, set well apart, straight when viewed from front; lower thighs, short, thick, muscular, sloping slightly to hock; shanks of medium length with good round bone; toes, long, clean, evenly and well spread; the back toe carried well backward and flat on the ground.

PLUMAGE: Hard, glossy, firm.

CARRIAGE: Bold, alert, quick and graceful in movement.

Note: See Instructions to Judges, paragraph "Quality of Feather," page 53.

OLD ENGLISH BLACK BREASTED RED GAMES AND GAME BANTAMS

COLOR OF MALE

COMB, FACE, WATTLES, AND EAR-LOBES: Bright red.
BEAK: Light horn.
HEAD: Plumage, orange red, free from dark feathers.

BLACK BREASTED RED OLD ENGLISH GAME COCK

BLACK BREASTED RED OLD ENGLISH GAME HEN

EYES: Red.

NECK: Hackle, orange red, free from dark feathers. Feathers on front of neck, black.

WINGS: Fronts, black; bows, lustrous deep red; coverts, lustrous bluish-black, forming wing-bar; primaries, black, lower webs edged with bay; secondaries, black, bay on outer web of surface to form wing-bay of same color.

BACK AND SADDLE: Lustrous deep red; saddle, lustrous orange red, free from dark feathers.

TAIL: Main-tail feathers, black, with lustrous greenish gloss.

BREAST: Black.

BODY AND STERN: Black.

LEGS AND TOES: Lower thighs, black; shanks and toes, pinkish white.

COLOR OF FEMALE

COMB, FACE, WATTLES, AND EAR-LOBES: Bright red.

BEAK: Light horn.

HEAD: Plumage, golden red.

EYES: Red.

NECK: Golden orange, striped with black. Feathers on front of neck, salmon.

WINGS: Fronts, bows and coverts, same color as described for back; primaries, dull black, the outer webs slightly edged with light brown stippling; secondaries, dull black, with outer webs finely stippled with light brown.

BACK: Web of feathers on surface, dull black, finely stippled with light brown, the light brown slightly predominating; importance is attached to fineness, sharp definition of stippling, evenness of color and freedom from shafting. The effect produced should not be suggestive of gray as one extreme to be avoided, or of red as the other. The unexposed portion of the feather to be dull black shading into slate.

TAIL: Main-tail feathers, dull black, except the two top feathers, which are stippled with light brown; coverts, same as back.

BREAST: Salmon, shading lighter at body, blending into body color.

BODY AND STERN: Ashy gray, except at sides, where surface color blends into that of wings and back.

LEGS AND TOES: Lower thighs, slaty black tinged with brown; shanks and toes, pinkish white.

OLD ENGLISH SPANGLED GAMES AND GAME BANTAMS

COLOR OF MALE

COMB, FACE, WATTLES AND EAR-LOBES: Bright red.

BEAK: Light horn.

HEAD: Plumage, dark red, feathers ending with small V-shaped white tips, a narrow black bar dividing the white from balance of feather.

EYES: Reddish bay.

NECK: Hackle, dark red, feathers ending with small diamond-shaped white spangles, a narrow black bar dividing the white from balance of feather, and extending upward, forming a narrow black stripe in center of feather.

WINGS: Shoulders, black, feathers ending with small diamond-shaped white tips; bows, dark red, feathers ending with small V-shaped white tips; coverts, lustrous black, forming a distinct bar across wing, each feather ending with a small sharply defined V-shaped white tip; primaries, black tipped with V-shaped white; secondaries, black with part of lower webs bay, forming wing-bay, remainder of secondaries ending with white tip.

BACK AND SADDLE: Dark red, feathers ending with small V-shaped white spangles, a narrow black bar dividing the white from balance of feather; saddle, dark red, feathers ending with small diamond-shaped white spangles, a narrow black bar dividing the white from the balance of the feather and extending upward, forming a narrow black stripe in center of feather.

TAIL: Main-tail feathers, black, each feather ending with a V-shaped white tip; sickles and coverts, lustrous greenish black, each feather ending with a V-shaped white tip.

BREAST: Lustrous black, feathers ending with V-shaped white tips.

BODY AND STERN: Body, black, feathers ending with small white tips; stern, black, tinged with white.

LEGS AND TOES: Lower thighs, black tipped with white; toes, pinkish white.

OLD ENGLISH BLACK BREASTED RED GAME BANTAM MALE

OLD ENGLISH BLACK BREASTED RED GAME BANTAM FEMALE

373-B

COLOR OF FEMALE

COMB, FACE, WATTLES AND EAR-LOBES: Bright red.

BEAK: Light horn.

HEAD: Plumage, golden red striped with black, feathers ending with small V-shaped white tips, a narrow black bar dividing the white from balance of feather.

EYES: Reddish bay.

NECK: Golden red, striped with black, feathers ending with small V-shaped white tips, a narrow black bar dividing the white from balance of feather; front of neck, reddish salmon, marked similar to breast.

WINGS: Fronts and bows, dull black, evenly stippled with medium shade of brown, the brown predominating, each feather ending with small V-shaped white tip, a narrow black bar dividing the white from balance of feather; coverts, dull black, evenly stippled with medium shade of brown, the brown predominating, each feather with a sharply defined V-shaped small white tip, a narrow black bar dividing the white from balance of feather; primaries, dull black, tipped with V-shaped white; secondaries, dull black, with lower web evenly mottled with medium brown, each feather ending with small V-shaped white tip, a narrow black bar dividing the white from balance of feather; importance is attached to fineness, evenness of color and freedom from shafting. The effect produced should not be suggestive of red.

BACK: Dull black, evenly stippled with a medium shade of brown, the brown predominating, each feather ending with V-shaped white tip, a narrow black bar dividing the white from balance of feather.

TAIL: Main-tail feathers, black, each feather ending with V-shaped white tip, the two top feathers evenly stippled with medium shade of brown, tipped with V-shaped white; coverts, dull black, stippled with a medium shade of brown, with brown predominating, feathers ending with small V-shaped white tips, a narrow black bar dividing the white from balance of feather.

BREAST: Rich salmon, shading lighter as it approaches the body, evenly stippled with brown, feathers tipped with small V-shaped white spangles, a narrow black bar dividing spangle from balance of feather.

BODY AND STERN : Salmon, evenly stippled with brown, feathers tipped with small V-shaped white spangles, a narrow black bar dividing spangle from remainder of feather.

LEGS AND TOES : Lower thighs, dull black evenly stippled with a medium shade of brown, each feather tipped with white; shanks and toes, pinkish white.

SPANGLED OLD ENGLISH GAME BANTAM FEATHERS

Male Plumage: (1) Hackle Feather, (2) Saddle Feather.
Female Plumage: (3) Back Feather, (4) Breast Feather, (5) Neck Feather, (front).

NOTE:

In all varieties except Black Breasted Red, the color in Old English Games and Game Bantams and in Modern Games and Game Bantams should be identical, except in color of legs and feet, which in Black Breasted Red, Golden and Silver Duckwings, Red Pyle and White Old English should be white.

ORIENTALS

Breeds	*Varieties*
SUMATRAS	Black
MALAYS	Black-Breasted Red
MALAY BANTAMS	Black-Breasted Red

BLACK SUMATRAS

The Black Sumatra fowl is a native of Sumatra, and, as far as known, is as pure blooded today as when first discovered on that island in the Far East many years ago. This is a fowl of graceful form and distinct carriage, with the richest of lustrous, greenish black plumage throughout. Its particular characteristic is the long, drooping tail of the male, which has an abundance of long sweeping sickles and coverts. Length and breadth of feather; single, double, or triple spurs on cocks, and practically no wattle development, are Sumatra breed characteristics.

ECONOMIC QUALITIES: Exhibition, and dual purpose fowl for the production of meat and eggs. Color of skin, yellow; color of egg shells, white.

Disqualifications

More than one-third white in ear-lobes; more than one-half inch of positive white in any part of surface plumage, or two or more feathers tipped or edged with positive white; shanks other than black or slate. (See General Disqualifications and Cutting for Defects.)

SHAPE OF MALE

COMB: Pea, small. (See Standard illustration, page 378.)

BEAK: Short, stout, well-curved.

HEAD: Short, round. (See standard illustration, page 378.)

EYES: Large, prominent.

WATTLES: Practically no development.

EAR-LOBES: Very small.

NECK: Rather long, well arched, throat full; hackle, full, long, flowing.

WINGS: Long, large, carried with fronts slightly raised, points of feathers folded closely together, slightly drooping.

BACK: Long, broad at shoulders, narrowing slightly and sloping gently to tail, with very long, full, flowing saddle feathers.

TAIL: Long, drooping, carried horizontally with abundance of feathers; sickles, long, broad and drooping; lesser sickles and coverts, abundant, long, broad and flowing, extending well onto main-tail. (See page 28, figures 30 and 31.)

377

SUMATRA MALE

SUMATRA FEMALE

BREAST: Broad, full, well-rounded.

BODY AND STERN: Body, moderately long, firm, muscular, tapering slightly to tail; stern, compact.

LEGS AND TOES: Legs, set well apart and straight when viewed from front; lower thighs, of medium length, strong; shanks, medium length; toes, long, straight, well-spread.

SHAPE OF FEMALE

COMB: Pea, small. (See Standard illustration, page 379.)

BEAK: Short, stout, well-curved.

HEAD: Short, round. (See Standard illustration, page 379.)

EYES: Large, prominent.

WATTLES: Very small.

EAR-LOBES: Very small.

NECK: Rather long, throat full; feathers, long.

WINGS: Long, large, points slightly drooping.

BACK: Long, broad at shoulders, narrowing slightly and sloping gently to tail.

TAIL: Long, large, carried at an angle of fifteen degrees above horizontal; coverts, abundant, long, broad and flowing, extending well onto main-tail. (See page 28, figures 30 and 31.)

BREAST: Broad, round, full.

BODY AND STERN: Body, moderately long, firm, muscular, tapering slightly to tail; stern, compact.

LEGS AND TOES: Legs, set well apart, straight when viewed from front; lower thighs, of medium length, large, strong; shanks, medium length; toes, straight, well-spread.

Note: See Instructions to Judges, paragraph "Quality of Feather," page 53.

COLOR OF MALE AND FEMALE

COMB, FACE, WATTLES AND EAR-LOBES: Gypsy color.

BEAK: Black.

EYES: Dark brown.

SHANKS AND TOES: Dark slate; bottoms of feet, yellow.

PLUMAGE: Very lustrous, greenish black throughout; under-color, dull black.

MALAYS

The Malay, as its name implies, originated in Asia, from which country it came to England as early as 1830. A giant among other breeds of poultry, it was given considerable prominence by early writers who regarded it as one of the old pure breeds of poultry. Its chief characteristics are great length of leg, and the sinister expression caused by a broad skull and projecting beetle eyebrows.

Black-Breasted Red Malays were admitted to the Standard in 1883.

ECONOMIC QUALITIES: Exhibition and table fowl, valuable for crossing with other breeds. Color of skin, yellow; color of egg shells, dark brown.

BLACK-BREASTED RED MALAYS

STANDARD WEIGHTS

Cock	9 lbs.	Hen	7 lbs.
Cockerel	7 lbs.	Pullet	5 lbs.

STANDARD HEIGHTS

Cock	26 in.	Hen	18 in.
Cockerel	18 in.	Pullet	15 in.

Disqualifications

Lopped combs; shanks or feet other than yellow; (See General Disqualifications and Cutting for Defects.)

SHAPE OF MALE

COMB: Rather small, resembling a strawberry in front, set well forward. If males are dubbed, deduct eight points.

BEAK: Thick, short, strong.

HEAD: Broad, long, crown heavy and projecting over eyes, giving a fierce, cruel expression; face and throat, bare of feathers.

EYES: Large.

WATTLE: Very small.

EAR-LOBES: Very small.

NECK: Long, nearly straight and upright; hackle, short, scanty.

WINGS: Rather short, large, stout, bony, very prominent at shoulders, carried compactly against sides; wing-points resting under saddle feathers, without drooping or being carried over back.

BACK: Rather long, slanting, rather convex in outline, tapering to tail, large and broad at shoulder; saddle, narrow, drooping; saddle feathers, short, scanty.

TAIL: Of medium length, drooping, carried below horizontal; well folded together; sickle feathers, curved, but not long.

BREAST: Broad, full; breast-bone, deep, prominent.

BODY AND STERN: Body, firm, muscular, broad, tapering toward tail; stern, well tucked up.

THIGHS AND SHANKS: Lower thighs, long, hard, round, set well apart; shanks, long, scales, smooth.

FEET: Flat, broad; toes, long, straight, well apart.

HARDNESS OF FEATHER: Feathers, short, lying close, hard, firm and strong.

SHAPE OF FEMALE

COMB: Rather small, resembling a strawberry in front, set well forward.

BEAK: Thick, short.

HEAD: Broad, long, crown heavy and projecting over eyes, giving a fierce, cruel expression; face and throat, bare of feathers.

EYES: Large.

WATTLES: Very small.

EAR-LOBES: Very small.

NECK: Long, nearly straight and upright; feathers short.

WINGS: Rather short, large, strong, bony, very prominent at shoulders, carried compactly against sides; wing-points resting under saddle feathers, without drooping or being carried over back.

BACK: Rather long, slanting, rather convex in outline, tapering to tail, large and broad at shoulders.

TAIL: Of medium length, drooping, carried slightly below the horizontal; closely folded.

BREAST: Broad, full; breast-bone, deep, prominent.

BODY AND STERN: Body, firm, muscular, broad, tapering toward tail; stern, well tucked up.

THIGHS AND SHANKS: Lower thighs, long, hard, round, set well apart; shanks, long, bony, strong, standing evenly apart; scales, smooth.

FEET: Flat, broad; toes, long, straight, well apart.

HARDNESS OF FEATHER: Feathers, short, lying close, hard, firm, strong.

Note: See Instructions to Judges, paragraph "Quality of Feather," page 53.

COLOR OF MALE

COMB, FACE, WATTLES AND EAR-LOBES: Bright red.

BEAK: Yellow.

HEAD: Plumage, reddish maroon.

EYES: Pearl.

NECK: Hackle, dark red, shading into reddish maroon; plumage on front of neck, black.

WINGS: Fronts, black; bows, a rich, glossy, dark red; coverts, glossy, greenish black, forming a wide bar across the wing; primaries, black, outer webs rich bay; secondaries, part of outer webs forming wing-bays, rich bay, the remainder of secondary feathers, black.

BACK AND SADDLE: Rich, glossy, dark reddish maroon; saddle feathers, rich, dark red.

TAIL: Main-tail feathers, black; sickle feathers and coverts, rich, greenish black.

BREAST: Glossy black.

BODY AND STERN: Black.

LEGS AND TOES: Lower thighs, black; shanks and feet, yellow.

UNDER-COLOR OF ALL SECTIONS: Slate tinged with brown.

COLOR OF FEMALE

COMB, FACE, WATTLES AND EAR-LOBES: Bright red.

BEAK: Yellow.

HEAD: Plumage, dark brown.

EYES: Pearl.

NECK: Dark brown striped with black; feathers on front of neck, cinnamon brown.

WINGS: Fronts, bows, coverts, and secondaries, brown; primaries, very dark brown.

BACK: Dark cinnamon brown.

TAIL: Very dark brown, approaching black.

BREAST: Cinnamon brown.
BODY AND STERN: Brown.
LEGS AND TOES: Lower thighs, brown; shanks and feet, yellow.
UNDER-COLOR OF ALL SECTIONS: Slate tinged with brown.

BLACK-BREASTED RED MALAY BANTAMS

STANDARD WEIGHTS

Cock ....26 oz.   Hen ....24 oz.
Cockerel ....24 oz.   Pullet ....22 oz.

Disqualifications

Same as for Malays except for weight. (See General Disqualifications and Cutting for Defects.)

SHAPE AND COLOR OF MALE AND FEMALE

The general shape and color requirements for Black-Breasted Red Malay Bantams is the same as for Malays.

ORNAMENTAL BANTAMS

FEATHER LEGGED

Breeds	*Varieties*
MILLE FLEUR	
SILKIES	{ Bearded Non-Bearded
BOOTED	White

CLEAN LEGGED

SEBRIGHTS	{ Golden Silver
ROSE-COMB	{ White Black
JAPANESE	{ Black-Tailed White Black Gray

ORNAMENTAL BANTAMS

Bantams are dwarf fowl that have existed for many centuries. The term "Bantam" was probably originally applied because of the fact that the first importation of dwarfed fowls came, so it has been recorded, from the District of "Bantam" in the Dutch East Indies, though the term "bantam" has always been associated with something small. Moubray, an English writer on poultry in 1854, wrote: "Bantam, a well-known small breed, originally from India, valued chiefly for its grotesque figure and delicate flesh."

The Japanese Bantams fit this description, for they constitute one of the curiosities among dwarf fowl. The disproportionately large comb, face, wings and tail of the male, and the remarkable shortness of the legs, are striking characteristics. The tail is distinguished by the long, sword-shaped sickles that are carried forward and upright to an unusual degree, accentuating the grotesque figure of the Japanese Bantam.

Many of the popular varieties of Bantams, however, originated, or were developed, in European and American countries.

Rose-Comb Bantams should be smaller counterparts of the graceful and sprightly Hamburgs, carrying, however, wings and tails somewhat larger in proportion to the body.

Sebright Bantams originated in England, the result of thirty years of selection in mating and breeding by the late Sir John Sebright. They are, perhaps, the greatest achievement of the fanciers' skill and art in producing specimens of both sexes that are marvels in diminutive size and laced plumage in all sections. The feathers of both male and female are exactly alike. The low carriage of wings and the well-spread tail add greatly to the striking appearance of the beautiful Sebright Bantam.

White-Booted are distinct from the White Cochin Bantams in that they possess an abundance of stiff feathers, pronounced vulture-hocks, and an upright and sprightly carriage.

Mille Fleur Bantams were introduced in 1911, a comparatively new variety in this country but well-known in Belgium, Germany, and England. The name means "Thousand Flowers." The tri-colored plumage is a most distinguishing feature. They were admitted to the Standard in 1914.

Silkies are a distinct race of fowls, differing in texture of plumage and color of skin from all other races of domesticated poultry. The feathers are not webbed and the plumage has the appearance of hair or down, a fixed characteristic of this breed. Silkies were known for several centuries in China and Japan, the latter country being accredited with the origin of the breed. Ancient writers referred to fowls with hair or wool instead of feathers, presumably the Silky fowl which has been bred and developed into the modern Silkies. Silkies lay well, but the eggs are small. Their chief value is for hatching and brooding purposes, especially to Bantam and Pheasant breeders. In general appearance they are short, having silky-feathered legs, broad backs and profuse plumage. The length of the webless feathers is a particularly desirable feature. They were admitted to the Standard in 1874.

Sebright, Rose-Comb and Black-Tailed Japanese Bantams were admitted to the Standard in 1874, Gray Japanese in 1914.

Ornamental Bantams are kept chiefly for pleasure and for exhibition purposes but they possess useful qualities as well, some of the varieties being exceptionally good layers. Japanese Bantams have yellow skin and lay brown-shelled eggs; Sebrights and Rose-Combs have white skin and lay white-shelled eggs. Silkies have a dark or gypsy skin and lay white eggs.

387

SEBRIGHT BANTAMS

Cocks or cockerels having hackle feathers extending over shoulders, or sickle feathers extending more than an inch and a half beyond tail proper; shanks other than slaty-blue. (See General Disqualifications and Cutting for Defects.)

STANDARD WEIGHTS

Cock	26 oz.	Hen	22 oz.
Cockerel	22 oz.	Pullet	20 oz.

SHAPE OF MALE

COMB: Rose; square in front, firm and even on head, terminating at rear in a spike, which inclines upward very slightly; top covered with small points; free from hollow center. (See Standard illustration, page 390.)

BEAK: Short, slightly curved.

HEAD: Large, round in front and carried well back. (See Standard illustration, page 390.)

EYES: Large, round, prominent.

WATTLES: Broad, well-rounded.

EAR-LOBES: Smooth.

NECK: Moderately short, tapering, well-arched, carried very far back; hen-feathered; free from hackle feathers.

WINGS: Large, carried low, but not so low as to conceal hocks; primaries and secondaries, broad, and overlapping in natural order when wing is folded.

BACK: Very short, feathers broad and well-rounded; free from saddle hangers.

TAIL: Full, well-expanded, carried at an angle of seventy degrees above the horizontal (see illustrations, page 28, figures 30 and 31); free from sickles; feathers broadest toward the ends, the two upper, which may be slightly curved, not extending more than one inch and a half beyond the others; coverts, straight, round at ends and lying close to sides of tail; main-tail feathers, broad and overlapping.

BREAST: Full, round, carried prominently forward.

BODY AND FLUFF: Body, compact, deep, short; fluff, short.

LEGS AND TOES: Legs set well apart, straight when viewed from front; lower thighs, very short, stout; shanks, short, rather slender; toes, straight, well-spread.

SHAPE OF FEMALE

COMB: Rose; similar to that of male, but very small. (See Standard illustration, page 391.)

BEAK: Short, slightly curved.

HEAD: Broad and well-rounded. (See Standard illustration, page 391.)

EYES: Large, round, prominent.

WATTLES: Small, well-rounded.

EAR-LOBES: Flat, smooth, small.

NECK: Moderately short, tapering, well-arched.

WINGS: Large, carried low, but not so low as to conceal hocks; primaries and secondaries, broad, and overlapping in natural order when wing is folded.

BACK: Short, tapering to tail, feathers broad and well-rounded.

TAIL: Full, well-expanded, carried at an angle of seventy degrees above the horizontal (see illustrations, page 28, figures 30 and 31); main-tail feathers, broad, and overlapping.

BREAST: Full, round, carried prominently forward.

BODY AND FLUFF: Body, compact, deep, short; fluff, short.

LEGS AND TOES: Legs, set well apart and straight when viewed from front; lower thighs, very short, stout; shanks, short, rather slender; toes, straight, well-spread.

Note: See Instructions to Judges, paragraph "Quality of Feather," (page 53.)

GOLDEN SEBRIGHT BANTAMS

COLOR OF MALE AND FEMALE

COMB AND FACE: Purplish red.

BEAK: Dark horn.

EYES: Brown.

WATTLES: Bright red.

EAR-LOBES: Purplish red.

SHANKS AND TOES: Slaty blue.

PLUMAGE: Surface throughout, golden bay, each feather

SILVER SEBRIGHT BANTAM MALE

SILVER SEBRIGHT BANTAM FEMALE

evenly and distinctly laced all around with a narrow edging of lustrous black.

UNDER-COLOR OF ALL SECTIONS: Slate.

SILVER SEBRIGHT BANTAMS
COLOR OF MALE AND FEMALE

COMB AND FACE: Purplish red.

BEAK: Dark horn.

EYES: Brown.

WATTLES: Bright red.

EAR-LOBES: Purplish red.

SHANKS AND TOES: Slaty blue.

PLUMAGE: Surface throughout, silvery-white, each feather evenly and distinctly laced all around with a narrow edging of lustrous black.

UNDER-COLOR OF ALL SECTIONS: Slate.

ROSE-COMB BANTAMS

STANDARD WEIGHTS

Cock ....26 oz.   Hen ....22 oz.
Cockerel ....22 oz.   Pullet ....20 oz.

SHAPE OF MALE

COMB: Rose; square in front, firm and even on head, terminating at rear in spike, which inclines upward very slightly; top covered with small points; free from hollow center. (See Standard illustration, page 394.)

BEAK: Short, slightly curved.

HEAD: Small, round, carried well backward. (See Standard illustration, page 394.)

EYES: Full, round, prominent.

WATTLES: Broad, thin, well-rounded.

EAR-LOBES: Large, flat, round, smooth, even, fitting closely to head.

NECK: Tapering, well-arched; hackle, full, long, flowing well over shoulders.

WINGS: Large, points carried low but not to conceal hocks; secondaries, slightly expanded.

BACK: Short, broad from shoulder to tail, having a short concave sweep.

TAIL: Large, full, well-expanded, carried at an angle of forty degrees above the horizontal (see illustrations, page 28, figure 30 and 31); main-tail feathers, broad and overlapping; sickles, long, broad, well-curved; coverts, broad, abundant.

BREAST: Full, round, carried prominently forward.

BODY AND FLUFF: Body short, fluff short.

LEGS AND TOES: Legs, set well apart, straight when viewed from front; lower thighs, short; shanks, smooth, short; toes, straight, well-spread.

SHAPE OF FEMALE

COMB: Rose; similar to that of male, but smaller. (See Standard illustration, page 395.)

BEAK: Short, slightly curved.

HEAD: Small, round. (See Standard illustration, page 395.)

393

ROSE-COMB BLACK BANTAM MALE

ROSE-COMB BLACK BANTAM FEMALE

EYES: Full, round, prominent.

WATTLES: Small, thin, well-rounded.

EAR-LOBES: Large, flat, round, smooth, even, fitting closely to head.

NECK: Short, tapering, well-arched.

WINGS: Large, points carried low, but not to conceal hocks.

BACK: Short, comparatively broad at shoulders, slightly tapering to tail.

TAIL: Large, full, well-expanded, carried at an angle of thirty-five degrees above the horizontal (see illustrations, page 28, figures 30 and 31); main-tail feathers, broad and overlapping; coverts, broad and abundant, extending well onto main-tail.

BREAST: Full, round, carried prominently forward.

BODY AND FLUFF: Body, compact, tapering toward tail; fluff, short.

LEGS AND TOES: Legs, set well apart, straight when viewed from front; lower thighs, short; shanks, smooth, short; toes, straight, well-spread.

Note: See Instructions to Judges, paragraph "Quality of Feather," page 53.

ROSE-COMB WHITE BANTAMS

Disqualifications

Shanks other than white or pinkish white. (See General Disqualifications and Cutting for Defects.)

COLOR OF MALE AND FEMALE

COMB, FACE, AND WATTLES: Bright red.

BEAK: Pinkish white.

EYES: Reddish bay.

EAR-LOBES: White.

SHANKS AND TOES: Pinkish white.

PLUMAGE: See description of White plumage color, page 63.

ROSE-COMB BLACK BANTAMS

Disqualifications

More than one-half inch of positive white in any part of plumage, or two or more feathers tipped or edged with positive white;

shanks other than black or dark leaden blue. (See General Disqualifications and Cutting for Defects.)

COLOR OF MALE AND FEMALE

COMB, FACE, AND WATTLES: Bright red.
BEAK: Black.
EYES: Brown.
EAR-LOBES: White.
SHANKS AND TOES: Black.
PLUMAGE: See description of Black plumage color, page 64.

BOOTED WHITE BANTAMS

Disqualifications

Absence of vulture hocks; shanks not feathered down the outer sides; shanks other than white; outer toes not feathered. (See General Disqualifications and Cutting for Defects.)

STANDARD WEIGHTS

Cock	26 oz.	Hen	22 oz.
Cockerel	22 oz.	Pullet	20 oz.

SHAPE OF MALE

COMB: Single; of medium size, firm and straight on head, with five well-defined points, evenly serrated.
BEAK: Short, slightly curved.
HEAD: Small, round, carried well back.
EYES: Full, round, prominent.
WATTLES: Broad, thin, well-rounded.
EAR-LOBES: Smooth, medium size.
NECK: Tapering, well-arched, with full, long hackle descending well over shoulders.
WINGS: Large, points carried rather low.
BACK: Comparatively broad at shoulders, short, saddle feathers, abundant, long.
TAIL: Full, well-expanded, carried at an angle of ninety degrees above the horizontal (see page 28, figures 30 and 31); sickles, long, well-curved; coverts, abundant, long.
BREAST: Full, round, prominent.
BODY AND FLUFF: Body, rather short and compact; fluff, moderately full.

LEGS AND TOES: Legs, set well apart, straight when viewed from front; lower thighs, long, well furnished with long, stiff feathers or vulture hocks, which almost touch the ground; shanks, long, heavily feathered on the outer sides; toes, straight; outer toes, heavily feathered to their extremities.

SHAPE OF FEMALE

COMB: Single; small, firm and straight on head, with five well-defined points, evenly serrated.

BEAK: Short, slightly curved.

HEAD: Small, round.

EYES: Full, round, prominent.

WATTLES: Small, well-rounded, thin.

EAR-LOBES: Flat, medium sized.

NECK: Of medium length, tapering, well-arched.

WINGS: Large, points carried rather low.

BACK: Short, comparatively broad at shoulders.

TAIL: Full, well-expanded, carried at an angle of seventy-five degrees above the horizontal. (See page 28, figures 30 and 31.)

BREAST: Full, round, prominent.

BODY AND FLUFF: Body, rather short and compact; fluff, moderately full.

LEGS AND TOES: Legs, set well apart, straight when viewed from front; lower thighs, long, well-furnished with long, stiff feathers or vulture hocks; shanks, long, heavily feathered on outer sides; toes, straight; outer toes, heavily feathered to their extremities.

Note: See Instructions to Judges, paragraph "Quality of Feather," page 53.

COLOR OF MALE AND FEMALE

COMB, FACE, WATTLES, AND EAR-LOBES: Bright red.

BEAK: Pinkish white.

EYES: Reddish bay.

SHANKS AND TOES: Pinkish white.

PLUMAGE: See description of White plumage color, page 63.

JAPANESE BANTAMS

Disqualifications
(See General Disqualifications and Cutting for Defects.)

STANDARD WEIGHTS

Cock	26 oz.	Hen	22 oz.
Cockerel	22 oz.	Pullet	20 oz.

SHAPE OF MALE

COMB: Single; large, firm and straight on head; evenly serrated, having five distinct points. (See Standard illustration, page 402.)

BEAK: Strong, well curved.

HEAD: Rather large and broad. (See Standard illustration, page 402.)

EYES: Large, round, and prominent.

WATTLES: Large, smooth.

EAR-LOBES: Large, smooth.

NECK: Rather short, curving prominently backward, with abundant hackle flowing well over shoulders.

WINGS: Large, long, points decidedly drooping.

BACK: Very short; saddle feathers, abundant.

TAIL: Very large, somewhat expanded, carried forward of perpendicular, so as to almost come in contact with back of head; sickles, long, very slightly upright, slightly curved.

BREAST: Very full, round, carried low.

BODY AND FLUFF: Body, rather short, deep and compact; fluff, short.

LEGS AND TOES: Legs, set well apart, straight when viewed from front; lower thighs, of medium size, short; shanks, very short, smooth; toes, straight, well spread.

SHAPE OF FEMALE

COMB: Single; large, firm and straight on head, evenly serrated, having five distinct points. (See Standard illustration, page 403.)

BEAK: Strong, well curved.

HEAD: Rather large and broad. (See Standard illustration, page 403.)

EYES: Large, round, prominent.

WATTLES: Of medium size, well-rounded.

EAR-LOBES: Of medium size, smooth.

NECK: Short, well-curved.

WINGS: Large, long, points decidedly drooping.

BACK: Short.

TAIL: Large, somewhat expanded, carried forward of perpendicular.

BREAST: Full, round, carried low.

BODY AND FLUFF: Body, rather short, deep and compact; fluff, short.

LEGS AND TOES: Legs, set well apart, straight when viewed from front; lower thighs, of medium size, short; shanks, very short, smooth; toes, straight, well-spread.

Note: See Instructions to Judges, paragraph "Quality of Feather," page 53.

BLACK-TAILED JAPANESE BANTAMS

Disqualifications

Shanks other than yellow. (See General Disqualifications and Cutting for Defects.)

COLOR OF MALE

COMB, FACE, WATTLES, AND EAR-LOBES: Bright red.

BEAK: Yellow.

HEAD: Plumage, silvery white.

EYES: Reddish bay.

NECK: Silvery white; plumage on front of neck, silvery white.

WINGS: Fronts, bows, and coverts, silvery white; primaries, black edged with white; secondaries, black, with wide edging of white on upper webs, lower webs white; wing, when folded, shows white only.

BACK AND SADDLE: White; saddle feathers, white.

TAIL: Main-tail feathers, black; sickles and coverts, black, edged with white.

BREAST: White.

BODY AND FLUFF: White.

LEGS AND TOES: Lower thighs, white; shanks and toes, yellow.

UNDER-COLOR OF ALL SECTIONS: Bluish white.

COLOR OF FEMALE

COMB, FACE, WATTLES, AND EAR-LOBES: Bright red.
BEAK: Yellow.
HEAD: Plumage, white.
EYES: Reddish bay.
NECK: White; feathers on front of neck, white.
WINGS: Fronts, bows, and coverts, white; primaries, black, edged with white; secondaries, black with wide edging of white on upper webs, lower webs white; wing, when folded, shows white only.
BACK: White.
TAIL: Main-tail feathers, black, two top feathers edged with white; coverts, black edged with white.
BREAST: White.
BODY AND FLUFF: White.
LEGS AND TOES: Lower thighs, white; shanks and toes, yellow.
UNDER-COLOR OF ALL SECTIONS: Bluish white.

WHITE JAPANESE BANTAMS

Disqualifications

Shanks other than yellow. (See General Disqualifications and Cutting for Defects.)

COLOR OF MALE AND FEMALE

COMB, FACE, WATTLES, AND EAR-LOBES: Bright red.
BEAK: Yellow.
EYES: Reddish bay.
SHANKS AND TOES: Yellow.
PLUMAGE: See description of White plumage color, page 63.

BLACK JAPANESE BANTAMS

Disqualifications

More than one-half inch of positive white in any part of plumage; or two or more feathers tipped or edged with positive white; shanks other than yellow or yellow shaded with black. (See General Disqualifications and Cutting for Defects.)

COLOR OF MALE AND FEMALE

COMB, FACE, WATTLES, AND EAR-LOBES: Bright red.
BEAK: Yellow.

BLACK-TAILED JAPANESE BANTAM MALE

BLACK-TAILED JAPANESE BANTAM FEMALE

403

EYES: Brown.
SHANKS AND TOES: Yellow.
PLUMAGE: Undercolor of all sections slate. See description of Black plumage color, page 64.

GRAY JAPANESE BANTAMS

Disqualifications

Shanks other than yellow or yellow shaded with black. (See General Disqualifications and Cutting for Defects.)

COLOR OF MALE

COMB, FACE, WATTLES, AND EAR-LOBES: Bright red.
BEAK: Yellow shaded with dark horn.
HEAD: Plumage, silvery gray.
EYES: Brown.
NECK: Hackle, silvery gray with narrow, dark stripe terminating in a point near lower extremity of feather; plumage on front of neck, same as breast.
WINGS: Fronts, black; bows, silvery white; coverts, glossy black; primaries and secondaries, black.
BACK AND SADDLE: Silvery gray; saddle, silvery gray with narrow dark stripe through middle of each feather, terminating in a point near its extremity.
TAIL: Main-tail feathers, black; sickles and tail coverts, glossy greenish black.
BREAST: Black, feathers laced with silvery gray.
BODY AND FLUFF: Black.
LEGS AND TOES: Lower thighs, black; shanks and toes, yellow.
UNDER-COLOR OF ALL SECTIONS: Dark slate.

COLOR OF FEMALE

COMB, FACE, WATTLES, AND EAR-LOBES: Bright red.
BEAK: Yellow, shaded with dark horn.
HEAD: Plumage, white.
EYES: Brown.
NECK: White, with narrow dark stripe through middle of each feather, terminating in a point near its lower extremity; feathers on front of neck, same as breast.
WINGS: Black.
BACK: Black.

TAIL: Black.

BREAST: Black, feathers laced with white.

BODY AND FLUFF: Black.

LEGS AND TOES: Lower thighs, black; shanks and toes, dusky yellow.

UNDER-COLOR OF ALL SECTIONS: Dark slate.

MILLE FLEUR BOOTED BANTAMS

Disqualifications

Absence of vulture-hocks; shanks not feathered down the outer sides; outer toes not feathered. (See General Disqualifications and Cutting for Defects.)

STANDARD WEIGHTS

Cock	26 oz.	Hen	22 oz.
Cockerel	22 oz.	Pullet	20 oz.

SHAPE OF MALE

COMB: Single; of medium size, firm and straight on head, evenly serrated. (See Standard illustration, page 408.)

BEAK: Short, slightly curved.

HEAD: Small, round, carried well back. (See Standard illustration, page 408.)

EYES: Full, round, prominent.

WATTLES: Broad, thin, well-rounded.

EAR-LOBES: Flat, almond shape.

BEARD (in bearded variety): Thick and full, extending back of eye, projecting from sides of face.

NECK: Tapering, well-arched, with full, long hackle, extending well over shoulders.

WINGS: Large, points carried rather low.

BACK: Short, forming a slight concave sweep to juncture of tail; saddle, long, abundant.

TAIL: Long, well-spread, carried very erect; sickles, medium in length, slightly curved; coverts, abundant.

BREAST: Full, round, carried well forward.

BODY AND FLUFF: Body, rather short and compact; fluff, moderately full.

LEGS AND TOES: Legs, set well apart, straight when viewed from front; lower thighs, medium in length, covered with long, stiff feathers, forming a vulture hock almost touching the ground; shanks, medium in length, heavily feathered on outer sides; toes, straight; outer toes, heavily feathered to their extremities.

SHAPE OF FEMALE

COMB: Single; firm, small and straight on head, evenly serrated. (See Standard illustration, page 409.)

BEAK: Short, slightly curved.

HEAD: Small, round, carried well back. (See Standard illustration, page 409.)

EYES: Full, round, prominent.

WATTLES: Small, well-rounded.

EAR-LOBES: Flat, almond shape.

BEARD (in bearded variety): Thick and full, extending back of eye, projecting from sides of face.

NECK: Medium in length, well-arched.

WINGS: Large, points carried rather low.

BACK: Short, forming a slight concave sweep to juncture of tail.

TAIL: Long, well-spread, carried very erect.

BREAST: Full, round, carried well forward.

BODY AND FLUFF: Body, rather short and compact; fluff, moderately full.

LEGS AND TOES: Legs, set well apart, straight when viewed from front; lower thighs, medium in length, covered with long, stiff feathers, forming a vulture-hock, almost touching the ground; shanks, medium in length, heavily feathered on outer sides; toes, straight; outer toes, heavily feathered to their extremities.

Note: See Instructions to Judges, paragraph "Quality of Feather," (page 53.)

COLOR OF MALE

COMB, FACE, WATTLES, AND EAR-LOBES: Bright red.

BEAK: Horn.

HEAD: Plumage, bright red, each feather tipped with a small white spangle, a narrow bar of black dividing the white spangle from balance of feather.

EYES: Reddish bay.

NECK: Plumage, rich, bright red, each feather having a greenish black stripe extending lengthwise through lower part of feather, terminating near end of feather; feathers tipped with diamond-shaped spangle of pure white; plumage on front of neck,

MILLE FLEUR BOOTED BANTAM MALE

MILLE FLEUR BOOTED BANTAM FEMALE

PLUMAGE OF MILLE FLEUR BANTAMS

1. Feather from neck of female.
2. Feather from back of female.
3. Feather from hackle of male.
4. Feather from saddle of male.
5. Feather from breast of male.
6. Feather from lower thigh of male.

same color as breast; in bearded variety, each feather of beard
tipped with white, balance of feather, red.(See page 410.)

WINGS: Fronts, black; bows, rich brilliant red, each feather
tipped with a pure white spangle; coverts, rich bay, each feather
having a V-shaped white spangle at end of feather, a crescent-
shaped bar of black dividing white spangle from balance of
feather, which is rich bay; primaries, inner webs black; outer
webs black, slightly edged with bay; lower portion of feather
edged with white; secondaries, outer webs bay, inner webs dull
black extending into outer webs near end of feathers, end of
feathers tipped with white.

BACK AND SADDLE: Rich bright red, each feather having a
greenish black stripe extending lengthwise through lower part of
feather and terminating near end of feather, end of feather
tipped with a diamond-shaped white spangle, the black stripe
broadening out to edge of feather where it meets white spangle.

TAIL: Main-tail feathers, black, each feather tipped with
white; coverts and sickles, greenish black, each feather tipped
with a V-shaped white spangle.

BREAST: Golden bay, each feather tipped with a V-shaped
white spangle, a crescent-shaped bar of black dividing white
spangle from balance of feather. (See page 410.)

BODY AND FLUFF: Body, plumage, same in color and markings
as breast; fluff, dull black, mottled with white.

LEGS AND TOES: Lower thighs, plumage, same in colors and
markings as breast; fluff, dull black, mottled with white; shanks
and toes, slaty blue; bottoms of feet, yellow; shanks and toe
feathers, black, tipped with white.

UNDER-COLOR OF ALL SECTIONS: Slate, shading to grayish
buff at base.

COLOR OF FEMALE

COMB, FACE, WATTLES, AND EAR-LOBES: Bright red.
BEAK: Horn.
HEAD: Plumage, rich, golden buff, each feather marked with
crescent-shaped spangle of black near end of feather, end of
feather tipped with a pure white V-shaped spangle.
EYES: Reddish bay.
NECK: Plumage, rich, golden buff, each feather marked with
a crescent-shaped spangle of black near end of feather, end of

feather tipped with a pure white diamond-shaped spangle; in bearded variety, each feather of beard tipped with white, balance of feather light golden buff; feathers on front of neck, same as breast.

WINGS: Fronts, bows, and coverts, rich, golden buff, each feather marked with crescent-shaped spangle of black near end of feather, end of feather tipped with a pure white V-shaped spangle; primaries, inner webs black, outer webs black, slightly edged with bay, lower portion of feathers edged with white; secondaries, outer webs light golden buff extending nearly to end of feathers; inner webs dull black, extending nearly to end of feathers and broadening out into outer webs nearly to end of feathers where it joins a spangle of white at tips.

BACK: Rich, golden buff, each feather marked with a crescent-shaped spangle of black near end of feather, end of feather tipped with a pure white diamond-shaped spangle. (See page 410.)

TAIL: Main-tail feathers, dull black, tipped with white; coverts, same as back.

BREAST: Same as back.

BODY AND FLUFF: Same as back.

LEGS AND TOES: Lower thighs, same as back; hock, same as back; shanks and toes, slaty blue; bottoms of feet, yellow; shank and toe feathering, dull black tipped with white.

UNDER-COLOR OF ALL SECTIONS: Slate, shading to grayish buff at base.

SILKIES NON-BEARDED AND BEARDED

Disqualifications

Absence of crest. Shanks not feathered down outer sides. Feathers not truly silky (except in primaries, secondaries, leg, toe and main-tail feathers).

Vulture hocks. See general disqualifications.

SHAPE OF MALE

COMB: Small, nearly round, surface covered with small corrugations.

CREST: Large, soft and full, standing upright with streamer feathers projecting and falling gracefully backward from crest.

BEAK: Short and stout, curving to point.

EYES: Large, full and round.

WATTLES: Medium length, concave outer surface, nearly semicircular. Very small, if any, on bearded variety.

EAR-LOBES: Flat, oval, smooth in texture.

NECK: Short with very full hackle flowing well over shoulders.

WING: Well rounded, small and short, carried nearly horizontally, well folded; primaries and secondaries having a shredded-like appearance and ends covered by lesser sickles and coverts.

BACK: Broad, short and rising gradually from middle of back towards tail.

TAIL: Short in appearance, very broad, well rounded and filled underneath with an abundance of soft, fluffy plumage.

BREAST: Carried forward, very full, well rounded and of great depth and width.

BODY AND FLUFF: Body of moderate length, broad, deep and well rounded from breast bone to stern and let down well between the legs.

LEGS AND TOES: Legs, set well apart, straight when viewed from the front; lower thighs, short, with abundance of silky fluff. Shanks moderately short and well feathered on outer sides with silky plumage. Five toes on each foot, the fifth toe well separated from the fourth and curving upward. Middle and outer toes well feathered. (Bare middle toe a serious defect.)

SILKIE MALE

SILKIE FEMALE

SHAPE OF FEMALE

COMB, BEAK, EYES, EAR-LOBES, NECK, WING, BACK, TAIL, BREAST, BODY AND FLUFF, LEGS AND TOES: As in the male.

CREST: Round, soft and full, standing upright.

WATTLES: Medium length, concave outer surface, nearly semi-circular (absence in bearded variety preferred).

COLOR OF MALE AND FEMALE

COMB, FACE AND WATTLES: Deep mulberry approaching black.

BEAK: Leaden blue.

EYES: Black.

EAR-LOBES: Light blue.

SHANKS AND TOES: Leaden blue.

SKIN: Dark blue.

PLUMAGE: White.

WEIGHTS: Cock 36 oz., hen 32 oz., cockerel 32 oz., pullet 28 oz.

SHAPE OF MALE AND FEMALE
BEARDED VARIETY

See above and

BEARD: Thick and full, extending back of eye, projecting from sides of face.

Disqualifications

Absence of beard. See Silkies and General Disqualifications.

CLASS XII.

MISCELLANEOUS

BREEDS..⎰ Sultans
⎱ Frizzles

SULTANS

A very old, ornamental race of poultry, listed in the first American Standard of Excellence in 1874. Sultans came to England in 1854 from Constantinople. They originated in Southeastern Europe, but were bred in Turkey under the name of "Sultan's Fowl," the breed evidently enjoying the favor of Turkish rulers, possibly due to their attractive appearance. They have for their most distinguishing characteristics the novel features of a full crest, muff, and beard, combined with vulture hocks and profuse shank and toe feathering.

ECONOMIC QUALITIES: Bred primarily for exhibition, the Sultan is not classed among production fowls, although the hens are good layers of medium-sized eggs. Color of skin, white; color of egg shells, white.

Disqualifications

Beak other than white or pale flesh color; large, red face; absence of beard; absence of vulture-hocks; shanks not feathered down outer sides. (See General Disqualifications and Cutting for Defects.)

SHAPE OF MALE

COMB: Very small, V-shaped.
CREST: Large, globular, and compact.
BEAK: Short, well-curved.
HEAD: Medium size.
NOSTRILS: Large.
EYES: Oval, prominent.
BEARD: Very full, joining muffs.
WATTLES: Small, round.
EAR-LOBES: Small, round, concealed by crest and muffs.
NECK: Short, arched, carried well back.
WINGS: Rather large, carried low.
BACK: Rather long, straight.
TAIL: Large, full abundantly furnished with sickles and coverts; carried erect.
BREAST: Deep and prominent.

BODY AND FLUFF: Body, very square, deep, compact, carried low.

LEGS AND TOES: Legs, set well apart, straight when viewed from front; lower thighs, very short, well-feathered with long full, vulture-hocks; shanks, short, heavily feathered down outer sides; toes, straight, five on each foot, the fifth toe distinct from the others, the middle and outer toes well-feathered.

SHAPE OF FEMALE

COMB: Very small, V-shaped.
CREST: Large, globular, and compact.
BEAK: Short, well-curved.
HEAD: Medium size.
NOSTRILS: Large.
EYES: Oval, prominent.
BEARD: Very full, joining muffs.
WATTLES: Small, round.
EAR-LOBES: Small, round, concealed by crest and muffs.
NECK: Short, arched, carried well back.
WINGS: Large, carried low.
BACK: Long and straight.
TAIL: Large, well-expanded, rather erect.
BREAST: Deep and prominent.
BODY AND FLUFF: Body, very square, compact, carried low.
LEGS AND TOES: Legs, set well apart, straight when viewed from front; lower thighs, very short, well feathered with long vulture-hocks; shanks, short, heavily feathered down outer sides; toes, straight, five on each foot, the fifth toe distinct from the others, the middle and outer toes well-feathered.
Note: See Instructions to Judges, paragraph "Quality of Feather," page 53.

COLOR OF MALE AND FEMALE

COMB AND FACE: Bright red; face covered by whiskers and almost invisible.
BEAK: Pale flesh color.
EYES: Reddish bay.
WATTLES AND EAR-LOBES: Bright red.
SHANKS AND TOES: Slaty blue.
PLUMAGE: See description of White plumage color, page 63.

FRIZZLE MALE

FRIZZLE FEMALE

FRIZZLES

Frizzles are one of our odd breeds, and but little is known about their origin. Charles Darwin classes them as "Frizzled or Caffie Fowls—not uncommon in India, and with feathers curling backwards and primary feathers of wing and tail imperfect." The main points for exhibition purposes are the curl, which is most pronounced on feathers not too broad; the purity of color in plumage, correctness in leg color; i. e., yellow legs for the white, red, or buff, and yellow or willow for other varieties.

ECONOMIC QUALITIES: General purpose fowl for production of meat and eggs. Color of skin, yellow; color of egg shells, brown.

NO SCALE OF POINTS
Disqualifications

Combs other than single; not matching in color of shanks or plumage when shown in pairs, trios, or pens; more than four toes. (See General Disqualifications and Cutting for Defects.)

MALE AND FEMALE

The feathers show a tendency to curve backward or upward at the ends, this curving at the ends being most noticeable in the hackle and saddle feathers, but the more all the feathers are curved, the better. Feathers curving upward on neck and back of head, after the style of the hooded pigeons, to be encouraged.

COLOR: Solid black, white, red, or bay admissible, provided the specimens match when shown in pairs, trios, and pens.

COMBS: Single.

DUCKS

Breeds	Varieties
PEKIN	
AYLESBURY	
ROUEN	
CAYUGA	
CALL	{ Gray { White
EAST INDIA	Black
MUSCOVY	{ Colored { White
SWEDISH	Blue
BUFF	
CRESTED	White
RUNNER	{ Fawn and White { White { Penciled

DUCKS

Ducks are not only popular for exhibition purposes, but useful and profitable for the production of meat and eggs. The many variations in size, type and color patterns give breeders of waterfowl a wide range from which to choose the variety most suitable to their needs. From the large, heavily-meated White Pekin to the racy Runner or from the large White Aylesbury or the massive, beautiful Rouen to the little Black East India, there is ample variety from which to choose.

The Crested Whites are very similar in type to the Pekins, but somewhat smaller in size and possess a crest which should be large and set firmly on the top of the head, without any inclination to fall over to one side.

The Muscovy originated in South America. It is a distinct race, and when crossed with other races of Ducks its progeny is sterile. The period of incubation for eggs of this variety is thirty-five days instead of twenty-eight, as with other races of ducks. The disproportion in sizes of drakes and ducks is remarkable, as the males are much larger than the females.

The Runners are very distinctive in type; in fact, type is the most important characteristic of the breed. In judging Runners, the typical shape must be given first consideration, and a ringed-in enclosure is advisable so that they can be judged "on the run" for correct carriage and gait which for Runners is a quick run, quite unlike the waddle of other ducks.

East Indias and Calls are the bantams of the Duck family. They should be small in size, the smaller the better, although type should not be sacrificed for smallness of size.

During the summer old drakes with the color pattern of the Rouen and Gray Call shed their showy male plumage and take on a plumage resembling that of the female. In the fall they moult again and take on the male plumage. Young drakes also carry the less showy female color before they take on adult plumage.

ECONOMIC QUALITIES: The skin of all domesticated races of ducks is more or less yellow, with the possible exception of the Aylesbury and Muscovy, the skin of which is pinkish white.

Indian Runners produce white eggs, although tinted eggs are common in some strains. Runner ducks are the greatest layers known for the weight and number of eggs produced yearly. The Cayuga and the Black East India lay a very characteristic egg. When production begins the eggs are practically black, but as production progresses the black pigment more or less disappears and the eggs are blue. The Rouen egg is blue-shelled, although white-shelled eggs are not uncommon.

The larger breeds of Ducks are noted for their market and table qualities.

PEKIN DUCKS

Disqualifications
Feathers other than white, or creamy white, in any part of plumage. (See General Disqualifications and Cutting for Defects.)

STANDARD WEIGHTS

Adult Drake	9 lbs.	Adult Duck	8 lbs.
Young Drake	8 lbs.	Young Duck	7 lbs.

SHAPE OF DRAKE AND DUCK

HEAD: Long, finely formed.

BILL: Of medium size, slightly convex between juncture of head and extremity of bill.

EYES: Large, deep set.

NECK: In drake, large and of medium length; in duck, of medium length; in both, carried well forward; arched.

WINGS: Short, carried closely and smoothly against sides.

BACK: Long, broad, with a slight depression from shoulder to tail.

TAIL: Rather erect, the sex feathers of drake being well-curled, hard and stiff.

BREAST: Broad, deep, prominent.

BODY AND KEEL: Body, long, broad, deep, carried just clear of ground; keel, straight, carried well forward; carriage, but slightly elevated in front, sloping toward rear.

LEGS AND TOES: Lower thighs and shanks, short, large, set well back; toes, straight, connected by web.

PEKIN DRAKE

PEKIN DUCK

COLOR OF DRAKE AND DUCK

BILL: Orange-yellow.

EYES: Deep leaden blue.

SHANKS AND TOES: Reddish orange.

PLUMAGE: Creamy white.

AYLESBURY DUCKS

Disqualifications

Feathers other than white in any part of plumage. (See General Disqualifications and Cutting for Defects.)

STANDARD WEIGHTS

Adult Drake.....................9 lbs.   Adult Duck.....................8 lbs.
Young Drake.....................8 lbs.   Young Duck.....................7 lbs.

SHAPE OF DRAKE AND DUCK

HEAD: Large, long, finely formed.

BILL: Long, broad, outline nearly straight from top of head to tip of bill.

EYES: Full, deep set.

NECK: Long, moderately thick, slightly curved.

WINGS: Strong, carried closely and smoothly against sides.

BACK: Long, broad on top, slightly convex.

TAIL: Slightly elevated, composed of stiff, hard feathers; sex feathers of drake, hard, well-curled.

BREAST: Deep, prominent, carried low.

BODY AND KEEL: Body, long, deep, broad; keel, long, straight, carried low; carriage, nearly horizontal.

LEGS AND TOES: Lower thighs, short, stout; shanks, strong; toes, straight, connected by web.

COLOR OF DRAKE AND DUCK

BILL: Pale flesh-color.

EYES: Deep leaden.

SHANKS AND TOES: Bright, light orange.

PLUMAGE: Web, quill, and fluff of feathers in all sections, pure white.

ROUEN DUCKS

Disqualifications

Bills, clear yellow, dark green, blue or lead coior; any approach to white ring on neck of duck; white feather or feathers in primaries. (See General Disqualifications and Cutting for Defects.)

STANDARD WEIGHTS

Adult Drake	9 lbs.	Adult Duck	8 lbs.
Young Drake	8 lbs.	Young Duck	7 lbs.

SHAPE OF DRAKE AND DUCK

HEAD: Full and round.

BILL: Long, broad, wider at extremity than at base; top slightly depressed from crown of head to tip of bill.

EYES: Bold, full.

NECK: Long, tapering, curved, erect.

WINGS: Short, carried smoothly against sides.

BACK: Long, broad, slightly arched.

TAIL: Slightly elevated; composed of hard, stiff feathers; sex feathers of drake, hard, well-curled.

BREAST: Broad, deep, carried low.

BODY AND KEEL: Body, long, deep, broad; keel, long, straight, carried low; carriage, nearly horizontal.

LEGS AND TOES: Lower thighs, short, large; shanks, short, large; toes, straight, connected by web.

COLOR OF DRAKE

HEAD: Plumage, rich, lustrous green.

BILL: Greenish yellow, without any other shade, except black bean at tip.

EYES: Dark brown.

NECK: Rich, lustrous green, with a distinct white ring on lower part, not quite meeting at back.

WINGS: Fronts and bows, slaty gray, gradually blending into lighter gray on bows; uppermost secondary coverts, slaty gray blending into lighter gray; upper secondaries, dark slaty gray; lower secondaries, dark slaty gray, the lower web having a broad band of iridescent blue, then a band of black, and ending in a narrow band of white; coverts, slate, with a band of white and

ROUEN DRAKE AND DUCK FEATHERS

(See page 431)

DRAKE PLUMAGE

1. Feather from breast.
2. Feather from rear and side of body.
3. Feather from breast at lower side.
4. Feather from main-tail.
5. Feather from upper wing-covert.
6. Feather from wing-bar (small).
7. Feather from main wing-bar (large).

FEMALE PLUMAGE

8. Feather from wing-front.
9. Feather from breast.
10. Feather from rump.
11. Feather from secondary covert. (Small feather from wing-bar.)
12. Feather from lower secondaries. (Large feather from wing-bar.)
13. Feather from upper secondary next to body.
14. Feather from shoulder covert.
15. Feather from wing primary.

FEATHERS FROM ROUEN DRAKE AND DUCK

(See page 430)

ROUEN DRAKE

ROUEN DUCK

ending in a narrow band of black; the overlapping of the coverts on the secondaries forming the wing-bar; primaries, slaty brown.

BACK: Upper part, ashy gray, mixed with green, becoming a rich, lustrous green on lower part of rump; shoulders, gray, finely streaked with wavy brown lines.

TAIL: Dark, ashy brown, outer web in old specimens edged with white; coverts, black, showing very rich purple reflections; tail, well supplied on outer side with solid, beetle-green feathers.

BREAST: Very rich purplish brown or claret, extending well down on breast and free from any other color.

BODY: Upper part, steel-gray; sides, steel-gray, very finely penciled across the feathers with glossy black, growing wider near the vent and ending in solid-greenish black, forming a distinct line of separation between the two colors.

LEGS AND TOES: Lower thighs, ashy gray; shanks and toes, orange, with brownish tinge.

COLOR OF DUCK

HEAD: Plumage, deep brown with two light tan stripes on each side, running from bill to point behind eyes.

BILL: Brownish orange, with dark blue blotch on upper part and black bean at tip.

EYES: Dark brown.

NECK: Mahogany brown, penciled with dark, lustrous brown.

WINGS: Fronts and bows, light brown with distinct pencilings of darker brown having a green sheen; uppermost secondary coverts, dark slaty brown, heavily penciled with a rich shade of lighter brown; upper secondaries, slaty brown, the lower web marked with lighter brown, lower secondaries, slaty, the lower web having a broad band of iridescent blue, then a band of black and ending in a narrow band of white; coverts, slate, with a band of white ending in a band of black; the overlapping of the coverts on the secondaries forming the wing-bar; primaries, brownish slate.

BACK: Rich mahogany brown, richly marked with wide pencilings of greenish black; shoulder-coverts, dark brown with distinct pencilings of light brown that conform to shape of feather.

TAIL: Mahogany brown, with a distinct, broad, wavy penciling of darker brown with greenish sheen; coverts, brown, with broad, distinct and regular pencilings of darker brown with greenish sheen.

BREAST: Rich, mahogany brown, with distinct, wide pencilings of light brown that conform to shape of feather.

BODY: Under part, light brown, each feather distinctly penciled with rich, dark brown to point of tail; sides, dark brown, with distinct pencilings of light brown that conform to shape of feather.

LEGS AND TOES: Lower thighs, dark brown, distinctly penciled; shanks and toes, dusky orange.

CAYUGA DUCKS

Disqualifications

White in any part of plumage. (See General Disqualifications and Cutting for Defects.)

STANDARD WEIGHTS

Adult Drake	8 lbs.	Adult Duck	7 lbs.
Young Drake	7 lbs.	Young Duck	6 lbs.

SHAPE OF DRAKE AND DUCK

HEAD: Long, finely formed.

BILL: Long, top line slightly depressed.

EYES: Full.

NECK: Of medium length, slightly arched.

WINGS: Short, folded closely and smoothly against sides.

BACK: Long, broad.

TAIL: Slightly elevated; composed of hard, stiff feathers; sex feathers of drake, hard, well-curled.

BREAST: Broad, full, prominent.

BODY: Long, broad, deep; carriage, nearly horizontal.

LEGS AND TOES: Lower thighs, short, large; shanks, of medium length and size; toes, straight, connected by web.

COLOR OF DRAKE AND DUCK

BILL: Black.

EYES: Dark brown.

SHANKS AND TOES: Very dark slate.

PLUMAGE: Lustrous, greenish black throughout.

435

CALL DUCKS

Disqualifications

(See General Disqualifications and Cutting for Defects.)

SHAPE OF DRAKE AND DUCK

HEAD: Small, slender.

BILL: Short, trim.

EYES: Of medium size.

NECK: Of medium length.

WINGS: Neat, closely folded.

BACK: Comparatively short.

TAIL: Slightly elevated; composed of hard, stiff feathers; sex feathers of drake, hard, well-curled.

BREAST: Round, full.

BODY: Short, compact, small—the smaller the better; carriage, nearly horizontal.

LEGS AND TOES: Lower thighs, short, plump; shanks, short; toes, straight, connected by web.

GRAY CALL DUCKS

Disqualifications

Any approach to white ring on neck of duck; one or more white primaries in either sex. (See General Disqualifications and Cutting for Defects.)

COLOR OF DRAKE

HEAD: Plumage, rich, lustrous green.

BILL: Greenish yellow.

EYES: Dark brown.

NECK: Lustrous green with a distinct, white ring on lower part, not quite meeting at back.

WINGS: Same markings and color patterns as given for Rouen Drakes, with a lighter ground color.

BACK: Ashy gray, mixed with green on upper part; on lower part and rump, rich, lustrous green.

TAIL: Dark, ashy brown; outer web in old specimens, edged with white; tail-coverts, black, showing rich purple reflections.

BREAST: Rich purplish brown or claret, extending well down on breast and free from any other color.

BODY: Under part and sides, steel-gray, finely and distinctly penciled with dull black, growing lighter near vent and ending in solid, beetle-green black, forming distinct line of separation between the two colors.

LEGS AND TOES: Lower thighs, ashy gray; shanks and toes, orange, with a brownish tinge.

COLOR OF DUCK

HEAD: Plumage, deep brown, with two light tan stripes on each side, running from bill to a point behind eyes.

BILL: Brownish orange.

EYES: Dark brown.

NECK: Light brown, penciled with dark, lustrous brown, free from any appearance of a white ring.

WINGS: The same markings and color pattern as given for Rouen ducks, with a lighter ground color.

BACK: Light brown, richly marked with green.

TAIL: Light brown, with distinct, broad, wavy penciling of dark, greenish brown; tail-coverts, brown, with broad, distinct and regular pencilings of dark brown or greenish brown.

BREAST: Dark brown, richly penciled with a lighter brown.

BODY: Under part and sides, light brown, each feather distinctly penciled with rich, dark brown to point of tail.

LEGS AND TOES: Lower thighs, dark brown, distinctly penciled; shanks and toes, dusky orange.

WHITE CALL DUCKS

Disqualifications

Feathers other than white or creamy white in any part of plumage. (See General Disqualifications and Cutting for Defects.)

COLOR OF DRAKE AND DUCK

BILL: Bright yellow.

EYES: Blue.

SHANKS AND TOES: Bright orange.

PLUMAGE: Web, quill and fluff of feathers in all sections, pure white.

BLACK EAST INDIA DUCKS

Disqualifications

White in any part of plumage. (See General Disqualifications and Cutting for Defects.)

SHAPE OF DRAKE AND DUCK

HEAD: Short.

BILL: Rather short.

EYES: Of medium size.

NECK: Short, nicely arched.

WINGS: Long, well-folded.

BACK: Of medium width, rather long.

TAIL: Slightly elevated, composed of short, stiff feathers; sex feathers of drake, hard, well-curled.

BREAST: Full, plump.

BODY: Long, comparatively small—the smaller the better; carriage, nearly horizontal.

LEGS AND TOES: Lower thighs, short, plump; shanks, short; toes, straight, connected by web.

COLOR OF DRAKE AND DUCK

BILL: Black.

EYES: Dark brown.

SHANKS AND TOES: Black.

PLUMAGE: Lustrous, greenish black.

MUSCOVY DUCKS

Disqualifications

(See General Disqualifications and Cutting for Defects.)

STANDARD WEIGHTS

Adult Drake................10 lbs.   Adult Duck ....7 lbs.

Young Drake .... 8 lbs.   Young Duck ....6 lbs.

SHAPE OF DRAKE AND DUCK

HEAD: Rather long; in drake, large, the top covered with long, crest-like feathers, which are elevated or depressed by the specimen when it becomes excited or alarmed; sides of head and face covered with caruncles—the larger, the better

BILL: Rather short, of medium width.

EYES: Of medium size, having slightly over-arched socket.

NECK: Of medium length, well-arched.

WINGS: Very long, stout.

BACK: Long, broad, somewhat flat.

TAIL: Rather long, with abundance of stiff plumage; sex feathers of drake, hard, well-curled.

BREAST: Broad, full.

BODY: Long, broad; carriage, nearly horizontal.

LEGS AND TOES: Lower thighs, very short, large; shanks, short, large; toes, straight, connected by web.

COLORED MUSCOVY DUCKS

Disqualifications

Smooth heads; plumage more than one-half white. (See General Disqualifications and Cutting for Defects.)

COLOR OF DRAKE AND DUCK

HEAD: Plumage, glossy black and white.

BILL: Pink, shaded with horn.

EYES: Brown.

FACE: Caruncles, red.

NECK: Black, may be slightly marked with white.

WINGS: Fronts, white; bows, black intermingled with a number of white feathers; primaries, black, with white feathers permissible; secondaries, black; coverts, rich, lustrous, greenish-black.

BACK: Lustrous, greenish black.

TAIL: Black.

BODY AND BREAST: Lustrous, greenish-black, broken with white—the blacker the plumage, the better.

LEGS AND TOES: Lower thighs, black; shanks and toes, varying from yellow to dark lead.

WHITE MUSCOVY DUCKS

Disqualifications

Smooth heads; feathers other than pure white in any part of plumage, except dark markings on head of young specimens. (See General Disqualifications and Cutting for Defects.)

COLOR OF DRAKE AND DUCK

BILL: Pinkish flesh-color.

EYES: Blue.

FACE: Caruncles, red.

SHANKS AND TOES: Pale orange.

PLUMAGE: Web, quill, and fluff of feathers in all sections, pure white.

BLUE SWEDISH DUCKS

Disqualifications

Yellow bills; absence of white in breast; feathers of any other color than blue forming one-fourth of plumage. (See General Disqualifications and Cutting for Defects.)

STANDARD WEIGHTS

Adult Drake	8 lbs.	Adult Duck	7 lbs.
Young Drake	6½ lbs.	Young Duck	5½ lbs.

SHAPE OF DRAKE AND DUCK

HEAD: Long, finely formed.

BILL: Of medium size; nearly straight in outline when viewed sidewise.

EYES: Full.

NECK: Long, slightly arched.

WINGS: Short, carried closely.

BACK: Long, broad, with slight slope from shoulders to tail.

TAIL: Slightly elevated; sex feathers of drake, hard, well-curled.

BREAST: Full, deep.

BODY: Broad, of medium length; carriage, nearly horizontal, somewhat elevated in front.

LEGS AND TOES: Lower thighs, short, stout; shanks, stout; toes, straight, connected by web.

COLOR OF DRAKE AND DUCK

HEAD: Drake, dark blue, sometimes approaching black, with a green sheen. Duck, same as general body color.

BILL: Drake, greenish blue. Duck, smutty brown, with a dark brown blotch, similar to Rouen blotch, only larger.

EYES: Dark brown.

WINGS: Two flight feathers, pure white; balance of wing, uniform with general plumage.

BREAST: Front part, pure white, forming heart-shaped spot about three by four inches in size, often extending upward to lower mandible.

SHANKS AND TOES: Reddish brown.

PLUMAGE: Uniform steel-blue throughout, except as noted.

BUFF DUCKS

Disqualifications

Color of plumage other than buff or seal-brown, except white feathers, which shall be considered a serious defect. (See General Disqualifications and Cutting for Defects.)

STANDARD WEIGHTS

Adult Drake	8 lbs.	Adult Duck	7 lbs.
Young Drake	7 lbs.	Young Duck	6 lbs.

SHAPE OF DRAKE AND DUCK

HEAD: Oval, fine, racy.

BILL: Moderate in length, straight in line from skull.

EYES: Full, prominent.

NECK: Fairly long and gracefully curved.

WINGS: Short; carried closely and smoothly against side.

BACK: Broad, long.

TAIL: Small, slightly elevated; sex feathers of drake, hard, well-curled.

BREAST: Broad, deep, prominent, carried moderately low.

BODY: Long, broad, deep.

LEGS AND TOES: Lower thighs and shanks, short, large, set well apart; toes, straight, connected by web.

COLOR OF DRAKE AND DUCK

BILL: Yellow in drake, brownish orange in duck, with dark bean.

EYES: Brown, with blue pupil.

SHANKS AND TOES: Orange yellow.

PLUMAGE: Surface throughout an even shade of rich fawn-buff, with the exception of head and upper portion of neck in drake, which should be seal-brown. Penciling to be considered a serious defect.

CRESTED WHITE DUCKS

Disqualifications

Absence of crest, or crest falling decidedly to one side; bills and legs other than yellow; feathers other than white or creamy white in any part of plumage. (See General Disqualifications and Cutting for Defects.)

STANDARD WEIGHTS

Adult Drake ....7 lbs.   Adult Duck ....6 lbs.
Young Drake ....6 lbs.   Young Duck ....5 lbs.

SHAPE OF DRAKE AND DUCK

HEAD: Of medium size.

BILL: Of medium size.

EYES: Large.

CREST: Large, well-balanced on crown of head.

NECK: Rather long; slightly arched.

WINGS: Of medium length, smooth folded.

BACK: Of medium length and width.

TAIL: Slightly elevated; composed of hard, stiff feathers; sex feathers of drake, hard, well-curled.

BREAST: Prominent, full.

BODY: Of medium length, plump; carriage, nearly horizontal.

LEGS AND TOES: Lower thighs, short, plump; shanks, short; toes, straight, connected by web.

COLOR OF DRAKE AND DUCK

BILL: Yellow.

EYES: Blue.

SHANKS AND TOES: Light orange.

PLUMAGE: Web, quill, and fluff of feathers in all sections, pure white.

RUNNER DUCKS

STANDARD WEIGHTS

Adult Drake ....4½ lbs.   Adult Duck 4   lbs.
Young Drake ....4 lbs.   Young Duck ....3½ lbs.

Disqualifications
(See General Disqualifications and Cutting for Defects.)

SHAPE OF DRAKE AND DUCK

HEAD: Long, flat, finely formed.

BILL: Strong at base, fairly broad and long, extending down from the skull in a straight line, giving it the appearance of a long wedge.

EYES: Set high in head.

NECK: Long, thin, line of neck almost straight.

WINGS: Of medium length, carried close to body.

BACK: Long, straight, narrow.

TAIL: Composed of hard, stiff feathers; sex feathers of drake, hard, well-curled.

BREAST: Full, but not rounded, showing but little suggestion of keel, carried well up.

BODY: Long, narrow, racy-looking; no indication of keel.

CARRIAGE: Very erect.

LEGS AND TOES: Legs of medium length; toes, straight, connected by web.

FAWN AND WHITE RUNNER

Disqualifications
Claret breast; blue wing-bars; absence of two or more primaries or secondaries. (See General Disqualifications and Cutting for Defects.)

COLOR OF DRAKE AND DUCK

HEAD: Fawn and white. A line of white divides the cap from the cheek markings behind the eyes, and a narrow line of white divides the base of the bill from the head markings.

BILL: Drake, yellow when young; greenish yellow when fully developed. Duck, yellow spotted with green when young; a dull green when fully matured. Black bean in both drake and duck.

EYES: Dark brown.

FAWN AND WHITE RUNNER DRAKE

FAWN AND WHITE RUNNER DUCK

NECK: The upper two-thirds, white, lower one-third fawn, sharply defined.

WINGS: Wing-bows and coverts, fawn; primaries and secondaries, white.

BACK: Even fawn throughout.

TAIL: Fawn.

BREAST: Fawn and white, divided about halfway between point of breast-bone and legs; upper half, fawn; lower half, white.

BODY AND FLUFF: White, except an indistinct line of fawn, which runs from base of tail to thigh.

LEGS AND TOES: Lower thighs, white; shanks and toes, orange-red.

WHITE RUNNER

Disqualifications

Color other than white or creamy white in any part of plumage; absence of two or more primaries or secondaries. (See General Disqualifications and Cutting for Defects.)

COLOR OF DRAKE AND DUCK

HEAD: White.

BILL: Yellow.

EYES: Leaden blue.

SHANKS AND TOES: Orange.

PLUMAGE: Web, quill, and fluff of feathers in all sections, pure white.

PENCILED RUNNER

Disqualifications

Blue wing-bar; claret breast; bright green head like Rouen; absence of two or more primaries or secondaries. (See General Disqualifications and Cutting for Defects.)

COLOR OF DRAKE

HEAD: Dull bronze-green, a narrow line of white extending to and encircling the eyes, dividing cap and cheek markings; head markings and bill divided by a narrow line of white; all markings clear cut.

BILL: Of young specimens, yellow; of matured, greenish yellow; bean, black.

EYES: Dark brown.

NECK: Upper two-thirds white, lower one-third medium fawn, sharply defined.

WINGS: Shoulders and top part of wings, fawn, same shade as breast; primaries and secondaries, white, the white extending up the lower part of wings to a point a little above the lower part of the body, forming an inverted V-shaped marking on the side of the body; the color of shoulders and top part of wings when folded come to a point in lower part of back, forming a heart-shape, like a heart pressed on the back.

BACK: Medium fawn; the feathers when examined closely show a soft fawn ground regularly marked with a slightly darker shade of fawn.

TAIL: Dull bronze-green.

BREAST: Medium fawn and white, evenly divided about half way between point of breast-bone and the legs; upper section, dark fawn, lower section, white.

BODY AND FLUFF: Body, medium fawn, same shade as breast; fluff, white except an indistinct line of fawn which runs from the base of tail to thighs.

SHANKS AND TOES: Orange-red.

COLOR OF DUCK

HEAD: Medium fawn; a line of white divides the cap and cheek markings, and a narrow line of white divides the base of bill from head markings.

BILL: Spotted with green when young; dull green when matured; bean, black.

EYES: Dark brown.

SHANKS AND TOES: Orange-red.

PLUMAGE: White markings same as drake, colored markings medium fawn throughout, surface color should be even, no fawn colored section being lighter or darker than another. The under-color a medium or darker shade of fawn, a light line of fawn color running around near the edge of each feather, the border or edge a darker shade. The penciling may be more prominent on the back and wings.

447

DUCKS

SCALE OF POINTS

	White		Other than White	
	Shape	Color	Shape	Color
1. Symmetry	4		4	
2. Weight	4		4	
3. Condition and Vigor	10		10	
4. Head	4	2	3	3
5. Bill	4	2	3	3
6. Eye	2	2	2	2
7. Neck	3	3	2	4
8. Wings	5	3	3	5
9. Back	8	4	6	6
10. Tail	2	2	1	3
11. Breast	12	4	6	10
12. Body	12	4	6	10
13. Legs and Feet	2	2	2	2
	72	28	52	48

GEESE

Breeds	*Varieties*
Toulouse	
Emden	
African	
Chinese	{ Brown { White
Canada	
Egyptian	
Sebastopol	

SCALE OF POINTS

	White Shape	White Color	Parti Color Shape	Parti Color Color
1. Symmetry	4		4	
2. Weight	4		4	
3. Condition and Vigor	10		10	
4. Head	7	3	6	4
5. Bill	4	2	3	3
6. Eye	2	2	2	2
7. Neck	6	2	4	4
8. Wings	6	4	4	6
9. Back	7	3	6	4
10. Tail	3	1	1	3
11. Breast	10	4	9	5
12. Body	10	3	8	5
13. Legs and Toes	2	1	2	1
	75	25	63	37

GEESE

The Toulouse, Emden, and African varieties are the heavy-weight breeds of the Goose family. The females should resemble the males in appearance, except that all females are somewhat smaller in size. The broad, flat back, deep, full, rounded breast, and long body give well-bred specimens the massive appearance required of such heavy, meat producing breeds.

Chinese Geese are essentially ornamental in appearance, of medium size, with long, arched necks, carried upright, and having a large knob at base of beak, characteristic of the breed.

Canada Geese, now domesticated, because ornamental as well as useful, are most frequently seen in public parks. Egyptian Geese differ in most respects from the other Standard varieties; smallness of size and a pugnacious disposition are characteristics of the breed.

The Sebastopol, one of the oldest domestic varieties of geese, reputed to have come originally from Turkey and the vicinity of the Black Sea, is bred both for ornament because of its odd and beautiful appearance, and also for its economic qualities being prolific, hardy, and excellent for the table. Gander and goose are similar except that the goose is somewhat smaller.

ECONOMIC QUALITIES: Raised primarily for meat and production of feathers.

TOULOUSE

Disqualifications

White feathers in primaries or secondaries; white around the bill in young specimens; absence of dewlap on mature males; any suggestion of knob on bill. (See General Disqualifications and Cutting for Defects.)

STANDARD WEIGHTS

Adult Gander	26 lbs.	Adult Goose	20 lbs.
Young Gander	20 lbs.	Young Goose	16 lbs.

SHAPE OF GANDER AND GOOSE

HEAD: Large, deep, short.
BILL: Comparatively short, stout.
EYES: Large, not too prominent.

NECK: Of medium length, rather stout, slightly arched; dewlap, pronounced on mature specimen.

WINGS: Large, strong, smoothly folded against sides.

BACK: Of good length, very broad and slightly arched.

TAIL: Comparatively short, well spread and carried slightly above horizontal; feathers, hard, stiff.

BREAST: Broad, full and very deep.

BODY: Large, square, broad, very deep and massive, compact; in fat specimens, almost touching the ground; keel, long, deep, well set, extending in an unbroken line from the front part of the abdomen well up on breast; stern, almost square.

LEGS AND TOES: Lower thighs and shanks, short, stout; toes, straight, connected by web.

COLOR OF GANDER AND GOOSE

HEAD: Gray.

BILL: Pale orange; bean, light horn, free from black in mature specimens.

EYES: Dark brown or hazel.

NECK: Dark blue-gray, shading to lighter gray as it approaches the back; front of neck, same as breast.

WINGS: Bows and coverts, dark gray, with very narrow edging of lighter gray; primaries, dark gray; secondaries, darker than primaries, with very narrow edging of lighter gray.

BACK: Dark gray.

TAIL: Gray and white, the ends tipped with white.

BREAST: Light gray.

BODY: Underneath, light gray, growing lighter until it becomes almost white on abdomen, the white extending back to and around tail; sides, light gray, becoming dark blue-gray over thighs, edged with lighter gray; white covering all lower posterior parts; from lower front view very little white visible.

LEGS AND TOES: Lower thighs, light gray; shanks and toes, deep reddish-orange.

EMDEN GEESE

Disqualifications

Feathers other than white in any part of plumage, except traces of gray in wings and backs of young specimens. (See General Disqualifications and Cutting for Defects.)

TOULOUSE GANDER

452

TOULOUSE GOOSE

STANDARD WEIGHTS

Adult Gander ....20 lbs.   Adult Goose ....18 lbs.
Young Gander ....18 lbs.   Young Goose ....16 lbs.

SHAPE OF GANDER AND GOOSE

HEAD: Rather large.
BILL: Of medium length and size; stout at base.
EYES: Large.
NECK: Rather long, carried quite upright.
WINGS: Large, well-rounded, strong, smoothly folded against sides.
BACK: Long and straight.
TAIL: Comparatively short; feathers, hard and stiff.
BREAST: Round, deep, full, without keel.
BODY: Long, broad, deep; in fat specimens almost touching the ground; abdomen, full and deep.
LEGS AND TOES: Lower thighs, short, large; shanks, short, stout; toes, straight, connected by web.

COLOR OF GANDER AND GOOSE

BILL: Orange.
EYES: Bright blue.
SHANKS AND TOES: Deep orange.
PLUMAGE: Pure white.

AFRICAN GEESE

Disqualifications

Bill and knob other than black; absence of knob in young, or absence of knob or dewlap in adult specimens; white feathers in primaries and secondaries. (See General Disqualifications and Cutting for Defects.)

STANDARD WEIGHTS

Adult Gander ....20 lbs.   Adult Goose ....18 lbs.
Young Gander ....16 lbs.   Young Goose ....14 lbs.

SHAPE OF GANDER AND GOOSE

HEAD: Broad, deep, large, with large knob, broad as head or slightly broader; heavy dewlap under throat, which in young specimens is but slightly developed.
KNOB: Large, broad as the head or slightly broader.

BILL: Rather large, stout at base.

EYES: Large.

NECK: Long, nicely arched; throat with well-developed dewlap.

WINGS: Large, strong, smoothly folded against sides.

BACK: Broad, moderately long, flat.

TAIL: Slightly elevated; composed of stiff, hard feathers.

BREAST: Full, well-rounded, carried forward.

BODY: Large, long, carried rather upright.

LEGS AND TOES: Lower thighs, short, stout; shanks, of medium length; toes, straight, connected by web.

COLOR OF GANDER AND GOOSE

HEAD: Light brown.

KNOB: Black.

BILL: Black.

EYES: Dark brown.

NECK: Very light ashy brown with distinct broad, dark brown stripe down center of the back of neck and extending its entire length; front of neck under mandible, very light ashy brown, gradually getting lighter in color until past the dewlap where it is almost cream in color, then gradually deepening in color as it approaches the breast.

WINGS: Bows, ashy brown, slightly edged with a lighter shade; coverts, ashy brown distinctly edged with a lighter shade; secondaries, dark slate distinctly edged with a lighter shade approaching white; primaries, dark slate; primary coverts, light slate.

BACK: Ashy brown.

TAIL: Ashy brown heavily edged with a shade approaching white; tail-coverts, white.

BREAST: Very light ashy brown shading to a lighter color under the body.

BODY AND FLUFF: Body, a lighter shade than the breast, gradually getting lighter as it approaches the fluff, which is so light as to approach white; sides of body, ashy brown, each feather edged with a lighter shade.

LEGS AND TOES: Lower thighs, upper part similar to sides of body, ashy brown edged with a lighter shade, lower part similar in color to under part of body; shanks and toes, dark orange.

AFRICAN GANDER

AFRICAN GOOSE

457

CHINESE GEESE

Disqualifications

Absence of knob. (See General Disqualifications and Cutting for Defects.)

STANDARD WEIGHTS

Adult Gander	............12 lbs.	Adult Goose	............10 lbs.
Young Gander	............10 lbs.	Young Goose	.... 8 lbs.

SHAPE OF GANDER AND GOOSE

HEAD: Of medium size, with large knob at base of bill.

KNOB: Round, large, the larger the better.

BILL: Of medium length, stout at base.

EYES: Large.

NECK: Long, gracefully arched, carried very upright.

WINGS: Large, strong, closely folded against sides, and carried high.

BACK: Rather short, of medium width, sloping from neck to tail.

BREAST: Round, full, carried well up.

BODY: Rather short, round, plump; carriage, upright.

LEGS AND TOES: Lower thighs, short, stout; shanks, of medium length; toes, straight, connected by web.

BROWN CHINESE

Disqualifications

Absence of knob; bill or knob other than dark slate or black; white feathers in primaries or secondaries. (See General Disqualifications and Cutting for Defects.)

COLOR OF GANDER AND GOOSE

HEAD: Dark russet brown on top; face, grayish fawn, extending just above eye, forming a distinct line of demarkation.

KNOB: Dark slate.

BILL: Black or dark slate.

EYES: Dark brown.

NECK: Fawn, with a distinct, dark, russet brown stripe down

the center of the back of neck and running its entire length; front of neck under mandible, light grayish fawn.

WINGS: Bows, medium russet brown, slightly edged with a lighter shade; coverts, russet brown, distinctly edged with a lighter shade approaching white; primaries, russet brown; primary coverts, russet brown.

BACK: Russet brown.

TAIL: Dark russet brown, heavily edged with a shade approaching white; tail-coverts, very light grayish fawn approaching white.

BREAST: Grayish fawn, shading to a lighter color under the body.

BODY AND FLUFF: Body, a lighter shade of grayish fawn than the breast, gradually getting lighter as it approaches the fluff, which is so light as to approach white.

LEGS AND TOES: Lower thighs, russet brown, edged with a lighter shade approaching white; shanks and toes, orange.

WHITE CHINESE

Disqualifications

Absence of knob; feathers other than pure white in any part of plumage. (See General Disqualifications and Cutting for Defects.)

COLOR OF GANDER AND GOOSE

KNOB: Orange.
BILL: Orange.
EYES: Light blue.
SHANKS AND TOES: Orange-yellow.
PLUMAGE: Pure white.

CANADA GEESE

Disqualifications

Clipped flights or pinioned wing to prevent flying shall not handicap the specimen. (See General Disqualifications and Cutting for Defects.)

WHITE CHINESE GANDER

WHITE CHINESE GOOSE

STANDARD WEIGHTS

Adult Gander ....12 lbs.   Adult Goose ....10 lbs.
Young Gander ....10 lbs.   Young Goose .... 8 lbs.

SHAPE OF GANDER AND GOOSE

HEAD: Rather small.

BILL: Small, tapering toward point.

EYES: Prominent.

NECK: Long, slender, snaky in appearance.

WINGS: Long, large, powerful.

BACK: Moderate in length and breadth, slightly arched from neck to tail.

TAIL: Composed of hard, stiff feathers.

BREAST: Full, broad—not deep.

BODY: Rather long.

LEGS AND TOES: Lower thighs, rather short; shanks, rather long; toes, straight, of medium length, connected by web.

COLOR OF GANDER AND GOOSE

HEAD: Black with white markings on each side of face which begin at a point in rear of skull and extend in a triangular form to meet under throat.

BILL: Black.

EYES: Black.

NECK: Black.

WINGS: Dark slaty gray edged with lighter gray; primaries, dusky black; secondaries, lighter than primaries, each feather edged with lighter gray.

BACK: Dark gray.

TAIL: Glossy black.

BREAST: Light gray, growing darker as it approaches legs.

BODY: Under part of body, from legs to tail, white.

LEGS AND TOES: Lower thighs, gray; shanks and toes, black.

EGYPTIAN GEESE

Disqualifications

Clipped flights or pinioned wing to prevent flying shall not handicap the specimen. (See General Disqualifications and Cutting for Defects.)

STANDARD WEIGHTS

Adult Gander	10 lbs.	Adult Goose	8 lbs.
Young Gander	8 lbs.	Young Goose	6 lbs.

SHAPE OF GANDER AND GOOSE

HEAD: Small, rather long.

BILL: Of medium length and size.

EYES: Prominent.

NECK: Of medium length, rather small.

WINGS: Large; on wing-joint, in place of the ordinary hard knobs, there are strong, white horny spurs, about five-eighths of an inch long.

BACK: Rather narrow, slightly arched from neck to tail.

TAIL: Composed of hard, stiff feathers.

BREAST: Full, round, not deep.

BODY: Rather long, somewhat small and slender.

LEGS AND TOES: Lower thighs, of medium length, stout; shanks, rather long; toes, straight, long, connected by web.

COLOR OF GANDER AND GOOSE

HEAD: Black and gray, with reddish brown patch around eyes.

BILL: Reddish purple.

EYES: Orange.

NECK: Gray and black.

WINGS: Shoulders, white with narrow black stripe or bar of rich metallic luster; primaries and secondaries, glossy black.

BACK: Gray and black.

TAIL: Glossy black.

BREAST: Center, rich reddish brown; remainder, gray.

BODY: Gray and black on upper parts; under parts, yellowish buff, distinctly and regularly penciled with black lines.

LEGS AND TOES: Lower thighs, pale buff; shanks and toes, reddish yellow.

SEBASTOPOL

Disqualifications

Entire lack of curled feathers on breast. Straight (normal) wing flights. (See General Disqualifications and Cutting for Defects.)

STANDARD WEIGHTS

Adult Gander	14 lbs.	Adult Goose	12 lbs.
Young Gander	12 lbs.	Young Goose	10 lbs.

SHAPE OF GANDER AND GOOSE

HEAD: Rather large.

BILL: Of medium length and size, stout at base.

EYES: Large and prominent.

NECK: Medium in length, carried upright. Feathers of head and upper neck smooth, of lower neck curled.

WINGS: Incapable of flight; primaries and secondaries much curled and twisted.

BACK: Short, straight, covered with profuse feathering, feathers very much curled and developed in length, in good specimens reaching to the ground. The curlier and longer, the better.

TAIL: Main-tail feathers long and very much curled and twisted.

BREAST: Round, deep, full, without keel, feathers very much curled, the curlier the better.

BODY: Round, broad, deep, profusely covered with long and much curled feathers.

LEGS AND TOES: Lower thighs, short, large, feathers curled; shanks short, stout; toes straight, connected by web.

COLOR OF GANDER AND GOOSE

BILL: Orange.

EYES: Bright blue.

SHANKS AND TOES: Deep orange.

PLUMAGE: Pure white. In young specimens traces of gray should not be cut.

TURKEYS

Varieties

Turkeys ....
{
Bronze
Narragansett
White Holland
Black
Slate
Bourbon Red
}

SCALE OF POINTS

Symmetry	4
Weight	12
Condition and Vigor	4
Head—Shape 2, Color 2..	4
Eyes—Shape 2, Color 2..	4
Throat-Wattle	4
Neck—Shape 3, Color 2..	5
Wings—Shape 4, Color 6...	10
Back—Shape 6, Color 6..	12
Tail—Shape 6, Color 8...	14
Breast—Shape 6, Color 5..	11
Body and Fluff—Shape 6, Color 5...	11
Legs and Toes—Shape 3, Color 2..	5
	——
	100

TURKEYS

Wild turkeys were found in great numbers by the pioneer settlers in the Eastern, Southern and Western sections of the United States. They also were plentiful in Mexico. The Turkey was introduced into Europe from America, so it is evident that it originated in this country. All the varieties listed in the Standard were produced in the United States, with the possible exception of the White Holland Turkey. The Bronze is the largest and heaviest variety.

"Size and weight" in Turkeys are of great importance. The body should be broad, round, and the breast full, which gives the male a very stately appearance. The legs and shanks must be large, straight, and well set. The head should be of good size, and the eyes possess a bold expression. The female Turkey is similar in all sections to the male, though smaller and finer in bone structure.

ECONOMIC QUALITIES: Turkeys are raised for their excellent market qualities, and are great foragers. Color of egg shells,—varying in color but all Turkey eggs show characteristic brown spots.

Disqualifications

Deformed wings. Decidedly crooked breastbone. (See General Disqualifications and Cutting for Defects.)

SHAPE OF MALE AND FEMALE

HEAD: Moderately long, deep, broad, carunculated, with tubular leader at base of beak, its size subject to extension or contraction, according to mood of specimen.

BEAK: Medium length, strong, curved, well set in head.

EYES: Full, oval, prominent.

THROAT-WATTLE: Heavily carunculated.

NECK: Moderately long, erect, gracefully curved, blending into back.

BEARD: Long, bristly, prominent in adult males; not required in females.

WINGS: Large, powerful, smoothly folded, carried well up on sides. Feathers broad and overlapping.

466

BACK: Broad, sloping from neck in a convex curve to tail.

TAIL: Rather long, feathers broad, carried low in a continued graceful curve in line with back; coverts, broad and abundant, extending well onto tail.

BREAST: Broad, deep, full, well-rounded, carried well forward and slightly above the horizontal. Keel medium in length, slightly convex, full-fleshed throughout its entire length.

BODY: Broad, deep, compact.

FLUFF: Moderately short.

LEGS AND TOES: Legs of medium length, strong, straight, set wide apart and well filled-out with flesh down to the hocks; shanks strong, of good substance and moderate in length. Toes, straight, strong and well-spread.

BRONZE TURKEYS

Disqualifications

White feathers in any part of plumage; wings showing one or more primary or secondary feathers clear black or brown, or absence of white or gray bars more than one-half the length of primaries; color of back, clear black; feather or feathers in tail or main-tail coverts, clear black, brown or gray; absence of black band and of white edging on back of female; white or gray bars showing on main-tail feathers beyond greater main-tail coverts, except the terminating wide edging of white; and complete absence of white edging on breast of female. (See General and Turkey Disqualifications, and Cutting for Defects.)

Note: The following defects should be cut severely: Absence of one or more primary or secondary wing feathers; absence of one or more center main-tail feathers; white or gray bars, other than the terminating wide edging of white, showing on base of main-tail feathers; absence of black bands on one or more of the large main-tail coverts; knob on the end of breastbone to be considered a very serious defect.

STANDARD WEIGHTS

Adult Tom	36 lbs.	Adult Hen	20 lbs.
Yearling Tom	33 lbs.	Yearling Hen	18 lbs.
Young Tom	25 lbs.	Young Hen	16 lbs.

When two specimens are both over Standard weight and equal in all other points, the one nearest Standard weight shall win.

BRONZE TURKEY MALE

BRONZE TURKEY FEMALE

COLOR OF MALE

HEAD: Red, changeable to bluish white.

BEAK: Light horn at tip, dark at base.

EYES: Dark brown.

THROAT-WATTLE: Red, changeable to bluish white.

NECK: Rich, brilliant, copperish bronze.

BEARD: Black.

WINGS: Fronts and bows, rich, brilliant, copperish bronze, ending in a narrow band of black; coverts, bright, rich copperish bronze, forming a beautiful broad, bronze band across wings when folded, feathers terminating in a distinct black band, forming a glossy, ribbon-like mark, which separates them from secondaries; primaries, each feather, throughout its entire length, alternately crossed with distinct, parallel black and white bars of equal width, running straight across the feathers; flight coverts, barred similar to primaries; secondaries, dull black, alternately crossed with distinct parallel black and white bars, the black bar taking on a rich bronze cast on the shorter top secondaries, the white bar becoming less distinct; an edging of brown in secondaries being very objectionable.

BACK: From neck to middle of back, a rich, brilliant copperish bronze, each feather terminating in a narrow black band, extending across end; from middle of back to tail-coverts, black, each feather having a broad, brilliant, copperish bronze band extending across it near the end, the more bronze the better, the feathers ending in a distinct black band, gradually narrowing as the tail coverts are approached.

TAIL: Main-tail and coverts, dull black, each feather evenly and distinctly marked transversely with parallel lines of brown; each feather having a wide, the wider the better, lustrous, copperish bronze band extending across the feather, bordered on each side by a narrow but distinct band of intense black; the feather terminating in a wide edging of pure white. The more distinct the colors throughout the whole plumage, the better.

BREAST: Unexposed portions of feathers black; exposed surface, rich, lustrous copperish bronze; each feather on lower part of breast approaching the body terminating in a distinct narrow, intense black band extending across the end.

BODY AND FLUFF: Body, black, each feather with a wide, brilliant copperish bronze band extending across it near the end, a narrow but distinct band of black bordering the bronze and terminating in a narrow edging of pure white; fluff, dull black.

LEGS AND TOES: Lower thighs dull black with slight edgings of grayish white with shanks and toes in young specimens dull black, changing to smoky pink with maturity.

COLOR OF FEMALE

BEAK, EYES, THROAT-WATTLE, LEGS AND TOES: Same as male.

PLUMAGE: Similar to that of male, except an edging of white on feathers of neck, back, wing-bows, wing-coverts, breast, and body, which edging should be narrow in front, gradually widening as it approaches the rear of the specimen.

NARRAGANSETT TURKEYS

Disqualifications

Wings showing one or more primary or secondary feathers clear black or brown, or absence of white or gray bars more than one-half of the length of primaries; white or gray bars showing on main-tail feathers beyond greater main-tail coverts, except terminating wide edging of white. (See General and Turkey Disqualifications and Cutting for Defects.)

Note: The following defects should be severely cut: Absence of one or more center main-tail feathers; white or gray bars, other than the terminating wide edging of steel-gray approaching white, showing on the base of main-tail feathers; decidedly crooked breast bones.

STANDARD WEIGHTS

Adult Tom	33 lbs.	Adult Hen	18 lbs.
Yearling Tom	30 lbs.	Yearling Hen	16 lbs.
Young Tom	23 lbs.	Young Hen	14 lbs.

COLOR OF MALE

HEAD: Red, changeable to bluish white.
BEAK: Horn.
EYES: Brown.
THROAT-WATTLE: Red, changeable to bluish white.
NECK: Upper part, black, each feather ending in a broad, steel-gray band; lower part, black, each feather ending in a broad, steel-gray band, edged with black, the edging of the black increasing as the body is approached.
BEARD: Black.

PLUMAGE OF NARRAGANSETT TURKEY, MALE

(See page 473)

(1) Feather from top-center of Back.

(2) Tail-Covert (short).

(3) Tail-Covert (long).

(4) Main-tail Feather (Middle of Tail).

(5) Feather from Breast near Wing-Front.

(6) Feather from Body below Wing.

(7) Wing (Middle Secondary).

(8) Wing (Middle Primary).

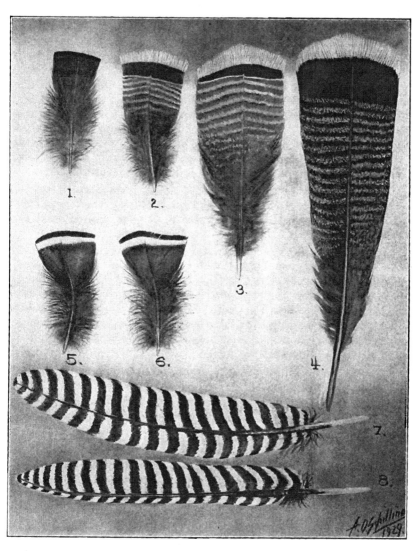

IDEAL FEATHERS OF THE NARRAGANSETT TURKEY MALE

(See page 472)

WINGS: Fronts and bows, light steel-gray ending in a narrow band of black; coverts, a light steel gray, forming a beautiful, broad steel-gray band across wings when folded, feathers terminating in a distinct black band, forming a glossy, ribbon-like mark, which separates them from secondaries; primaries, each feather, throughout its entire length, alternately crossed with distinct, parallel black and white bars of equal width, running straight across feathers; flight coverts, barred similar to primaries; secondaries, alternately crossed with distinct parallel black and white bars, the black bar taking on a light steel-gray cast on the shorter top secondaries; the white bar becoming less distinct; an edging of brown in secondaries being very objectionable.

BACK: Rich, metallic black, free from bronze cast; saddle, black, each feather ending in a broad, steel-gray band approaching white, the light band increasing as the tail-coverts are approached.

TAIL: Main-tail, dull black, each feather regularly penciled with parallel lines of light brown, ending in a broad band of metallic black, free from bronze cast, edged with steel-gray approaching white; coverts and lesser coverts, dull black, each feather regularly penciled with parallel lines of light brown, having a wide band of metallic black, free from bronze cast, extending across it near the end, terminating in a wide edging of light steel-gray approaching white.

BREAST: Metallic black, free from bronze cast, each feather ending in a broad, light steel-gray band edged with black.

BODY AND FLUFF: Body, metallic black, free from bronze cast, each feather ending in a broad, light steel-gray band edged with black; fluff, slate.

LEGS AND TOES: Lower thighs, rich metallic black, free from bronze cast, each feather ending in a light steel-gray band edged with black; shanks and toes, in mature specimens, deep salmon; in young specimens, dark, approaching salmon.

COLOR OF FEMALE

BEAK, EYES, THROAT-WATTLE, LEGS AND TOES: Same as male.

PLUMAGE: Similar to that of male, except an edging of light, steel-gray approaching white on feathers of back, wing-bows, wing-coverts, breast and body, which edging should be narrow in front gradually widening as it approaches the rear.

WHITE HOLLAND TURKEYS

Disqualifications

(See General and Turkey Disqualifications and Cutting for Defects.)

STANDARD WEIGHTS

Adult Tom	33 lbs.	Adult Hen	18 lbs.
Yearling Tom	30 lbs.	Yearling Hen	16 lbs.
Young Tom	23 lbs.	Young Hen	14 lbs.

COLOR OF MALE AND FEMALE

HEAD: Red, changeable to bluish white.
BEAK: Horn.
EYES: Dark brown.
THROAT-WATTLE: Red, changeable to pinkish white.
SHANKS AND TOES: Pinkish white.
PLUMAGE: Web, fluff, and quill of feathers in all sections, pure white, except beard, which is deep black.

BLACK TURKEYS

Disqualifications

Feathers other than black in any part of plumage; a slight brown tinge in tails of females not to disqualify. (See General and Turkey Disqualifications, and Cutting for Defects.)

STANDARD WEIGHTS

Adult Tom	33 lbs.	Adult Hen	18 lbs.
Yearling Tom	30 lbs.	Yearling Hen	16 lbs.
Young Tom	23 lbs.	Young Hen	14 lbs.

COLOR OF MALE AND FEMALE

HEAD: Red, changeable to bluish white.
BEAK: Slaty black.
EYES: Dark brown.
THROAT-WATTLE: Red, changeable to bluish white.
SHANKS AND TOES: Pink in adults, slaty black in young.
PLUMAGE: Surface, lustrous, greenish black throughout; under-color, dull black; beard black.

BOURBON RED TURKEY MALE

BOURBON RED TURKEY FEMALE

SLATE TURKEYS

Disqualifications

Feathers other than slaty or ashy blue, which may be dotted with black, in any part of plumage. (See General and Turkey Disqualifications, and Cutting for Defects.)

STANDARD WEIGHTS

Adult Tom............................33 lbs.	Adult Hen ....18 lbs.
Yearling Tom ....30 lbs.	Yearling Hen ....16 lbs.
Young Tom............................23 lbs.	Young Hen............................14 lbs.

COLOR OF MALE AND FEMALE

HEAD: Red, changeable to bluish white.
BEAK: Horn.
EYES: Dark brown.
THROAT-WATTLE: Red, changeable to bluish white.
SHANKS AND TOES: Pink in adults, deep pink in young.
PLUMAGE: Slaty blue, beard, black.

BOURBON RED TURKEYS

Disqualifications

More than one-third any other color than white showing in either primaries, secondaries, or main-tail feathers. (See General and Turkey Disqualifications, and Cutting for Defects.)

Note: The following defects should be cut severely: mealy backs, bibs, black barring on body plumage, more than one-third of wing feathers showing pronounced rustiness, black edging on body plumage of females.

STANDARD WEIGHTS

Adult Tom............................33 lbs.	Adult Hen ....18 lbs.
Yearling Tom ....30 lbs.	Yearling Hen ....16 lbs.
Young Tom............................23 lbs.	Young Hen............................14 lbs.

COLOR OF MALE

HEAD: Red, changeable to bluish white.
BEAK: Light horn at tip, darker at base.

EYES: Dark brown.

THROAT-WATTLE: Red, changeable to bluish white.

NECK: Rich, dark, chestnut mahogany.

BEARD: Black.

WINGS: Fronts and bows, rich dark chestnut mahogany; primaries and secondaries, pure white.

BACK: Deep, brownish red.

TAIL: Pure white, with a dimly outlined bar of soft red crossing each main-tail feather near the end; coverts deep brownish red.

BREAST: Rich, dark chestnut mahogany, feathers having a very narrow edging of lustrous black.

BODY AND FLUFF: Body, deep, brownish red; fluff, a lighter shade of same color.

LEGS AND TOES: Lower thighs, dark chestnut mahogany; shanks and toes, reddish pink in adults; deep reddish horn in young.

UNDER-COLOR OF ALL SECTIONS: Red, shading to light salmon at base.

COLOR OF FEMALE

Similar to that of male, except breast, which has narrow, threadlike edging of white.

CONTENTS

Page

Page

Page

Page

H

I

J

L

Page

M

Page

R

W

CPSIA information can be obtained at www.ICGtesting.com
Printed in the USA
LVOW090750191111

255585LV00005B/53/P